Surviving the Americas

SURVIVING THE AMERICAS

Garifuna Persistence from Nicaragua to New York City

Serena Cosgrove, José Idiáquez, Leonard Joseph Bent, and Andrew Gorvetzian

In gratitude,
Serena (on behalf for all four authors)

University of
CINCINNATI | PRESS

About the University of Cincinnati Press

The University of Cincinnati Press is committed to publishing rigorous, peer-reviewed, leading scholarship accessibly to stimulate dialog among the academy, public intellectuals and lay practitioners. The Press endeavors to erase disciplinary boundaries in order to cast fresh light on common problems in our global community. Building on the university's long- standing tradition of social responsibility to the citizens of Cincinnati, state of Ohio, and the world, the Press publishes books on topics that expose and resolve disparities at every level of society and have local, national and global impact.

The University of Cincinnati Press, Cincinnati 45221
Copyright © 2021

Published in 2020

ISBN 978-1-947602-11-3 (hardback)
ISBN 978-1-947602-12-0 (e-book, PDF)
ISBN 978-1-947602-10-6 (e-book, EPUB)

Names: Cosgrove, Serena, 1963– author. | Idiáquez, José, author. | Joseph Bent, Leonard, author. | Gorvetzian, Andrew (Andrew James), author.
Title: Surviving the Americas : Garifuna persistence from Nicaragua to New York City / Serena Cosgrove, José Idiáquez, Leonard Joseph Bent, and Andrew Gorvetzian.
Description: Cincinnati, Ohio : The University of Cincinnati Press, 2021. | Includes bibliographical references and index.
Identifiers: LCCN 2019045946 (print) | LCCN 2019045947 (ebook) | ISBN 9781947602113 (hardback) | ISBN 9781947602106 (epub) | ISBN 9781947602120 (pdf)
Subjects: LCSH: Garifuna (Caribbean people)—Nicaragua—Social conditions. | Garifuna (Caribbean people)—New York (State)—New York—Social conditions.
Classification: LCC F1505.2.C3 C67 2020 (print) | LCC F1505.2.C3 (ebook) | DDC 305.896/9720747—dc23
LC record available at https://lccn.loc.gov/2019045946
LC ebook record available at https://lccn.loc.gov/2019045947

Designed and produced for UC Press by Julie Rushing and Jennifer Flint
Typeset in: Adobe Text Pro and Hypatia Sans Pro
Printed in the United States of America
First Printing
Cover image of Garifuna Dancers during Caribbean Day 2018 in NYC by mais_nyc, via Flickr, https://www.flickr.com/photos/urbanprose/27655637897 /in/album-72157696976161514/. CC-BY SA 2.0.

We dedicate this book (and all royalties it may generate)
to increasing educational opportunities for the Garifuna people in Nicaragua,
whose persistence is hope for the entire world.
Seremein. Gracias. Thank you.

Table of Contents

Central America

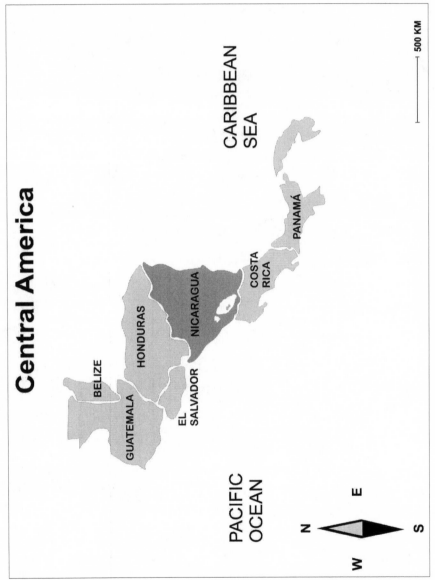

PACIFIC OCEAN

CARIBBEAN SEA

BELIZE

GUATEMALA

HONDURAS

EL SALVADOR

NICARAGUA

COSTA RICA

PANAMÁ

500 KM

N E S W

Courtesy of the Universidad Centroamericana-Managua.

Garifuna Timeline

Prepared by Isabeau J. Belisle Dempsey

Entries specific to Nicaragua are indicated in bold.

1200   Some Caribs migrate from the Guianas region of northern South America to the island of St. Vincent, integrating with the Arawaks that inhabit it.[1]

1502   Christopher Columbus's fourth voyage reaches the coast of Honduras, and he travels south to Panamá.

1500s The Arawaks are forced to labor in mines by the Spanish, where many of them die from overwork, starvation, and disease.[2]

1512   The king of Spain authorizes the enslavement of Caribs from St. Vincent and the Lesser Antilles. The Caribs on St. Vincent had been largely left alone due to two reasons: St. Vincent did not have precious metals to entice the Spanish, and the Caribs were far fiercer and defensive against incursions than the "gentle" Arawak.[3]

1525   Spain begins its conquest of Honduras.

1600s The northern coast of Honduras is claimed by British buccaneers.

1625   The French, under Belain d'Esnambuc, arrive to St. Vincent to settle alongside the British, leading to increasing tension with the Caribs. Eventually, the Caribs attack the English settlement on the island.[4]

1626   The French and English ally to ambush the Caribs and massacre them in retaliation.[5]

1629   **English Puritans colonize the island of Providencia, 110 miles off the coast of Nicaragua. Africans also settled the island alongside the Puritans.[6]**

1635   Two Spanish ships wreck on the coast of St. Vincent. West African slaves on the ships escape onto the island and begin to integrate with the Carib Indian population;[7] their mixing leads to the emergence of the Garifuna or Black Caribs.

1641   **The Spanish invade the Providencia colony and destroy it, capturing many English and African settlers in the process. Some of the African settlers escape to the Nicaraguan mainland and join the Miskitu who live there. Other Africans arrive to the area around this time fleeing slavery, either having escaped from shipwrecks off the coast or from other areas of the Caribbean and Central America.[8]**

1652   The first Jesuit priest, Father André Déjan, arrives to St. Vincent from France.[9]

1653	A second Jesuit priest, Father Pierre Aubergeon, arrives to replace Fr. Déjan.[10]
1654	Black Caribs attack and kill the two Jesuit priests and their assistant.[11]
1660	Both France and England recognize St. Vincent as belonging to the Black Caribs.[12]
1674	Black Caribs on St. Vincent and Dominica ally with France to attack English settlements.[13]
1675	Another ship wrecks on the coast of St. Vincent, bringing another wave of African slaves to the island.
1700s	**By the mid-eighteenth century, there are several "Anglo-dominated British/African/Amerindian communities" along the Caribbean coast. Some of the biggest settlements include Bluefields, Corn Island, Pearl Key Lagoon, Cabo Gracias a Dios, Black River, Bragmans Bluff, and Punta Gorda.[14]**
1723	Two British ships arrive to St. Vincent to declare the islanders "natural-born subjects of Great Britain" and begin the British settlement process.[15]
1747	**The British government places the Mosquitia under control of the governor of Jamaica to oversee the settlements. The British governor existed alongside the Miskitu king who continued to preside over the Miskitu kingdom. The British imported Africans through Jamaica to labor alongside the Amerindians in fishing, lumbering cedar, and mahogany, and working sugar, cotton, and indigo plantations.[16]**
1748	The French and English ratify their recognition of the Black Caribs' rights to St. Vincent.[17]
1757	**The population of the Mosquito Shore is recorded as consisting of "154 white persons, 190 free 'mulattoes' and 'mustees,' 20 freed slaves, and 780 African and Amerindian slaves."[18]**
1763	The Seven Years War ends with the Treaty of Paris, giving England "colonial supremacy" in the Caribbean and transferring the ownership of St. Vincent island from the French to the English. This transference occurred without consulting the Black Carib population, whom the French and English both supposedly recognized as owning the island.[19]
1772	In an effort to continue resisting the British, the Black Caribs seek out the French as allies, citing years of "protestations of friendship"; however, the Count of Nozières rebuked their advances to "discourage the [Black Caribs] from undertaking violent Measures."[20]
1779–1783	The Black Caribs are left to run the island, in spite of hostilities from local French authorities.[21]
1783–1787	**The Treaty of Versailles (1783) and the Convention of London (1786) are signed between Britain and Spain, wherein the British government agrees to withdraw their colonists from the Mosquito Coast and relinquish their**

superintendency. The settlers leave in 1787. Many of their slaves and other settlers of color either stayed in Nicaragua or soon returned. The largest settlement of these former English families of color is led by Col. Robert Hodgson Jr. and is established in Bluefields Lagoon.[22]

1784	St. Vincent is formally placed back under British rule.[23]
1795	The Black Caribs declare war on the British, leading multiple attacks against them.[24]
1796	Following several minor engagements, the Black Caribs lead a "full-scale rebellion" against the British that is ultimately unsuccessful.[25]
1797	In the wake of their defeat, the Black Caribs are exiled to Roatán Island, off the coast of modern Honduras, by the British in an effort to prevent any future uprisings or conflicts. From there, the Garifuna begin to expand to the Central American coastline,[26] arriving in modern Honduras and migrating from there.[27]
1802	The Black Caribs arrive to the territory of British Honduras (modern Belize).[28]
1807	Britain abolishes the slave trade, leading to an increase of Black Carib laborers in British Honduras.[29]
1832	Three counterrevolutionary armies with the prominent presence of Black Caribs and in alliance with Manuel José Arce attack Francisco Morazán, president of the Federation of Central American States. These attacks are defeated by Morazán, and the Black Caribs flee the Central American Federation to British Honduras where they are welcomed by laborers already present there.[30]
1833	By this time, many Garifuna[31] men are laboring alongside slaves in British logging camps, and in an effort to dissuade any potential alliances between the two groups, the British purposefully employed a "'divide and rule' strategy."[32]
1836	Black Caribs begin to migrate to other Central American territories, particularly Guatemala and Honduras.[33]
1844	**The Mosquito Coast is designated a British protectorate, and the new consul general, Patrick Walker, takes up post in Bluefields.[34]**
1845	**Miskitu King George is crowned at age fourteen and establishes his residence in Bluefields.[35]**
1849	**The Moravian Church arrives to the Mosquito Coast, particularly embedding itself into Bluefields and Pearl Lagoon. Most of the missionaries are German, and are accompanied by Jamaican colleagues. These missionaries begin to set up schools and gain significant power, influencing local politics and even gaining seats in the government. The Moravian Church "functioned as the national church of the Mosquitia."[36]**

1860s   A census estimates nearly a quarter of the Black Carib population lives throughout Central America, mostly as labor migrants. The government of the Central American Federation decides to deny Black Caribs titles to land they had settled in southern Belize in order to maintain their availability as wage laborers.[37]

1860   **The Treaty of Managua is signed, and Great Britain recognizes Nicaragua's sovereignty over the southern part of the Mosquito Coast and renounces the British protectorate there.**[38]

1860s–1870s Garifuna from Honduras arrive to Nicaragua as seasonal migrant workers to labor as mahogany cutters.[39]

1881   **The "Great Awakening" occurs: large numbers of *costeños* (those who live on the coast), of all ethnic groups, convert to Christianity. From 1879 to 1894 membership to the Moravian Church increases drastically.**[40]

1890s   U.S. fruit companies begin to buy up coastal land to establish banana plantations along the Caribbean coast of Central America. Black Caribs form a large portion of these companies' laborers. By 1915, Black Caribs make up 10 percent of the Standard Fruit Company's employees.[41]

1890s   **The United States takes an interest in production of crops and extraction of raw materials in the Mosquito Reserve, investing in bananas, lumber, rubber, gold mining, coconuts, as well as transportation and commercial business. By 1894, the U.S. capital investment totaled at least $2 million.**[42]

1892   **The Moravian Church opens a high school in Bluefields. They strive to reinforce British patriotism over the costeños' cultural ways.**[43]

1894   **The Mosquito Coast reserve is annexed from the Indigenous communities by the state of Nicaragua in what is called "the Reincorporation" (by the Nicaraguan government) or "the Overthrow" (by the costeños). Military troops occupied Bluefields.**[44]

1896   **La Fe is founded by Lino López.**[45]

1900s   Wage labor becomes the basis of Garifuna economy, particularly emphasizing horticulture and fishing for those still living among their communities.[46] This era also saw the evolution of (Belizean) Garifuna's ethnic identity in an effort to escape their position at the bottom of the social stratification system; they began to refer to themselves as Caribs as compared to Black Caribs, to distance themselves from their African heritage.[47]

1900   **The Zelaya government demands that all schools be taught exclusively in Spanish; unable to comply with this requirement, the Moravians close schools on the coast.**[48]

1905   **Brown Bank is founded in the Pearl Lagoon basin, comprising one of the Garifuna communities that will eventually be located there.**[49]

1906   **La Fe is founded by Lino López, who arrived to the territory from Brown Bank.**[50]

1908	John Sambola arrives from Honduras and founds San Vicente, previously known as Square Point.[51]
1912	John Sambola establishes Orinoco. According to the story, John went out for a hunt one day and left the care of his five children in the hands of his brother, Basilio, who also had daughters. One of John's daughters got into an altercation with her cousin, and Basilio punished John's daughter, but not his own. When John returned from the hunt and learned of this unequal treatment, he confronted Basilio. Shortly after, he left San Vicente for a farm located on the territory that would later be Orinoco.[52]
1929	The Honduran government passes an immigration law that prohibited, among other races, Black migrants from entering the country, with national rhetoric targeting West Indians in particular. This law is ratified in 1934.[53]
1960s	Seeking employment, many Garifuna men and women begin to migrate to the United States, particularly in Los Angeles, New York City, and Chicago.[54]
1970s	The National Agrarian Office or *Instituto Nacional Agrario* (INA) issues titles of occupation to Garifuna communities attempting to formalize land holdings; however, titles of occupation do not grant ownership over the land nor right to harvest.[55]
1978	Garifuna leaders in Honduras found the Black Fraternal Organization of Honduras or *Organización Fraternal Negra Hondureña* (OFRANEH), which defends the cultural and territorial rights of Honduran Garifuna people.
1979	The triumph of the Sandinista revolution on July 19, 1979, overthrows the Somoza dynasty.
1980s	From the early 1980s until 1990, the counterrevolutionary war affects the whole country, including the Caribbean coast.
1981	Belize gains independence from Britain; the National Garifuna Council (NGC) is founded in the Garifuna settlement of Dangriga, Belize, and begins to defend the Garifuna against the ethnic and racial discrimination they have faced in Belize.
1982	The *traslado* occurs. This was the collective relocation of communities from along the Río Coco, on the Nicaraguan-Honduran border, a decision by the Nicaraguan government with military backing.[56]
1987	The Caribbean coast "counterrevolutionaries" lay down their arms and sign a peace accord with the Sandinistas.
1987–1990	Autonomy Law 28 is passed in 1987 and begins to be implemented in 1990. It creates two regional governments (one in the north and one in the south on the Caribbean coast) with their own respective structures of forty-five members each with five legislators to the National Assembly in Managua.

1990s   The Garifuna in Honduras begin to protest against tourism development, as "the battle over tourism is a battle over land."[57] A communal land titling program begins, with the goal of awarding Garifuna communities full land titles (titles of *dominio pleno*). As of 2018, fifty-two communal and cooperative titles had been granted. These titles exclude ancestral territory.[58]

1992   The Garifuna are admitted to the World Council of Indigenous Peoples after overcoming resistance to their admission because they are also racially Black people in the Americas.[59]

1995   Honduras recognizes the Garifuna's rights as Indigenous peoples and their claims to territory with the signing of the International Labour Organization's Convention on Indigenous and Tribal Peoples in Independent Countries (ILO 169).[60]

2001   The Garifuna of Sambo Creek, Honduras, occupy territory that they claim was stolen, and present a petition for the land to the Inter-American Commission on Human Rights.[61] UNESCO declares Garifuna culture as a Masterpiece of the Oral and Intangible Heritage of Humanity.[62]

2001   **The Mayagna—an Indigenous people on the Caribbean coast of Nicaragua—win a landmark case against the government of Nicaragua in which the Inter-American Court of Human Rights decides they have rights to their communally held land in northeastern Nicaragua.**

2002   **The Nicaraguan government passes Law 445 for Communal Land Titling with five phases that are supposed to lead to the demarcation, legalization, and clearing of outside settlers from Indigenous, Afro-Indigenous, and Afro-descendant communal lands on the Caribbean coast.**

2005   The Inter-American Human Rights Court rules in favor of the Sambo Creek community in a land reclamation case.[63]

2007   The United Nations passes the Declaration on the Rights of Indigenous Peoples, which aims to grant full and equal human rights to Indigenous peoples. Through this convention, along with ILO 169, the Garifuna's human rights are reinforced.[64]

2019   The National Autonomous University of Honduras or *Universidad Nacional Autónoma de Hondura*s creates the first Garifuna Academy as part of their Head Office for Scientific University Research.

Welcoming: *Garifuna Hospitality*

Serena Cosgrove and José Idiáquez

Welcome to Orinoco

Welcome to Orinoco, a village that peeks out from the shore of Pearl Lagoon, on the southern Caribbean coast of Nicaragua, against a backdrop of lush, verdant green, appearing to bob up and down like a buoy as the *panga* speedboat triumphs over the wind and waves to draw close.[1] At the same moment the panga slows down in its approach to the pier after the three-hour journey from Bluefields through mangroves, rivers, and the open water of the lagoon, the sight of a Claro cellphone tower and a busy commercial dock are the first signs that the Garifuna people living in Orinoco are facing changes, stemming from a complex process of modernization, globalization, and incorporation into a neoliberal economy that has brought opportunities and challenges to the entire Pearl Lagoon region. Yet, even with the challenges, many things that distinguish the Garifuna from other groups on the Caribbean coast of Nicaragua endure: special dishes—often prepared from produce grown on family plots on communal land; reverence for the land and sea that have sustained them; dancing, drumming, and making music that evoke the rituals of their ancestors; and for many, a recognition that today's persistence is thanks to ancestors who came before.

We're a bit of a rag-tag team at the moment as we unsteadily make our way off the boat onto the pier; the wind was fierce this trip and blew up a lot of water on the passengers so all of us are wet and a little sore from the pounding of the boat as it made its way through the waves. Leonard Joseph Bent, or Leonard as he is called, is the first to alight. His family is from Orinoco; as a child, he spent his vacations with his grandmother in Orinoco. Today he lives in Bluefields where he has just retired as a sociology professor at the Bluefields Indian and Caribbean University (BICU). Like so many other Garifuna we've met over the years, Leonard is rooted in his community but doesn't live there. His life is routed through other places. Living in Bluefields and working along the length of the Caribbean coast of Nicaragua, he still comes home regularly to visit family and celebrate community festivals and attend funerals. Second to make it successfully off the boat is Andrew Gorvetzian (we call him Andy), a former student of Serena's who had the grave misfortune to have her as a professor at Seattle University and became interested in field research and Central America. His amusement at the anthropological methods we use (seems like a lot of just hanging out and gossiping) has turned to fascination and a keen desire to study this discipline in graduate school. José Idiáquez, known to us as Father Chepe, is the third one of us to get off the boat. He's simultaneously relieved the boat ride is over, and glad to be back in the community where he lived for two years in the early 1990s when he carried out fieldwork for his master's thesis about Garifuna spirituality. His silent questions are: "Will I recognize Orinoco? What is similar? What has changed? Will old friends recognize me?" Serena Cosgrove is the last off the boat. Even though she is happy to have arrived safely to Orinoco, part of her wants the panga ride to go on forever: the beauty, rough ride, and isolation of the journey make her yearn to know what lies further ahead. Yet, the social scientist within her knows that this project will only unfold if we build relationships in the community. That evening as we're laughing over dinner with our welcoming host, Miss Rebecca, our research group recognizes the feeling: we're home and give thanks for having arrived safe and sound. The goal of this preface is to tell you a little bit about how this project came to absorb us and to introduce ourselves, the authors.

Welcome to these pages. This book is about the Nicaraguan Garifuna, about five thousand people who live primarily on the Caribbean coast of the country, who are part of the pan-Garifuna community of Central America and beyond. Little has been written in English about the Garifuna in Nicaragua. This is our attempt to invite you into our learning, unlearning, and relearning about what it means to be Garifuna today in Nicaragua. The Garifuna are a Central American, Afro-Indigenous people born of the Caribbean and watched over by loyal ancestors. Worldwide the pan-Garifuna community numbers about three hundred to four hundred thousand; they inhabit communities along the Caribbean coast of Central America, including one hundred thousand who live in the United States and Canada.[2] The Garifuna are a hybrid group who emerged as a people a couple of hundred years ago on the Caribbean island of St. Vincent from the intermarriage of shipwrecked West Africans destined to be sold as slaves, escaped slaves, and local Indigenous groups, the Arawak and Red Caribs. The Garifuna ended up in Honduras when exiled there by the British in 1796, and their diaspora continued from there to include Garifuna communities along the Caribbean coast of Central America, including Nicaragua, the focus of this book. The diasporic movement of Garifunas seeking work and moving around the region is a constant trait; it is described frequently in the historical accounts and also in present-day scholarship.

The Nicaraguan Garifuna and their persistence as a people inspire this research project and ethnography; though they form part of the pan-Garifuna community and share many practices with the broader Garifuna community, their story is different from other Garifuna communities given the particular historical, political, and economic context of the Nicaraguan Caribbean coast. Little has been published internationally about the Nicaraguan Garifuna as the major scholarship about the Garifuna has focused on Honduras and Belize. This book expands research and scholarship about the coastal populations of the Nicaraguan Caribbean because most of the research that has been carried out has focused on Indigenous or Afro-descendant or Creole communities, not on the Afro-Indigenous group called the Garifuna. This book focuses on the Garifuna in Nicaragua, an Afro-Indigenous community that is often ignored, even discriminated against by other groups on the Caribbean coast, for its small size, isolation, and marginalization.

We are honored to have been invited into the Garifuna community of Orinoco and other communities on Pearl Lagoon, Garifuna communities in Honduras, and Garifuna communities in the New York City area where we have observed their sustained persistence to embrace what it means to be Garifuna. These conversations, relationships, scary boat trips, and interminable rides in 4x4 vehicles have become a hemispheric journey. In Orinoco, folks talked about the other Garifuna communities on Pearl Lagoon. So, we visited Marshall Point, Brown Bank, San Vicente, and La Fe. This raised questions in turn about all the youth and adults who have left their communities for Bluefields and other cities in Nicaragua as well as other parts of the Americas. From questions about who are the Nicaraguan Garifuna and how have they persisted since arriving in Nicaragua in the early 1900s, this research opened up new venues: what does Garifuna culture look like in other places? Will it resemble what we've come to know and love in Orinoco? So, we visited with Garifuna in other parts of Nicaragua, spent time in Honduras where the Garifuna originally landed in Central America back in the 1700s, and began to carry out research with Garifuna organizations, leaders, and people in the Bronx and then Brooklyn, most of whom were from Garifuna communities in Honduras. We use the term transmigration to refer to Garifuna migration because often they maintain relationships with communities of origin through regular visits home, donations to community priorities, or choosing to retire in their communities of origin after decades working abroad.[3]

In the course of the research and writing of this book, which started in 2015 and has involved more than nine months of fieldwork (see chapter 7 for more information about our research methods), we have spent the majority of our time with Garifuna communities in Nicaragua and visited Garifuna communities in other

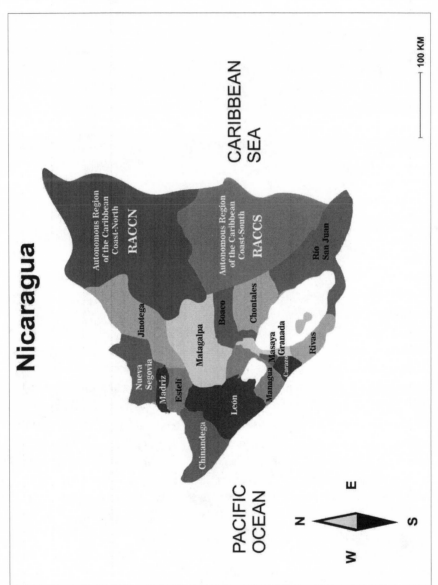

Nicaragua

Courtesy of the Universidad Centroamericana-Managua.

countries while becoming more and more concerned about the current political crisis unfolding in Nicaragua and how it is affecting minoritized groups like the Garifuna on the Caribbean coast. Though not the focus of this book, many were surprised by the protests calling for Nicaraguan President, Daniel Ortega, to step down. Our research team, on the other hand, hasn't been surprised at all because we've been carrying out research in a different Nicaragua: the Nicaraguan Caribbean, the part of the country that is used primarily for natural resource extraction, and where settlers—peasants, farmers, and land investors—are moving onto the land of local communities at an unprecedented rate. We've been documenting these tensions for a while, tracking examples of disillusionment, distrust, apathy, and even fear of the government.

Why Nicaragua? Why the Caribbean coast? Why the Nicaraguan Garifuna? Nicaragua is the second poorest country in the Americas after Haiti, and the poorest region of Nicaragua is the Caribbean coast. "The [Nicaraguan Caribbean] coast is also an ethnically diverse region, where indigenous peoples, afro-descendants, and mestizos coexist, comprising 12 percent of the country's population."[4] The Caribbean coast is home to at least six different ethnic groups including Afro-descendent Creoles, Afro-Indigenous Garifuna, and Miskitu, Mayagna, and Rama Indigenous groups along with mestizos from the Pacific coast. Annexed by the Nicaraguan state in 1894, the Caribbean coast retains a legal status of autonomy, recognized officially as two autonomous regions, south and north,[5] called the Autonomous Region of the Caribbean Coast–South (RACCS for its acronym in Spanish) and the Autonomous Region of the Caribbean Coast–North (RACCN). A common theme throughout the history of the Caribbean coast of Nicaragua is the extraction of natural resources or taking of Caribbean territories for colonial, neocolonial, or national interests. Though not the focus of this book, this is exemplified by the different international interests and national elites who have attempted to build a canal through the southern region of the coast to connect to Lake Nicaragua and out to the Pacific coast. In the mid-nineteenth century, U.S. mercenary William Walker declared himself president of Nicaragua in order to grant concessions for the building of a canal. Though this did not happen, Nicaragua was considered as a site for a canal up until the decision to build the Panama Canal in the early twentieth century. However, in 2013, the Nicaraguan government signed a contract with Wang Jing, a Chinese billionaire, to give his company rights to build an interoceanic canal across the country that would be bigger than the Panama Canal. "More than half of the canal route, 52% of its length, crosses the lands of indigenous and Afro-descendant people of the Caribbean Coast, specifically the territory of the Rama and Kriol people and of the Bluefields Creole community. The canal would also cross the territory of five indigenous communities on the Pacific coast side of the country."[6] Though construction has not moved forward, this plan has led to government repression of civilian protests, and multiple scientific research projects about the dangers of the project, and the deterritorialization of local Indigenous and Creole communities and communal lands.

Despite numerous legal protections on paper, 70 percent of Caribbean coast inhabitants live in extreme poverty and continue to face significant social and economic disadvantages.[7] Even with abundant natural and cultural diversity, the Caribbean coast suffers from isolation, poverty, and natural resource exploitation and depletion often exacerbated by state occlusion and foreign economic investment. The Nicaraguan Garifuna, in particular, have faced more isolation and discrimination than other groups on the Caribbean coast due to their late arrival to the coast (early 1900s) and their social position as rural and inferior to other groups on the coast. Furthermore, the inhabitants of Orinoco and the surrounding Garifuna communities of Pearl Lagoon find themselves confronting extractive market forces that have not brought corresponding benefits, but rather raised difficult questions for the Garifuna communities about how they will adapt and survive in this unfolding context. And yet, even with centuries of challenges and a current situation plagued by state repression, political uncertainty, poverty, and livelihood pressures, the Garifuna persist. This persistence is synergistic and flexible as the community changes to adapt to new challenges.

On our first trip as a research team—Father Chepe's first trip back to Orinoco since 1992—his former host mother told him, "this is not the same Orinoco that you knew in 1992."[8] Chepe's first trip to Orinoco from the capital of Managua took thirty-three hours in 1992. He took a bus at three in the morning that left Managua to cross the entire country on an unpaved road. When he arrived in El Rama in the afternoon, he boarded the Bluefields Express, a ferry that only left once it was full. He slung a hammock, patiently waiting for the boat to fill before it began to float slowly down the Rio Escondido. Once the ferry arrived in Bluefields, it was on to a sailboat that curved through narrow river channels and across Pearl Lagoon for another fourteen hours on the way to Orinoco. Just as with our 2015 journey, though, Father Chepe's first journey came to its end at the sight of Orinoco, a small village on the edge of the lagoon. Chepe found a small, economically impoverished town without electricity; nonetheless, the vibrancy of the community's commitment to Garifuna spiritual, environmental, and livelihood practices illuminated the small town. Like the Orinoco of 1992, which had survived the 1980s conflict between the Sandinistas and the Counterrevolutionary forces or *Contras*, the communities of Pearl Lagoon continue to face multifaceted and fast-moving changes signaling their incorporation into a globalized and interconnected world. Facing these changes requires adaptation and agility, stewarding natural resources, reminding neighbors to thank their ancestors, and negotiating with children to visit the bush and not just watch television. This is the persistence at the heart of the Garifuna people who continue to hear the beat of ancestor drums today.

SU–UCA–BICU

As a research team, our engagement with Orinoco and other Garifuna communities throughout the Americas has deep roots, but it was the relationship between our universities that brought us together and catalyzed this present research project. Our engagement with these issues emerges from the strategic partnership between two Jesuit universities, Seattle University (SU) and the Universidad Centroamericana (UCA) in Managua, and the partnership between the UCA and the Bluefields Indian and Caribbean University (BICU), a thriving public college system with eight branch campuses serving the Caribbean coast of Nicaragua.

For over twenty years, SU faculty and staff have participated in annual immersion trips to Nicaragua, slowly developing contacts and friendships with UCA professors and local nongovernmental organizations (NGOs). When Seattle University made global engagement a strategic priority in 2010, it made sense to learn more about the Universidad Centroamericana in Managua, their mission, and the possible interest at UCA in expanding exchanges and collaborations between faculty, staff, and students of both universities. Our two universities signed a memorandum of understanding in 2013, which in turn led to the creation of Seattle University's Central America Initiative, and soon after, we were making plans to try and get Father Chepe back to Orinoco. Our first step was to go to Bluefields to meet with the rector of the Bluefields Indian and Caribbean University, and that is when we met Leonard who had been teaching and leading community development and outreach efforts at BICU. Immediately, the conversation was alive with shared interest and a desire to see if the Garifuna communities of Pearl Lagoon might want to talk to us about persistence, survival, and cultural flourishing in the twenty-first century.

Why were Seattle University, the Universidad Centroamericana, and the Bluefields Indian and Caribbean University interested in a research project with the Garifuna? Jesuit universities like SU and the UCA form part of a global network of more than 190 colleges and universities animated by the teachings of St. Ignatius who founded the Jesuit order in 1534; within the Jesuit order and emergent for many member universities, there is an awareness of the importance of learning and sharing with other Jesuit universities around the world. Given the speed of communication and globalization today, our graduates need to be prepared for a world in which intercultural competencies and knowledge of other languages and cultures are needed to thrive in today's world. Furthermore, problems that the world faces today, such as poverty, environmental devastation, climate change, extremism, fascism, and conflict, will only be overcome through collaboration across difference at the global scale. Today, there is now a flourishing set of conversations going on between Jesuit universities in the global south and global north, and south-south and north-north.

In this vein, the UCA has been collaborating with the BICU since 2013 to see how they can support education on the Caribbean coast and help assure that degree programs at the BICU—such as Environmental Engineering, which doesn't have sufficient infrastructure for laboratories—can use UCA installations, for example. The BICU, on the other hand, is a public university with eight campuses on the Caribbean coast of Nicaragua (Bluefields, Puerto Cabezas, Rama, Corn Island, Pearl Lagoon, Waspam, Bonanza, and Paiwas), and given the population it serves, the communities of the Caribbean coast of Nicaragua, learning from Indigenous, Afro-Indigenous, and Afro-descendent communities is vital for a successful university. The BICU has been working to connect their curricular offerings with the needs of communities in the region to address the problem that once students from the communities graduate, they aren't able to find employment in their communities and end up seeking work in other places. This contributes to the youth drain of rural communities on the Caribbean coast. Both the BICU and the UCA recognize that offering degree programs that generate employment for graduates or address community needs in their communities of origin is an important step for universities to make to address the pressures of outbound migration, acculturation, and income generation that confront youth today on the Caribbean coast.

Relevance of Research

Given our universities' commitment to serving communities on the margins, this research with Nicaraguan Garifuna communities is obviously of great interest to the long-term inclusion and diversity efforts of all three universities. We also found it important to listen to community members about their priorities for their communities so that this research can be relevant to the communities where we've been carrying out the research. We explore this in greater detail in chapter 7 "Unlearning/Relearning: Decolonial Methodologies," in which we describe how our research serves Orinoco and other Garifuna communities, but suffice it to say that from the makeup of our research team, which includes a Garifuna researcher as well as a Nicaraguan researcher with years of work on the Caribbean coast to discussions of how this research can best serve the needs of the communities, we have come to two main uses for this research. First, this research about Garifuna persistence serves to raise awareness about the existence of the Garifuna in Nicaragua and brings attention to the persistence of Nicaraguan Garifuna communities even in the face of centuries of abandonment and discrimination by foreign colonial and neocolonial interests as well as internal colonization promoted by the Nicaraguan government. The survival of Indigenous, Afro-Indigenous, and Afro-descendant cultures, their persistence, the fact that they have not disappeared, is quite an achievement that this research attempts to convey. It is a Nicaraguan story that has not been broadly told. Second, though not the focus of this ethnography, this research about an understudied group, the Nicaraguan Garifuna, has generated important insights for our three universities about how small cultural groups persist and reconfirms our commitment to inclusion efforts and responsive programming in our respective institutions.

Regarding how this research is relevant to you, the reader, it depends on your location. Are you reading this book from the global north? If so, this book can provide you with insight into two issues that are vital to your society right now, the inclusion of people who have been historically dispossessed within the boundaries of your own countries, and the debates around immigration. Reading about the persistence of the Garifuna and how they re-create their cultural practices today is one example of how Indigenous groups around the world are persisting in the face of a colonizing past and a postcolonial present. It opens up the possibility that maybe a decolonial future awaits. Furthermore, if you're reading this book from the global north, you are aware of the debates around immigration. This book will serve to put a human set of experiences on the polemics, stereotypes, and statistics related to immigration. Many of the Central American Garifuna who have come to the United States, for example, regularly travel back to communities of origin: their main interest is a looping around the Americas to generate income and return home and then travel out again. Some came with visas and others came without. They made their way to the United States as part of their duty to their families and ancestors. As you read about Miss Rebecca and how warmly she received us into her house in Orinoco, consider how you have received immigrants from Central America and the Caribbean into your community.

Are you from the global south? Many of the same takeaways may apply to you. If you are from a privileged background or a dominant ethnicity, maybe you'll see how the inclusion of Indigenous or marginalized communities in your country could lead to new forms of leadership and contributions. Maybe this book will help humanize the immense contributions of Indigenous and Afro-descendant peoples and their ways of life. If you are from a marginalized background yourself, maybe this book will inspire your own persistence. Sometimes life's hardships can be survived, sometimes they can be resisted, and sometimes they can be converted into motivation to overcome the challenges that face us.

In this book, it is our aim to apply critical social theory in new ways so that the stories with which our research partners have honored us and the ethnographic detail we've written down coalesce into a resonant, thrumming *canto* to the persistence of Garifuna communities in Nicaragua, Central America, and the United States today.

Reading This Book

We have structured our book according to what it means to be Garifuna in Nicaragua and in the diaspora today. Garifuna sociologist, Leonard Joseph, opens the book with an introduction about what it means to be Garifuna. Simultaneously personal and ethnographic, Leonard introduces us to what it means to have grown up Garifuna. He also introduces us to the Garifuna communities of Pearl Lagoon to the north of Bluefields on the Caribbean coast of Nicaragua.

Rooted in the cultural practices of the Garifuna and routed through Central America and the United States, chapter 1 tells the history of the Garifuna and provides definitions and theories to analyze and celebrate Garifuna history both for the Nicaraguan Garifuna and other Garifuna communities in Central America.

Chapter 2 provides the main theoretical framework for the book: a decolonial intersectionality that simultaneously explains marginalization and agency. Applied to the Garifuna, this framework allows us to trace what forces they have survived and how they've persisted. Today, the Garifuna thrive through the use of strategies such as articulation, performance, and translation: three practical ways they (re)make and (re)create cultural practices, nurturing their connection to land, sea, and their ancestors.

Chapter 3 explores the source-touchstone of land, sea, and natural resources, the *root* of Garifuna culture, through observations and conversations with community members. Integral to most definitions of being Indigenous as well as what it means to be Afro-descendent, land—where ancestors are buried—and land and the nearby sea—where one was born and/or raised, where one learned to farm and fish, where today's community members and ancestors are/were nourished—is held communally by the Garifuna and worked by kin groups. In Nicaragua, these communal and ancestral lands are protected under the constitution and other laws, but like many other places in the world, Indigenous lands are vulnerable to settler incursion and extractive practices by elites, state interests, and international companies. Furthermore, these global/local, economic, and extractive processes are affecting Garifuna communities in Nicaragua and Honduras and further intensifying pressures to immigrate to cities and the United States.

The importance of nature is indispensable to Garifuna spirituality. Chapter 4 describes the spiritual practices of the Nicaraguan Garifuna in historical, diasporic, and present-day perspective. It is the believing in one's ancestors and honoring them that connects the Garifuna to each other, whether they are in Nicaragua, Honduras, Belize, or the United States, and it is honoring the ancestors that keeps the Garifuna returning home (where ancestors are buried) as often as possible as well as strengthening their connection and commitment to the stewardship of the land where their ancestors lived.

Chapter 5 focuses on the persistence of Garifuna youth who are pushed to leave the community if they are to support elders and survive themselves. "Should I stay or should I go?" is a constant refrain for Garifuna youth in Orinoco and the other Pearl Lagoon communities as they choose *routes* out of the community: ship out on cruise ships, seek employment in Central American cities, or emigrate out of the region to earn a living and support their parents.

Chapter 6 is particularly relevant for readers in the United States and other parts of the global north who want to understand dynamics behind Central American immigration to the United States. This ethnographic chapter introduces us to many men and women and their experiences of being Garifuna in diaspora. We argue that one of the keys to Garifuna persistence is the ability to survive and thrive in diaspora. Based on interviews with Garifuna families who live (or who have lived) in the New York City area, most of whom originally emigrated from Honduras, this ethnographic chapter explores the junctures and disjunctures of cultural persistence at great distances from communities of origin.

When Father Chepe and Serena studied social anthropology in the 1990s, research methods were often relegated to a paragraph in the introduction or a footnote that was seldom read. Given both the possibility of the impossible—that Indigenous cultures do persist (and even thrive) under the yoke of colonization (and its modern manifestations)—as well as the politics of fieldwork—centuries of colonial agendas being replicated sometimes (un)knowingly by social scientists—we dedicate chapter 7 to critically unpacking our research methods. Decolonial methods, critical reflexivity, and research with community participation are necessary for accompanying peoples on the margins.

Surviving the Americas

Garifuna Communities of the Caribbean Coast of Nicaragua

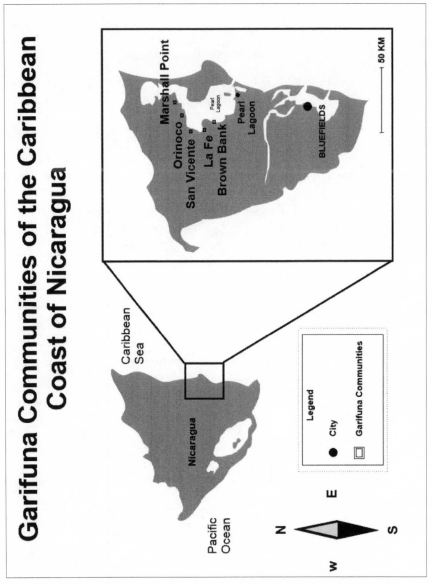

Courtesy of the Universidad Centroamericana-Managua.

Being Garifuna

Leonard Joseph Bent

The Founding of Orinoco and Garifuna Communities in Nicaragua

When I was growing up, I would hear the people saying that my great-great-grand-father was the founder of Orinoco, and that knowledge built a sense of pride and self-esteem in me. The founding of Orinoco all began when his father, my great-great-great-grandfather Joseph Sambola—because of the turmoil from the civil war in Honduras—decided to move out with his wife, Yape, nine sons, and two daughters, and sail southward, entering the Mosquitia Territory (today the Caribbean coast of Nicaragua). They arrived after two nights of travel to the Port of Graytown, south of Bluefields, an important port at that time.

According to my great-uncle Ivan and my great-aunt Marta, when great-great-great-grandfather Joseph Sambola reached Graytown, he and his family spent two to three months there, but they did not like the place, and so they decided to sail up north to Bluefields, the main city on the east coast of Nicaragua. There they met a kind old man, who gave them a place to stay, but they did not like the place either, because the water was deep and great-great-great-grandma Yape was afraid that her children would drown. And so they decided to move north, canoeing up rivers and across the lagoon, reaching the northern part of Pearl Lagoon, where they met another kind old man, who gave them a piece of land to live on. This place they liked, because the soil was good, so they decided to stay. This place's first name was Square Point, and later was given the name of San Vicente (St. Vincent), in honor of the place where the Ancestors came from, located in the Lesser Antilles Islands, or West Indies.

My great-uncle went on to say that the family lived lovingly and peacefully together in San Vicente for quite a long time. Joseph's sons and daughters got married and built themselves a family. John Sambola's wife Mrs. Marianna died in San Vicente, and that brought some sadness into the family. At one moment, there was an incident that took place between John's children and Joseph Jr.'s children that great-great-grandfather John did not like. And so, for the sake of peace and for the harmony of the family, he decided to leave the community and establish himself with his five daughters and the children of his stepdaughters on a little farm that

3

his good friend Mr. Garth gave him. This place first was known as Bear Point, and later on, great-great-grandfather John gave it the name of Orinoco in honor of the River Orinoco located in Venezuela, which is a name given by the Arawak people, a language that was also spoken by the natives in St. Vincent at the arrival of the Africans from Western Africa. Later on, Garifuna people came from nearby communities like Lauba, San Vicente, La Fe, and even Honduras and established themselves in the community. According to the information given, Orinoco was founded in the year 1912, around the same time of the founding of other Garifuna communities that still surround the Pearl Lagoon today. It changes a bit from person to person, but they say the years of founding are San Vicente in 1908, Brown Bank in 1905, and La Fe in 1906.

My Childhood and Youth

During my childhood it was delightful for me to visit the communities. It was so good and enjoyable to see and be near nature. I can remember when leaving Bluefields in my father's little dugout boat, or my uncle's barge boat, to go to Pearl Lagoon and then to Orinoco, Brown Bank, La Fe, San Vicente, or Marshall Point, we would pass by areas rich in flora with leafy vegetation. We could see a lot of *yolillos* (yolk trees), mangroves, lilies, orchids, coco plum, pine trees, maypole trees, oak trees, and other timber trees. We would also pass by areas rich in fauna, observing pelicans, albatross, herons, crocodiles, alligators, howler monkeys, squirrel, varieties of birds, and some snakes (poisonous and nonpoisonous ones).

We would ride across wide rivers and narrow rivers with crystal waters. In some areas we would take our bucket and fetch water to drink, so fresh and clean. When getting in the lagoon in the Pearl Lagoon area, the water was crystal clear and turquoise. We could see to the bottom where white sand and green grass served as food for manatees and fish. In the lagoon there were varieties of fish in abundance—snook, copper mouth, bass, catfish, jack, mackerel, tarpon, shark, swordfish, junefish, dolphins, turtle, and stingray.

Travelling from Pearl Lagoon to Orinoco for us kids was sometimes scary, and sometimes full of joy. It was scary during the months of June through December, because of the bad weather with boisterous waves that would threaten our boat, and then enjoyable during January through May because of the calm lagoon. We usually traveled during the day, but sometimes went at night. If we traveled at night, then our compass would be the North Star that led directly to Orinoco. The distance between Pearl Lagoon and Orinoco is approximately fifteen kilometers across the open waters of the lagoon.

When arriving to Orinoco, practically the entire community would come to the landing to receive us and give us warm embraces of welcome, and inquire about how family members who were left behind were doing. There would be long conversations, accompanied by meals with hot herbal tea. Orinoco was a small, quiet community. I still remember that during my childhood, the community had only two divisions (what some today call neighborhoods). There was the exclusive Up Town, where the founder of Orinoco, John Sambola, and his family lived, and the Down Town, where newer community members had built their homes. Great-great-grandfather John Sambola selected a certain portion of land and provided it to people and families who were migrating to the community in search of a place to live. As families continued arriving in Orinoco, the descendants of Ancestor John continued with the practice of their Father, since they had learned to be hospitable like him. The family name of the first family was Sambola, then came other families: Flores, Velásquez, Arana, Zenón, and Estrada. These first arrivals included approximately two hundred people, then López, Casildo, González, Crisanto, and Centen arrived, and today the community has approximately two thousand people and continues to grow. Almost 80 percent of the population of Orinoco has a family bond with one of these families.

I remember that most of the houses were built of a certain kind of palm tree, called Sconfra (by its name in English), or of a kind of wild cane. One of these materials was used to lift the walls, which were then lined with mud, creating a kind of adobe house. The roof was lined with palm so skillfully that not even a drop of water entered when it rained. Later the adobe houses were replaced by wooden houses, mostly with palm roofs and raised on stilts, with their detached kitchens and hearths that used firewood cut from fallen and dried trees. The atmosphere of the houses was fresh, clean, and spacious enough to accommodate the whole family in a comfortable way; there was always joy inside those houses.

Coming to spend holidays in Orinoco was a lot of fun. To the east of the community (on the way to Marshall Point), about fifty meters from my grandmother's house was a stream of crystalline waters with a sandy bottom and small stones. We considered it a beauty, the best pool that could be found throughout the region. For a large part of the day we stayed there, hanging and swaying on vines and then jumping into the water. At other times we walked to the shore of the beach when our uncles, aunts, and community members went fishing. When they threw the nets to catch the abundant *chacalines* (shrimp) that jumped on the beach, we captured them and did what we called "play cook." We got yucca, malanga, banana, and breadfruit, which we cooked in coconut milk with shrimp and fish. When it was time to eat, our dishes were accompanied by *ereba* or *bami* (cassava bread). We caught the fish from along the shore, and what a life we had: our vacations meant enjoying everything to the fullest.

I remember very well that in Orinoco during the time of my childhood and youth, the community lived by the value of "hand go and hand come." This was a practice of mutual help in which all families and the community supported each other, a community participation that was cheerful and conscious. It was a family subsistence economy characterized by fishing, agriculture, and hunting. These practices were carried out in a sustainable manner, making use of only what was necessary. There was no practice of exploitation, but rather taking only what was needed. I still remember how the men would throw nets from the shore into the water to get the shrimp that arrived in abundance. It was not necessary to climb into the boats, though when they did use the boats, shrimp fishing was done on the shore of the community and with appropriate nets, catching a quantity considered suitable for consumption. The aquatic and wild life was rich; natural resources existed in abundance. How I long for those times.

I liked to come to Orinoco to be with my great-grandmother, whom I considered a beautiful and affectionate person. I still carry her image in my mind. She was a woman who took care of herself in such a way that even at one hundred she looked pretty young, smiling brightly, sometimes with her pipe in her mouth. In the evening, sitting on the railing of the house and contemplating the vast lagoon of crystalline waters, with eyes fixed south toward Pearl Lagoon and west toward La Fe and San Vicente, we talked, us young people and Grama Daa (the nickname of great-grandmother Susan Flores Sambola). She would tell us stories told by her father and her grandfather about the life and culture of the Garifuna. She told us about our origins on the Island of San Vicente—she told us that the community of San Vicente in Pearl Lagoon, was thusly named in order to remember the Island where they came from—and how the ancestors migrated to Honduras, and her grandfather, who was a lover of peace and desire for the well-being of the family, decided to come to Nicaragua. She spoke of the lived experiences of the ancestors in San Vicente, then in Honduras. She spoke of their struggles for survival. She talked about the difficulties they went through and how they had to leave relatives behind. She also told us stories and riddles. Usually the session ended with songs and music sung by our uncles, who with their banjos and handmade guitars filled the evening with song.

At night, under the light of the lamp, with the smell of tobacco from the cigars that some smoked with a cup of tea of aromatic leaves (like sweet lemon, orange, cow foot, basil, lemon grass, and mint), accompanied with bread made of wheat flour, coconut milk, and coconut hatch, the family gathered to discuss the experiences of the day. They talked about those who went to the field to sow, about how many yucca bushes or malanga or *quiquisque* they planted. They talked about how many pieces of land they managed to use, and the time they spent working. They shared experiences about how many snakes they saw and killed, that they saw a deer and let it escape, or that they caught the smell of a herd of wild boar and so they had to take precautions in case these animals came to attack them. Those who went fishing talked about how many fish they caught, how many got away, and how some large fish challenged them during their catches. They talked about who was the most expert in fishing. But they also talked about how the moon, the stars, and the wind were signals to make weather predictions for the next day, and if conditions would be good to sail the next day or not. There was talk about ancestors and wisdom instilled through oral tradition. There was always an elder who gave the final directions that were put to the vote on who would take part in the activities of the next day. In the conversation they emphasized the importance of the unity that must exist between them.

During the night and especially during the moonlit nights, we listened to the guitars, banjos, and the singing of the adults who began to celebrate or simply animate the atmosphere in the community. It served as a relaxing moment after a day of work either on the lagoon or in the bush. And on special occasions there was also the sound of the drum, which was played as a reminder of community life and to strengthen the spirituality that our ancestors instilled in us. I remember the song: "Saraya Bungiu, Saraya Bungiu." I have only recently understood what it means: God has risen, God has risen.

The elders spoke among themselves in the Garifuna language; however, when they spoke to us, they spoke in Creole English, and this had a negative influence on communication to such a degree that I did not learn the Garifuna language. Furthermore, there are almost no books or documents written in Garifuna of their lived experience, as the system of transmission of culture and history was oral.

When our ancestors were in Honduras, we followed the Catholic religion. However, due to the presence of the Anglican Church, which arrived before Catholicism to Orinoco, we began to practice this religion. When Catholicism was established in the Pearl Lagoon region, the majority returned to profess the Catholic religion, combining with it myths, legends, rites, and practices that came from San Vicente to Honduras and then to Nicaragua.

How can I forget the positive influence of the Catholic and Anglican Churches in the lives of the community? We participated in the masses celebrated by priests who came from Bluefields or Delegates of the Word who lived in the community. There was respect for the sacredness of Sundays, and there was a collective aware-ness that all families should participate in the masses. Sundays were set aside to worship God, and to communicate with ancestors through reflection and dialogue within the family. There was a silence in the community, and if people left their homes it was to visit relatives, sick people, or the cemetery where the ancestors rest. Prayer was something important in the home. There was a need to pray for food and before going to bed to seek the protection of God and the ancestors over us and in rising to thank God and the ancestors for the new day.

My great-grandmother Daa talked to us a lot about God, saying that He was our creator, and that He created everything for us to enjoy, but in a good way: that we should not be selfish, but always think of others. She told us that the Garifuna are a very spiritual people and that this manifests itself through the respect we must have toward nature and the respect we must have among ourselves. She told us that, as human beings created by God, we have to practice and foster a good relationship between ourselves and nature. Garifuna spirituality is based on the unity between us, and the respect we must have toward nature. Great-grandma Daa said that it is this legacy that our ancestors left us. That is why there was always a practice of taking from nature only what is necessary. Older adults told us that we must take care of nature, not destroy it. Another important lesson about the ancestors that both great-grandmother Daa and the elders of the community told us was that when they went to their resting places, they still protect us from where they are. They told us that they watch us so that nothing and nobody hurts us, and that if we want protection, we must respect and honor their memories.

In the community we celebrated ceremonies and rituals inherited from the ancestors that originated in Africa, the homeland, myths that reminded us of where we come from. Some examples were: the *walagallo* ceremony or *dügü*. This ceremony is performed when Western medicine can no longer do anything for the health of a community member. As part of spirituality, through dreams, ancestors communicate with sick people or relatives of sick people, orienting them about how to perform this ceremony to heal the evil they suffer. This ceremony was only done during a person's illness. The combination of faith in the healer, who is known as the *sukia* or *buyei*, , and in the sacred sound of the drum, which penetrates the deepest part of the being, cured the sick of the ills they suffered. Great-great-grandfather John Sambola was a buyei, a man of many sciences (a man with high science), and there were other relatives who were buyei.

The spirituality of our ancestors was also reflected in the death ceremony, which did not commemorate the end of life, but the continuity of life, as one dies to live a different life. I remember how when a person died, there was a lot of respect for the dead. The first sign was solidarity toward the family of the deceased. There were people who voluntarily prepared the dead for their journey to eternity. The families of the community shared with the family of the dead to make food, bread, and drinks for people who would come to their house to express condolences and spend the night in vigil. Almost all the men in the community organized to build the coffin and others to dig the grave and prepare the deceased's resting place. After the nine days of death, the "nine night" ceremony was held. In this ceremony, there were religious songs, people congregated to talk about the person who had gone and remember them, and then relatives would share their experiences about the meeting that they had had with the dead in their dreams. At midnight, as was the custom, they placed the body on the bed and bid their final goodbyes to the dead as they went to their eternal rest, where they would continue to protect the community.

Cemeteries were considered sacred places, and they had to be kept clean and well cared for, because in that place rest the ancestors who protect us. At the head was the ancestor John Sambola, the one who carried the greatest respect, and the one who forged a community for the people. Another important aspect is the deep respect for the elderly in the community. They were central figures in the community—the people with the highest level of knowledge—and they were the living books to be consulted.

I remember when ethical, moral, and cultural values were the note of the day. These were community, collective work, humility, community justice, respect, tolerance, self-esteem, solidarity, hope, and courtesy. Not only relatives were responsible for the formation of the personality of individuals, but the entire community felt responsible for individual and collective formation. The process of education and socialization transcended the family. The entire community was involved, since one of the essential aspects of Garifuna spirituality is unity.

And how could I not remember the succulent dishes prepared by our grandmother and aunts during our visits to the community? Ancestral culture always manifested itself in food, based on products from the land and the lagoon like fish, malangas, bananas, and cassava. With the products that nature and work in the countryside offered us, we were able to feed and strengthen ourselves, so that people in the community lived a long life. Some foods of the ancestors were bami or ereba, also known as cassava bread, a kind of food that can last for months and was a meal for long trips outside the community. Bami is the word that the Garifuna communities of Pearl Lagoon call this staple, whereas in the broader Garifuna diaspora, it is called ereba. The *judut* meal was made with bananas and fish in sauce. The *pulali* was a kind of sweet atole or gruel, prepared with flour and dumplings. The *cuncante* was a dried banana atole made with flour. The *fufu* was a kind of dumpling prepared with crushed malanga or banana and cooked in coconut milk with seafood. Some drinks were made with rice and ginger, and there was the medicinal *giffiti*, an alcoholic beverage made with rum and herbs, that was consumed in moderation, especially during the walagallo ceremony.

In Orinoco, young people enjoyed good childhoods, and they spent their time in schools, working around the home, fishing, and spending time in the bush. They used their time well, and were productive. Always attentive and willing to collaborate in areas where they were useful. We also had our space for sports; the most interesting were baseball and volleyball.

It should be noted here that before 1979 on the Atlantic coast, today known as the Caribbean coast of Nicaragua, the economic system imposed was that of an enclave of the United States. In this model, U.S. companies received land concessions without having to pay taxes to the government and imported their own infrastructure to extract natural resources or grow bananas in order to then sell the products outside of the country. The natural resources (the bush, the sea, and the minerals) were exploited by transnational corporations through economic concessions, which included a cheap workforce that enjoyed few social services. The results were poverty, at times extreme poverty, and disease. Resource exploitation was less in Pearl Lagoon and the surrounding communities due to the good practices that existed there; since the natural resources were used in a sustainable manner, there was a common awareness that there should be a harmonious relationship between human beings and nature, which was one of the main teachings of the ancestors.

What Does It Mean to Be Garifuna Today?
And What Is Orinoco Like Today?

The Garifuna are a population that over the years have managed to survive through adversities due to our persistence and resistance. We have adapted to the different situations that life poses. From our adversaries we have appropriated the practices that we consider positive for our own human and community development.

After the death of my great-grandmother Susan Flores (Daa), who died at 104, I stopped going to Orinoco on a regular basis. Now that I have begun to return, I see some things are similar, but I also see changes in the land, and in spiritual and cultural practices. The physical transformations can be seen in the water of the lagoon where the community was first established. The water becomes cloudy during the winter, a product of the land erosion caused by the abundant logging by timber companies, in addition to the advance of the agricultural frontier with *colonos* (mestizo settlers migrating to the Caribbean coast of Nicaragua from the Pacific) who occupy communal lands to establish cattle farms, and unscrupulous landowners who have established large commercial farms in the area. The Orinoco community itself has grown territorially. There has also been physical growth for the new Garifuna families that have become independent from their relatives and have sought their own places or spaces to settle. Whereas before Orinoco had two neighborhoods, it currently has five neighborhoods. Many houses that had been built with local materials, such as wood and palm leaf roofs, have been replaced by concrete houses, and many of them resemble urban houses and buildings. About 60 percent of the homes are made of concrete now, made mostly by those who left the community with two objectives in mind: those who go away to work so they can earn money to come back and build a vacation home in Orinoco, or those who do it to save money so that they would come back to invest in a small business in the community.

In terms of social dynamics, when I return to the community of Orinoco, I find that it has been growing in population, a product of the growth of the families themselves that have sons and daughters who have formed their own homes. Population growth is a complex issue, and the increase is due in part to the many births that result from the lack of birth control and sex education for youth and adults both at home and in schools. On the other hand, there are human settlements on the periphery of the community. Some of these are colonos who have invaded Garifuna lands, while other *campesinos* have been warmly received in the community and have established good relations with the community.

Due to population growth, we find a community with little space between homes: fenced properties with few recreational spaces. Now many families think in individual terms (my lot or piece of property) and no longer think in collective terms nor in terms of a community that has the teachings of the ancestors. Many of the homes are built upon pieces of land inherited from ancestors, but in Orinoco there are fences now that surrounded those pieces of land, dividing the families from one another. Companies that sell timber and fishery products have been established in the Pearl Lagoon basin. As part of their regular operations, these companies provide financial resources on the basis of personal and collective credit and equipment such as fishing tools and equipment for sawing wood, then they buy products by volume from the community. I find that the commercial relationship has impacted the subsistence economy of families, since these resources have severely affected local resource management over time. Companies installed in the area do not have enough capacity to employ a good number of residents of the communities, so young people have found themselves having to migrate to Bluefields, Managua, or Corn Island, or shipping out on cruise ships in search of work.

In relation to the spiritual transformation that is happening today in Orinoco, I see that globalization, internal colonialism, and neoliberalism are permeating the identity and culture of the Garifuna People of Orinoco and surrounding communities. The most valuable ancestral practice of mutual help and the unity and respect toward nature are being attacked by individualism, selfishness, and greed, which characterize this new order. Elders are leaving us, and in relation to the generational change, little emphasis is placed at home on the relationship between God, human beings, and nature, as that relationship is replaced by a more material culture. The love of nature has been relegated behind the love of money, which promotes those with economic resources, so nature is exploited and not taken care of due to the pursuit of financial gain.

We find today a community where ancestral worship has not disappeared, but has been pushed to the background. Many youth are closing themselves off to the spaces where the ancestors can reveal themselves in dreams. Our ceremonies and rituals inherited from the ancestors are hardly practiced. They do not have the same values as before, and in many cases they are unknown to the new generation. Ancestral cultural values of great importance are not integrated into the educational system.

The community is bombarded by ultraconservative religious ideologies that reject the spirituality and many of the cultural practices of the Garifuna people. Before, there were only two churches, the Catholic and Anglican, which were respectful of the spirituality of the people, and the Garifuna people had fused elements of these churches with our ancestral religion. Today there are five new churches competing to establish themselves in the community. Our ritual ceremonies and our myths are no longer practiced with that previous fervor, and this is partly due to the fear that believers of these new religions have of being punished for doing so. But it is also due to the lack of unity and solidarity, practices that connected our identity in the community. There was a time before where the resources and the will necessary to carry out these ceremonies were jointly assumed by the families. Now it is not the case, and the ceremonies such as the walagallo or dügü or the "nine night" are seen as too expensive, and many families do not have the economic means to perform them.

What Are the Other Garifuna Communities of Pearl Lagoon Like Today?

Orinoco, a town of some 1,600 residents at the northern tip of the Pearl Lagoon, shares its struggle with the other, smaller Garifuna communities that surround Pearl Lagoon, yet there are some notable differences between Orinoco and these smaller communities. Brown Bank, La Fe, San Vicente, and Marshall Point all share a proximity to the lagoon that serves as the primary means of subsistence. Many men and women spend their days in rowboats or pangas with outboard engines or trudging through waist-high water, fishing for turtle, crab, and shrimp in the lagoon. Concrete homes, an immediate indicator of migration and economic growth via remittances that are a common sight in Orinoco, are few and far between in these smaller communities. Whereas over 60 percent of the houses

Figure 1. Garifuna Communities in Nicaragua
(information gathered in situ by Leonard Joseph Bent in September 2019)

Name of community	Date of founding	Name of founder	Present-day population	Present-day number of houses
Orinoco	1912	John Sambola	1,600	153
Marshall Point		Unknown	50	11
La Fe	1906	Lino López	180	35
San Vicente	1908	Joseph Sambola	47	14
Brown Bank	1905	Fedrick Blandford	187	35

in Orinoco are made from concrete, these smaller, more isolated communities are over 80 percent homes made of wood, raised on large posts and roofed with dry palm branches. As residents of these communities rely very little on remittances sent back from those who have migrated out of the communities, they find subsistence in the lagoon and earn small amounts of additional income from food raised on the land. The land is a key connection to the ancestors, as the land they are on today comes from the first inhabitants of the land. Furthermore, the land serves as a key space within which community ties are maintained. "Separation from *solar* to *solar* does not exist, because we are interconnected, we're one family," noted a community member in La Fe.[1] While all of the communities have *solares familiares* (family plots) on which they produce cassava, coconut, plantains, watermelon, squash, avocado, and other staples, the smaller communities have not built fences around these plots as has occurred in Orinoco. However, the challenges of declining community solidarity as noted in Orinoco still impact the fence-free land. As one woman in La Fe explained, "Before, we used to practice the hand-to-hand system, you give to me and I give to you. We still practice this a little but not as it was in the time of the ancestors. They were different than us."[2]

The promulgation of Law 445, which recognized Afro-Indigenous rights to communal land ownership of the Caribbean coast of Nicaragua, was cited in all of the communities as crucial legal support for their ancestral claims to these territories. However, they all also commented on the arrival of colonos to their lands, with ensuing tensions over different ways of relating to the land. Whereas many of the Garifuna rotated land to be used in a given growing season, intentionally leaving some land fallow in order to regenerate the fertility of the soil for future seasons as their ancestors did, many of the colonos come with strong commercial interests that clash with that particular relationship with the land. The overexploitation of land in search of commercial profits has reduced the quality of land available for production of important staples. Furthermore, when members of the community come together to try to prevent these exploitative practices, they confront the repressive forces of the Nicaraguan state. In one of the communities, a community member complained of a moment when "we stopped a shipment of *granadillo* wood that had been illegally harvested, and when we complained to the police, they threatened us instead of protecting us and our land."[3]

The challenge of the colonos is exaggerated by a sense of lost connection with the ancestors. As multiple community members in San Vicente and La Fe expressed, "We didn't learn the language, because our ancestors didn't teach it to us, and that led to our challenges today. . ." Another noted, "I wish the ancestors were alive so I could ask them so many things. . ."[4] Though the smaller Garifuna communities surrounding Pearl Lagoon still live on land inherited by their ancestors and this land is free of the fences that serve as a symbol of the fraying of Garifuna unity in Orinoco, significant challenges remain in Brown Bank, La Fe, and San Vicente. However, many still proudly profess their Garifuna heritage, and sustain themselves with the same food as their ancestors, grown on land that connects them across time.

Conclusion

Although we are experiencing these transformations, I can proudly say that we are a people with a positive culture. Our music, our dance, our drums, generate positive energy. We have a positive outlook. We believe in life here and after and have a positive attitude toward life. We do not see life as without hope. We see life with hope, and we see the future with hope. We believe that we will live forever. We believe in the ancestors. We believe that they are watching over us from the "place of the ancestors."

We the Garifuna people are proud of our identity. Historically the different groups of peoples on the Caribbean coast of Nicaragua have been discriminated against, and this is common knowledge for those of us who are from here. However, the Garifuna people pay less attention to this national attitude toward us, and this is because we are strongly identified with our culture. We love our culture, we love who we are and hold it in high self-esteem, which is manifested in our history, dance, songs, food, and rituals. Over the years, because of this discriminatory behavior toward us, we find that some people are ashamed, and some even hide their identity. Yet today there is a process of cultural revitalization that is being carried out by the various nations or peoples. This process is moving more rapidly among us than that of other cultures, and this is so because we value strongly our cultural heritage and ancestral knowledge.

Our identity as a people is more ingrained among us, the Garifuna. There is no border. We the Garifuna people from Honduras, Belize, Guatemala, the Bronx, and Nicaragua are one people. We are one great family. We interact naturally as a big brotherhood and sisterhood. We are the same people, the same family, and the sense of unity prevails in us.

We are a people with strong spirituality. Because of the Spanish colonization in Honduras, with their dominant Catholic religion, the majority of Garifunas are Catholic. However, the Catholicism practiced by the Garifuna is different from the Catholicism practiced by mestizos, since it is a blending of Catholicism with African and Indigenous religion. It is a survival mechanism in which the Garifuna people camouflage their religion with that of Catholicism. For example, we have a ceremony called dügü also known as walagallo. It is a ceremony of the ancestors combined with Catholic religion. Another example is the use of the drums in church worship. The drums for us the Garifuna people have a different meaning than that of the mestizo Catholics. A Garifuna mass is different from a mestizo mass.

Knowing my identity has allowed me to have greater clarity about the spirit of persistence that characterizes us as a people. This tells me that in spite of the fact that we are small in number, we are a great people and have a lot to offer to the world. We are a people, with cultural and spiritual values, which can be shared with other cultures. The struggle of our ancestors has taught us to value life in its fullness, to love nature, to be mutually supportive, and to have a sense of solidarity. Knowing our identity has helped us to choose the side of the weak and the outcast.

Despite threats from globalization and neocolonialism, Orinoco and its surrounding communities can get up again as always, but we will need solidarity and accompaniment. Let us make our spirit of persistence and resistance not only serve to accommodate survival, but to serve as an inspiration for a significant change in the lives of communities, and an example of struggle for other peoples who need to get ahead in the middle of adverse situations.

The struggle for true freedom against the evil force that has camouflaged itself as benevolent in the last three decades has come. We need to overturn the forces that marginalize, discriminate, exploit, and rip away the resources that the people need for their survival. The task is arduous and needs the participation of all of us. We need to take a stand. Now is the time for radical solidarity and radical transformation, and it all begins with each one of us. Each one of us needs to empty ourselves to find a space for that solidarity. So, brothers and sisters, it doesn't matter where you come from, you have a role to play in Garifuna persistence.

CHAPTER ONE

Persisting: *Garifuna Histories*

Serena Cosgrove and José Idiáquez

"I will shamelessly state that I want to stand rooted to the earth, growing outward, in a dialogue that is not unfixed, or destabilised, or blowing rootless in the winds of a globalised scape. Instead of a place that is rootless, I want to take root, and to regrow into a voice that is earthed."[1]
—IRENE WATSON, "Aboriginal Sovereignties: Past, Present and Future (Im)Possibilities"

"Given the crises facing an unequal, overpopulated, environmentally ravaged planet today, the survival of small societies that maintain, or at least aspire to, some degree of social balance and responsible local attachment is, in itself, an achievement."[2]
— JAMES CLIFFORD, *Returns: Becoming Indigenous in the Twenty-First Century*

Introduction

We're writing about an impossibility that is a possibility. Groups like the Garifuna of Nicaragua have faced and continue to face a series of obstacles; certainly, the slave trade and the disastrous effects of colonization placed limits on their survival as a people as well as the marginalization and repression of the present-day government of Nicaragua. And yet, they persist. Today, there are five Garifuna villages or communities in Nicaragua—Orinoco, San Vicente, La Fe, Marshall Point, and Brown Bank—around the Pearl Lagoon basin, north of Bluefields, and today as in the past, there is extensive outbound migration seeking employment. It is estimated that the entire Nicaraguan Garifuna population numbers around five to six thousand with most Garifuna living in Bluefields, Managua, and other places in Nicaragua. There are Garifuna communities in Honduras, Guatemala, and Belize; there are 100,000 to 200,000 Garifuna in the United States,[3] most of them living in the Bronx and Brooklyn in New York City with Garifuna strongholds also in New Orleans, Houston, and Los Angeles.[4]

Throughout this book, we refer to the Garifuna as an Afro-Indigenous people— both an Indigenous and an Afro-descendant people—with an attachment to the natural world of Pearl Lagoon where their ancestors are buried. The specific and localized or spatially situated part of their identity is particularly important for the Garifuna in Nicaragua because they have a spiritual and a livelihoods connection to the land and sea—something that is informed by both their Indigenous and Afro-descendant heritage. The term Indigenous is itself informed by a rich debate, and multiple overlapping definitions exist: some created by original peoples themselves (peoples living in places before colonizers arrived) and others by international agencies attempting to protect Indigenous rights. Commonalities between the definitions include a long-term commitment to a place and ways of knowing and being in the world that are different than Western ones. Linda Tuhiwai Smith, a Maori researcher, explains that Indigenous peoples "is a term that internationalizes the experiences, the issues and the struggles of some of the world's colonized peoples. . . They share experiences as peoples who have been subjected to colonization of their lands and cultures, and the denial of their sovereignty, by a colonizing society."[5] The plural of people, peoples, is important to the definition precisely because there is such a range of groups who identify as Indigenous: it is not one people we are talking about but many peoples. James Clifford adds that Indigenous peoples "are defined by long attachment to a locale and by violent histories of occupation, expropriation, and marginalization."[6] Key parts of this definition include common experiences of colonization and exclusionary treatment by colonizers.

Afro-descendant means that the people come from the involuntary diaspora of enslavement set in motion by the slave trade of the European colonial powers. "A review of the political economy of the European slave trade reveals that it was an inhuman act, precisely designed to create wealth for Europeans through exploitation of Africans. The slave trade also involved selling Africans as instruments of labor and as capital to finance the industrial revolution in Europe."[7] Between the fifteenth and nineteenth centuries, between 15 to 25 million West and Central African men, women, and children were brought to the Americas as part of the Atlantic slave trade.[8] This diaspora—an inhuman and horrific economic project that forcibly moved millions of people from their communities of origin into enslavement—has had global impacts whose effects are still felt today. "In using diaspora as a conceptual tool authors usually denote dispersed groups of African descent, descendants of peoples removed from the African continent who are racially Black."[9] The widespread contributions to Latin America and the Caribbean by peoples of African origin are significant "seeds of ancestral knowledge, philosophy, memory, and tradition, of resistance, and of and for life."[10] Because the Garifuna have their roots in both Afro-descendant and Indigenous cultures, they sometimes emphasize different aspects of their identities over others. For example, "Some evidence indicates that Garifuna have at times emphasized the indigenous component of their ancestry. Other evidence—such as Garifuna participation in

Marcus Garvey's Universal Negro Improvement Association in the 1920s suggests that at different moments they have adopted a Black racial identity."[11] In the case of the Garifuna in Nicaragua, identity as an Afro-Indigenous group is further complicated by the diversity of different ethnicities on the Caribbean coast. This is informed by the history of Indigenous leadership under the Miskitu, the role of the British challenging the Spanish for control over the Nicaraguan Caribbean coast, and the emergence of the ethnic group, the Creoles—descended from the progeny of British colonists and people of African descent. Explained in further detail below, this array of ethnicities is comprised of the following groups who live on the Caribbean coast today: Indigenous groups—Miskitu, Rama, Mayagna (formerly Sumo), and others, the Creoles, mestizos from the Pacific coast, and the Garifuna. Interestingly, the Garifuna share indigeneity with some groups and Afro-descendant identity with others; this, in turn, creates similarities and differences, points of convergence and divergence of identities and interests with all of these groups as we discuss below.

Our unpacking of what it means to be Garifuna today in Nicaragua comes from historical sources and our research participants. Some of our primary research protagonists from Orinoco, Nicaragua, include Mateo, Eric, Rebecca, and Kelsey, to mention a few.[12] To appreciate Mateo's healing powers as a bush doctor, it's vital to keep in mind that he never got the opportunity to go to school due to poverty and that he came of age during the Counterrevolutionary or Contra war (1980–1990). Mateo's life has been deeply marked by the Sandinista revolution, contradictory state policies, war, and exclusion. On a personal level, he struggled to find his path before he entered into ritual practices of ancestor worship, which entail daily contact with his ancestors and their guiding knowledge of the natural world and medicinal plants. Today he is a healer and spiritual leader in the community, and yet, he does not have a diploma or formal recognition for his skills. To appreciate Garifuna spirituality, as we learned, it's important to visit Mateo on the land his family cultivates outside Orinoco.

Similarly, comprehending the realities confronting Garifuna youth—such as Eric and Orson—requires understanding that the only way the elders can live in the community is for the youth to leave the community by "shipping out" on cruise boats, finding employment in call centers in Bluefields or Managua, or working in a hotel at a distant tourist destination—what Clifford calls "indigenous commuting"—to send money home.[13] This journeying to and fro, out and back, is an important component of Garifuna persistence. Though it means leaving (and looping back for visits), many have to leave to support those who stay, such as the elders and children.

Through our conversations with women community leaders in Orinoco, we've come to see that similar to Garifuna communities in other parts of Central

America,[14] the Garifuna in Nicaragua also have strong models of women's leadership. At the family and community level, women form strong bonds to support community survival when male family members are off earning money. Women participate in fishing and farming, frequently heading out of the village on foot or up the river in their dories to check on gardens. There are present-day challenges with gendered effects. Depredatory extractive practices have decimated fish and lobster stock which in turn have taken away Garifuna traditional income-generation activities, leaving some men playing cards on the dock. Garifuna women, on the other hand, take on entrepreneurial activities such as running stores and small hostels, and continue their farming in the bush to sustain their families. This dynamic was described to us by Kelsey, the daughter of a long line of Garifuna *sukias* (spiritual leaders), owner of a small hotel in Orinoco, and animator of the women's group that makes and sells traditional Garifuna food. In some cases, the inactivity of men and the attendant loss of income have led to alcoholism or use of other drugs, which can lead to increased levels of gender-based violence; in other cases, unemployment has led to new entrepreneurial developments such as Eric's drumming school and performances or Miss Rebecca's guest house.

This book aims to illuminate the Nicaraguan Garifuna journey to the impossible: their cultural persistence in the face of great odds. This chapter provides the reader with the historical context and the analytical framework to understand the "tensions, resonances, transformations, resistances, and complicities"[15] that emerge when analyzing the ethnographic data we've gathered about Garifuna everyday life, survival, and persistence in the Pearl Lagoon of Nicaragua and beyond.

A History of the Garifuna, a Different History of Nicaragua

For Nicaragua, history is usually told by mestizo (European descendant or mixed race) elites from the Pacific side of the country who have benefited from a dominant ideology that Nicaragua is universally mestizo.[16] Today, mestizos on the Pacific side of the country continue to administer and perpetuate a status quo that keeps the poor, Indigenous, and Afro-descendant communities at the margins, many of whom live on the Caribbean side of the country. On the Caribbean coast of Nicaragua, it is common to hear Afro-descendant people or Creoles, Indigenous people, and the Garifuna refer to the mestizos from the Pacific coast as *Pañas* or Spaniards, a sharp reminder that many on the Caribbean coast see mestizos from the Pacific coast as present-day conquerors and colonizers. In fact, mestizo migration to the Caribbean coast is on the rise throughout Central America: "This internal migration, leading to illegal land occupations in the newly demarcated and titled areas of indigenous and afro-descendant peoples, has created significant tensions and conflicts [on the coast]."[17]

Today's tensions have deep historical roots. The Garifuna became a people through the very emergence of the modern world system. Their ethnogenesis—or birth story as a people—is powerful and compelling: they are a hybrid culture from the island of St. Vincent in the Caribbean, born of the Indigenous Carib and Arawak peoples and shipwrecked West Africans intended to be sold as slaves in the Americas. "As early as 1612, European writers noted the appearance of a large number of Africans among the Carib war and trading parties. This population of Africans was progressively augmented by the wreck of one or several slave ships (for which several dates are given—1635, 1675, and 1742) and by the integration of African maroons from neighboring islands."[18] Survivors freed themselves from the wreckage of the ships and swam to shore. Kidnapped Africans destined for Caribbean plantations were abruptly thrown onto the shores and mercy of the Island Caribs of St. Vincent, an island, named but ignored by the Spanish. "Out of this sudden co-presence, an encounter not chosen by either group, a new synthetic ethnicity and religion—what Mary Helms (1969) called a 'colonial tribe'—was born."[19] People of African descent intermarried with Indigenous Red Caribs and Arawaks on the island and the first Garifuna were born. This co-existence led to intermarriage and children and the Garifuna as a people emerged, speaking Garifuna—a language informed by Indigenous Caribbean languages and by Yoruba in Western Africa, practicing a spirituality informed by the worship of ancestors, honoring the land and sea that had saved them, and demonstrating a fierce commitment to freedom and repudiation of slavery.[20]

During French and British disputes over St. Vincent, the Garifuna refused to leave their lands that had been taken from the French and given to the British in the Treaty of Paris in 1763.[21] This led to Garifuna conflict with the British who forcibly removed them from St. Vincent, first imprisoning them on the nearby, desolate island of Baliceaux, and then exiling them to Roatan off the coast of Honduras "some 1,700 miles to the northwest."[22] Authors Matthei and Smith summarize this period "as an ill-fated armed insurrection against the British colonizers... which resulted in their forced exile to a small island off the coast of Central America."[23] Very relevant to this book about the Garifuna of Nicaragua, the story of the Garifuna as a people or nation contains their most characteristic trait: a people born in movement, a diasporic people who continue their journey as time goes by. A little over two thousand Garifuna—including men, women, and children—arrived to Honduras, though it is believed that the pre-conflict population was between eight and nine thousand.[24] Upon arrival on Roatan, the Garifuna soon made their way to the coast of the Honduran mainland seeking fertile land for gardens and crops. Though many stayed in Honduras, the Garifuna continued to seek cultivatable land to grow cassava and access to the sea where they could fish;

this led to the eventual dispersal of the Garifuna along much of the Caribbean coast of Central America.[25]

When the Garifuna refer to the land, rivers, sea, and their ancestors, they do it with reverence and veneration. These are vital elements of their culture that have motivated their persistence and supported their survivance: the land bequeathed to them by watchful ancestors that has given them shelter and sustenance, the rivers and sea that have witnessed their trials and tribulations as well as providing them with sustenance, and their ancestors who watch over them. These phenomena are interconnected. The land holds the remains of the ancestors, and the accompaniment of the ancestors is also manifest through the bounty of land, rivers, and sea.

After Central American independence in the early 1800s, some Garifuna leaders in Honduras clashed with leaders of the Central American federation; thus began the movement of Garifuna to British Honduras, or what is today known as Belize, because the country was still under British rule.[26] During different periods of tension with the Honduran state, kin groups of Garifuna would leave for Nicaragua, Guatemala, and Belize: "It is likely that as [they] spread along the coast they moved in extended family groups headed by a 'captain' as they had on St. Vincent."[27] In the late nineteenth and early twentieth centuries, the first Garifuna families came to the Pearl Lagoon basin, north of Bluefields, on the Caribbean coast of Nicaragua as recounted by Leonard in the introduction of this book. "From [the] region [of the Caribbean coast of Honduras], sometimes known as Costa Arriba, Juan Sambola (possibly a descendant of the [Garifuna] war leader from St. Vincent) travelled to the shores of Pearl Lagoon to found the first Garifuna settlements in Nicaragua."[28] The Garifuna on the Caribbean coast of Nicaragua founded an initial community and then a second one as the families grew. "[Garifuna] migration to Pearl Lagoon in Nicaragua accelerated after 1870. Workers who went to the sawmills maintained a semi-permanent residence."[29]

The Garifuna in Nicaragua manage multiple and intersecting identities—being Indigenous and Afro-descendant, being primarily rural, being relative newcomers to the Nicaraguan Caribbean coast compared to other coastal ethnicities—and today they find themselves at the bottom of the social hierarchy on the Caribbean coast as Pacific-coast mestizos and urban, Afro-descendant Creoles occupy many of the jobs and hold most of the power on the coast. Though the next chapter further explores the present-day manifestations of discrimination and exclusion faced by the Garifuna, there is a long and complex history to power, race, and ethnicity on the Caribbean coast.

The social hierarchy of Nicaragua's Caribbean coast has evolved over the centuries, and its unique history emerges through Miskitu Indigenous leadership and the power struggle for control between British and Spanish colonial interests. Upon early contact with the colonial powers, the major population on the Caribbean coast was comprised of the Miskitu Indigenous people. Though they had primarily dedicated themselves to hunting, gathering, fishing, and some agricultural practices, the Miskitu were able to take advantage of British pirates and then British colonial interests on the coast to get arms and munitions as well as access to British goods, becoming intermediaries selling British goods to other Indigenous groups and rural Miskitu.[30] As the British continued to invest in the Caribbean while the Spanish controlled the Pacific side of the country, the British needed allies on the Caribbean coast. Access to British guns as well as political and military support were used by the Miskitu to gain military advantage over the other groups of the Caribbean coast.[31] The British exercised their control over the Caribbean coast through the Kingdom of Mosquitia, a series of Miskitu kings who ruled the Caribbean coast and were educated in England and other places in the Caribbean such as Jamaica. "From early on—as early as 1657—the Miskitu believed that for an individual to be a legitimate King, he had to be recognized by the British."[32]

This set of events differentiates the Nicaraguan Caribbean from other Central American countries like Honduras and Costa Rica, for example, where Spanish dominance was established early on. Furthermore, the emergence of the Afro-descendant Creoles on the Caribbean coast of Nicaragua added further complexity to the social hierarchy on the coast. The Afro-descendant Creoles were the progeny of the British and Afro-descendant people who had made their way to Nicaragua. "Creole culture formed within the tiny British-dominated slave society of the Mosquito Coast in the eighteenth century, nearly 150 years before the emergence of the now-dominant Nicaraguan national culture."[33] This group thought of themselves as British and superior to groups like the Garifuna or other groups on the coast. These original Creoles had economic power from the British and their language was English. Gordon argues that "it seems probable that only the lighter-skinned mixed elite were considered Creole initially; however, by mid-century [1800s] the term had been extended to encompass the entire free English Creole-speaking nonwhite population born in the Americas and living in the Mosquitia,"[34] which explains why the Garifuna felt so much pressure to learn English. When the Garifuna arrived in the early twentieth century to Nicaragua, not only did they occupy the lowest rungs on the social hierarchy, but they soon found themselves facing assimilation pressures they had not faced in Honduras where there were so many Garifuna communities.

The English exercised their control over the coast through the Miskitu kings until 1894 when the Nicaraguan state "reincorporated" the Mosquitia—Caribbean region of Nicaragua—under President Zelaya as part of a negotiated settlement with the British. However, during the mid- to late nineteenth century, the United States began to intervene in Nicaragua, both on the Pacific and Caribbean sides of the country. The role of the United States in the politics of Nicaragua has its roots in mid-eighteenth-century Manifest Destiny ideologies and the invasion of Nicaragua by U.S. mercenary William Walker, who declared himself president of Nicaragua in 1855 and (unsuccessfully) prepared to build a canal connecting the Caribbean to the Pacific across the country.[35] Walker eventually earned the enmity of all the Central American governments and was executed in Honduras. Nonetheless, U.S. military intervention and economic investment in agricultural and natural resource extraction on the Nicaraguan Caribbean coast expanded in the late nineteenth century and continued to grow into the twentieth century.[36] As Creoles in Bluefields gained opportunities in the city and mestizos from Managua moved into Bluefields, U.S. investment replaced the role of the British. Gordon corroborates this, saying, "The Nicaraguan state and U.S. capital operated in a relatively coordinated fashion, due in large part to Nicaragua's position as a client state of U.S. imperialism."[37] As described by Leonard in the introduction, the U.S. enclave system thrived for the early part of the twentieth century in close coordination with the Somoza dynasty of Nicaraguan strong-arm leaders. The enclave system meant that U.S. companies brought in their own infrastructure and exercised territorial control based on tax-free concessions for mining, banana plantations, timber extraction, and fishing. These companies had their own stores, schools, and churches and benefited immensely from a disenfranchised and ill-paid workforce of local people who received no social benefits individually as well as the fact that these companies invested little in local communities.

Early banana companies were abandoned during the civil war between the Somoza regime and guerrilla leader Augusto Cesar Sandino in the late 1920s and 1930s. Sandino fought against Somoza and the U.S. Marines; Sandino was very critical of the U.S. enclave model on the Caribbean coast and how it contributed to the poverty of the region. In response, the Nicaraguan National Guard took repressive measures against the Miskitu due to the presence of Sandino and his troops. Even though many banana companies closed, foreign investment expanded into timber extraction on the Caribbean coast.

Throughout the 1960s, the Nicaraguan National Guard under the Somoza regime—with support from the United States—moved over fifty thousand Miskitu to increase the workforce in other places on the coast for resource extraction. In turn, this led to an upsurge in cattle ranching by the Somoza dynasty and cronies on the Caribbean coast. Somoza and U.S. economic interests kept expanding extractive processes and generating significant profit for themselves. There were periodic protests and struggles on the Caribbean coast for rights, self-determination, and land throughout the twentieth century, which culminated in a lot of support for the Sandinista revolution in the 1970s. The Somoza dynasty was overthrown on July 19, 1979. Most Nicaraguans—including communities on the Caribbean coast—were initially pleased with these events. In the long run, the history of isolation and exclusion on the Caribbean coast was exacerbated by the 1979 Sandinista revolution and the ensuing effects of U.S. foreign policy that armed and supported the counterrevolution to fight the Sandinistas in the 1980s with military aid and money for the counterrevolution under President Reagan.[38]

Initially, it didn't take long for the mestizo revolutionaries of the Pacific coast to begin to alienate their Caribbean coastal comrades with declarations about turning Indigenous people into farmers. In fact, Daniel Ortega, then commander of the Sandinista revolution, declared that "indigenous peoples no longer existed in Nicaragua because the revolution represented the end of every type of ethnic or racist discrimination. The miskitos were no longer indigenous; they were Nicaraguans" and would do better to join a mass organization such as a union, farming association, or other committee than continuing to see themselves as Miskitu.[39] Other researchers sustain this interpretation; Gordon goes as far as to say that the Sandinistas were no different than the Somoza dynasty in how they viewed the Caribbean coast: "In the immediate post-Triumph era, the Sandinistas shared many of the same ideas about the Atlantic Coast held by other groups of Nicaraguan Mestizos. For them it was a vast, almost uninhabited, area rich in natural resources."[40] Not just Sandinista leaders but Sandinista troops were also not sensitive to coastal realities and mores. Mestizo soldiers didn't know the coast, they often didn't trust people from the coast, and given the vertical and centralized control of Managua, troops began to commit errors and abuses. Coastal organizations were relegated to an inferior level and were even accused of betraying the revolution when demanding Indigenous rights. Many people on the Caribbean coast began to leave for Honduras and Costa Rica to arm and organize against the Sandinistas.

Though not initially disillusioned by the Sandinistas, the Garifuna communities of Pearl Lagoon weren't able to enjoy the promises of the revolution such as social and human investments in development and autonomy of Indigenous communities due to the counterrevolutionary or Contra war that unfolded around them in the 1980s. Supported by the United States, counterrevolutionaries or Contras used low-intensity conflict strategies that put communities like Orinoco at risk because of their isolation and relative lack of defense. This led to many deaths in the community and a total death toll of eight thousand civilians across the country by counterrevolutionary forces.[41] The Garifuna took the side of the Sandinista government, and as the conflict unfolded between the Sandinistas and the counterrevolution, many Garifuna lost their lives. By the time the conflict was ending on the coast in the late 1980s, Pearl Lagoon and its Garifuna communities were soon relegated to the same isolation and abandonment to which they had been subject for the preceding century. The so-called Caribbean counterrevolutionaries did lay down their arms and sign a peace accord in 1987 with the Sandinistas. At this time the Sandinista government recognized that mistakes had been made on the Caribbean coast: they had never really gotten to know the Caribbean coast; the vertical nature of the Sandinista state made the coastal people feel excluded; the Sandinista collective model of production didn't work for the coast either; and many people on the coast were excluded from opportunities to get formal sector jobs because they didn't have party connections.

With the 1987 signing of a peace accord with the Caribbean coastal groups who had fought the Sandinistas, the Nicaraguan government committed itself to respecting the autonomy of the Caribbean coast. Autonomy Law 28 was passed in 1987 and was first implemented in 1990: there were two regional governments (one in the north and one in the south on the Caribbean coast) with their own respective structures of forty-five members, each with five legislators to the National Assembly in Managua. Lauded as innovative and inclusive for its attempt to respect the different ethnic groups on the coast,[42] Autonomy Law 28, however, faced multiple challenges from the beginning.

Sandinista leaders chose to support the advancement of the agricultural frontier in which farmers from the Pacific coast expanded cattle raising and agricultural production into Indigenous coastal territories supposedly protected by Autonomy Law 28 passed in 1987, which we describe in further detail in chapter 3 about the Garifuna and their relationship to the land. In 1990, the conflict with the Contras ended and the Sandinistas lost presidential elections; formal political power moved from the Sandinistas to the opposition. A series of neoliberal presidents—Violeta Barrios de Chamorro, Arnoldo Alemán, and Enrique Bolaños—implemented structural adjustment policies that involved privatizing state industries and decreasing social services. The Sandinistas, in turn, stayed active politically by "governing from below," using their social base to boycott the neoliberal reforms. This led to a negotiation or power sharing agreement with the right, which allowed Sandinista leaders to benefit from the cuts. The Sandinistas returned to power in 2007, and instead of moving forward with a reengagement with coastal autonomy and the formal titling of costeños' territory, the titling process has never been completed. Even with the positive change that autonomy laws could mean for the Garifuna and other groups in Nicaragua with long histories of community connection to the lands they inhabited, "closer inspection reveals the stubborn persistence (at least in Nicaragua) of official discourses of mestizo nationalism that continue to place limits on the political inclusion of black and indigenous costeños."[43] This entails a double tragedy for the Garifuna: state priorities don't include Indigenous communities' land claims and development needs on a macro-level, *and* on the micro-level state-sponsored support of mestizo farmers from the Pacific side of the country is directly taking land away from Garifuna communities.

Today's situation on the Caribbean coast of Nicaragua is exacerbated by the depletion of the fishing industry to the detriment of artisanal, local fishing practices from the Garifuna communities on one hand, and illegal land grabs by mestizo settlers on the other. This, in turn, has contributed to increased poverty and exclusion for the Garifuna communities, which has led to renewed diasporic economic arrangements as communal lands get occupied by settlers and rural families are forced to send family members abroad to earn income. These economic and political developments, with their historical roots in tensions between the colonizing forces of the Spanish and the British on the Caribbean coast of Nicaragua, unfolded in a place with pre-existing complex ethnic relations. All of this then paved the way for the neocolonial expansion of U.S. military, political, and economic interests in the eighteenth, nineteenth, and twentieth centuries, engendering a postcolonial present in which a repressive national mestizo government continues to promote internal colonization and the extractive practices of the past in Caribbean communities rich in natural resources yet marginalized by structures such as location, ethnicity, and poverty. Today, the Nicaraguan government is "a self-interested entity that maximizes power in the hands of the president and offers public officials an easy path to enrichment in exchange for their loyalty."[44]

A Theory of Persistence

Our learning with the Garifuna can help other researchers and readers alike celebrate the survival of the group, comprehend the need for solidarity given the history of exclusion, and consider what well-meaning people from more privileged spaces can learn from this persistence. For all of these reasons, this book uses a grounded analysis emerging from ongoing conversations with Garifuna research participants analyzed against a context of historical events and processes, political ramifications, and exogenous economic interests.[45] This book invites the reader into life in Orinoco and the other Garifuna communities of Pearl Lagoon with descriptions of the places and people who live there, yet it is simultaneously presented against the historical background that has shaped the community, and it takes the side of the community against the forces that would see its vitality fade. This book is political precisely because it centers the Garifuna and their persistence in the face of centuries of marginalization and exclusion that have included attempted enslavement, displacement, settler incursion, discrimination, and uneven and repressive state policies in the present day. And especially for an Afro-Indigenous group like the Garifuna, an historical context and critical analysis are necessary so the reader can understand the continuities, breaks, junctures, and disjunctures of the *longue durée* "reaching before and after colonization" of the *survivance* and *persistence* of Indigenous peoples.[46] These two terms appear frequently throughout the text of this book along with other strategies that Indigenous groups use to live well and sustain cultural practices.

Survivance: it is more than mere survival, which given the obstacles Indigenous communities have faced since colonization is remarkable itself. Survivance isn't just physical survival; it is cultural and epistemic survival as well. It is continuing to think outside the box of Western cultural imperialism. Survivance is a term taken up by Anishanaabe novelist Gerald Vizenor, who defines "Native survivance [as] an active sense of presence over absence, deracination, and oblivion; survivance is the continuance of stories, not a mere reaction, however pertinent."[47] In the case of small, rural communities on the Caribbean coast of Nicaragua today who are facing a repressive "neoliberal state, capitalist intensification, and drug war militarization,"[48] it would be easy to assume the worst, but these communities are persisting. For Indigenous peoples, survivance is more than physical survival; it's persistence. *Persistence*—obviously a related concept—can be found in between survivance and resistance and also embraces them both. Persistence is a conscious community commitment to what has existed before and a vision for how it continues to unfold *a pesar de* (even with all of) the dispossession, genocide, and attempts at assimilation that have been enforced by colonial and modern nation states.

In Central America and the Caribbean, colonization can best be summed up as the conquest, expropriation, and imposed imperial governance of European countries on the peoples inhabiting the region linking North America to South America. "Colonization almost invariably implies a relation of structural domination, and a suppression—often violent—of the heterogeneity of the subject(s) in question."[49] In Central America and the Caribbean, colonization involved *mestizaje*—the mixing of Spanish, British, and French people, for example, with local Indigenous and Afro-descendent peoples. Mestizaje, hybridity, and creolization "are rather unsatisfactory ways of naming the processes of cultural mutation and restless (dis)continuity that exceed racial discourse and avoid capture by its agents."[50] There are contradictions inherent in the term mestizaje: it simultaneously includes homogenization and differentiation,[51] sad histories of rape and forced acculturation, as well as emergent, resurgent, and creative new combinations and options. As Wade warns, "Scholars have recognised that mestizaje does not have a single meaning within the Latin American context, and contains within it tensions between sameness and difference, and between inclusion and exclusion."[52] Through these processes of "mutation" and "mixing"—often forced and violent—colonizers created and then imposed a stratification of society in which the representatives of colonial nation-states held power; they, in turn, were served by a mestizo set of elites who, upon independence in the 1800s, then came to rule over the poor, Indigenous, and Black communities in their countries with their own discourse of power to justify their actions.[53] It is worthwhile to note that this discourse contains the narrative of acculturation for Indigenous and Afro-descendent groups: "To expect that the Indian will be emancipated through a steady crossing of the aboriginal race with white immigrants is an anti-sociological naiveté,"[54] or in other words the creation and imposition of racist categories. "It is worth noting that, while scholars may cast mestizaje as subversive hybridity, in the Latin American context this is generally tempered with a recognition that mestizaje may work as an ideology of oppression, marginalising black and indigenous populations."[55]

Many of the opportunities and challenges that face the Garifuna today arise out of processes and relations set in motion in different epochs and places. The colonial model of extraction and exclusion gets replicated in new iterations of coloniality—often referred to as neocolonialism and internal colonization. Neocolonialism describes how other countries—often those in the global north, such as the United States—impose their agendas and political, economic, and territorial interests on other countries near and far. Neocolonialism can include the burden of disadvantageous trade agreements by countries in the global north imposed on the global south; it also encompasses the imposition of exogenous or outside agendas, aid, policies, military aid, and programming on countries or communities. With internal colonization, national governments and domestic economic elites implement the model vis-à-vis their own territories and peoples, which involves state-sponsored enforced acculturation and (at the least state-encouraged) settler incursion of farmers onto Indigenous and Afro-Indigenous land. These relations manifest today in Orinoco in the form of settler colonialism, defined by Australian cultural studies professor Lisa Slater as "the dispossession and replacement of Indigenous peoples that is justified by narratives of European progress and supremacy."[56] These different phases of coloniality—colonization, internal or settler colonization, and neocolonialism—comprise some of the different challenges the Garifuna have had to face since their emergence as a people. Decoloniality, on the other hand, is an umbrella term that includes decolonization and also refers to the broader processes of persistence and resurgence of Indigenous peoples and their allies today. We see this in Indigenous groups who refuse to acculturate and still re-create their culturally mediated ways of knowing. We see this in how some Indigenous groups steward natural resources, including land, sea, rivers, flora, fauna, and non-living beings such as spirits and ancestors. Similarly, Garifuna commitment to the land and the ocean was enabled by the place where they found themselves and the local peoples who received them, and it was strengthened by a new generation of ancestors who were born and buried on St. Vincent.

Persistence is the illuminating theme of this book. It's a celebration of the persistence of the Garifuna and many other marginalized groups in the Americas who have not been disappeared or annihilated by the array of forces they've had to confront over the centuries. In fact, this isn't just about a few practices surviving; it's about a radical resurgence of Indigenous actions, beliefs, and knowledges that respond to other logics that aren't Western or Eurocentric.[57] This resurgence is an interstitial opening, a decolonial crack, a persistent fissure in the colonial construction of power relations today.[58] This book argues that the persistence of the Garifuna contradicts coloniality—past and present—and exemplifies living into decoloniality, which means resisting the worldview that Western knowledge or Western ways of being are the only way of being; it means persisting with one's Indigenous practices and relationships to land and ancestors: what Mignolo and Walsh call choosing "other logics of thought, knowledge, and living in co-relation."[59]

Cultural "Roots" and Diasporic "Routes"

The Garifuna emerge historically and survive today as a people due to "the roots and routes" of globalization and colonization;[60] in the case of the Garifuna, these processes have catalyzed movements and displacements around the Atlantic Ocean, the Caribbean, Central America, and North America. Historical migrations happened over time so that today Garifuna people can be found on the Caribbean coast of Costa Rica, Nicaragua, Honduras, Guatemala, and Belize as well as in the United States. Mapping this journeying requires the analytical concept diaspora, an evocative, underutilized concept that describes the forced spread of people and "break(s) the dogmatic focus on discrete *national* dynamics."[61] Diaspora is the displacement of people, across great distances, due to forces not of their choosing; it is the interests of colonial and neocolonial powers that have created a situation so calamitous that people must move or die or not have the resources they need to survive; it is the people who are forced to move; it is also the survivance, persistence, and resistance of those who have to move. Clifford affirms the aptness of "diaspora" and how it can describe peoples' connections to the land they have had to leave: "Diaspora gets somewhat closer to a sociospatial reality of connectedness-in-dispersion. . . The goal of an actual return remains alive, and it takes concrete political form in land claims and repatriations. At the same time, many people give up the idea of a physical return to traditional communities, and land, focusing instead on ceremonial observations, seasonal visits to reservations or 'country' and symbolic tokens or performances of tradition."[62] Interestingly, the Garifuna, whose roots often require routes that loop between communities of origin and other places where they've traveled for work, family, or political commitments, embody what Glick-Schiller refers to as "transmigrants" who are simultaneously engaged in their new countries and firmly committed to maintaining economic, political, and familial links with their home communities.[63] Transmigration is more than the unilinear movement of migration; transmigrants "maintain connections, build institutions, conduct transactions, and influence local and national events in the countries from which they have emigrated."[64] Garifuna transmigration is exemplified by Nicaraguan Garifuna immigration to Costa Rica and Honduran Garifuna immigration to the United States. Given the poverty, settler incursion, and loss of subsistence livelihoods due to environmental devastation, many Garifuna youth choose to seek educational opportunities and employment elsewhere given concerns about the quality of education in the community and the lack of income-generating opportunities in Orinoco. This displacement does not mean that Garifuna identity is necessarily lessened or diluted as often employment-seeking youth connect with other community members and perform Garifuna traditions and practices in their new locations. We saw this when we visited Little Corn Island off the Caribbean coast of Nicaragua and witnessed Garifuna youth working in small hotels and restaurants on Little Corn Island presenting Garifuna traditional dances and drumming every Wednesday evening. We've also observed this dynamic through the experiences of Garifuna youth living in the United States who replicate Garifuna practices there and embrace learning about their culture when they visit their communities of origin in Central America. Often, youth do not return to live permanently in the community, yet many come home for Holy Week, Christmas, and other Garifuna holidays, what Clifford sums up as "a lot of coming and going."[65] This simultaneous rooting in Garifuna practices and routing away and back again are strategies and trajectories that exemplify Garifuna persistence. This is persistence. This is resurgence, and this is also accommodation. They leave to seek education and income-generating opportunities and then they come home. Again and again.

In fact, the Garifuna are born out of diaspora and continue to live in diaspora today; they are a diasporic people. As important as the concept of diaspora is for understanding the Garifuna, it is important to remember that the Garifuna aren't just leaving their communities capriciously; they are leaving because of an economic, social, and political context that requires they leave in order to sustain the community. As portrayed in this chapter, a set of power relations and its historical roots provide important insights into the indiscriminate driving forces of diaspora.

The critical connection between Afro-Indigenous roots and diasporic routes holds together the commitment to land, sea, and other natural resource stewardship and the commuting important for articulation and continued survival. Gegeo explores this tension in an important article about Pacific Islander Indigeneity and place: at times Indigenous peoples must sacrifice "place" for "space" for multiple reasons, not limited to forced migration but also including voluntary relocation for work or school.[66] Rather than essentializing an Indigenous person as tied to land or community of origin, the work of Gegeo and others distinguishes between place and space: Indigenous understandings of land and culture may be more about understandings or commitments rather than GPS locations. "For to recognize a specifically indigenous dialectic of dwelling and traveling requires more than simply unmaking the exoticist/colonialist concept of the homebody native, always firmly at home, in his place or her place... The contrast between colonial fixity and postcolonial mobility, between indigenous roots and diasporic routes, can't be allowed to harden into an opposition or a before-after scenario in which cosmopolitan equals modern."[67] This tension holds as we walk from Orinoco to Marshall Point and see the "private property: no trespassing signs" that mestizo settlers have put up; it also holds as we talk with Garifuna families in the Bronx. In neighborhoods of New York City, for example, the Garifuna are concurrently rooted—to home communities on the Caribbean coast—and routed—across the Americas seeking economic stability and opportunities for their children.

Conclusion

The histories and concepts laid out in this chapter aim to elucidate a present-day set of forces informed by a history of globalization, colonialization, neocolonialism, and postcolonial negotiations toward a decolonial future. Many people with privilege—particularly Euro-descendant people both in Latin America and the global north—have directly or indirectly benefited from these forces. It is important to reflect on one's own complicity. "As [Irene] Watson [Aboriginal legal theorist] advises, we need to stay with the discomfort, thoughtfully meditate upon how settler colonialism reproduces subjects who desire the comforts and security of exclusive possession and limits our capacities to reimagine belonging, and thus social justice."[68] This uncomfortable space—this *aporia*—might just ease us into a decolonial era of co-responsibility and sharing so there can be a more inclusive future for humanity.

Framing: *Decolonial Intersectionality*

Serena Cosgrove

"The buck stops not at the top but at the bottom, a bottom which is often gendered, classed, and frequently racialized."[1]

—KIMBERLÉ CRENSHAW, *Background Paper for the Expert Meeting of the Gender-Related Aspects of Race Discrimination*

Introduction

This chapter acquaints you with the main theoretical framing for the book: a decolonial intersectionality that simultaneously explains marginalization *and* agency through the *longue dure*é of conquest, colonization, and modernity. *Decoloniality* locates us in historical movements that include coloniality and modernity and is animated by the persistence and resistance of Indigenous, Afro-Indigenous, and Afro-descendant peoples who bear the brunt of these processes. *Intersectionality*—rooted in Black feminist legal theory—is a lens or way of analyzing a given reality that facilitates seeing how the combined effects of difference, such as race, ethnicity/Indigeneity, location, gender, and socioeconomic class, compound exclusion and marginalization while simultaneously inspiring agency and motivation to fight back, resist, and persist. Together these terms, what I call *decolonial intersectionality*, facilitate understanding how Garifuna communities negotiate multiple forms of social difference that exacerbate their exclusion—Afro-descendent, Indigenous, poor, and isolated in rural, coastal communities—against a set of power relations informed by imperialism and the colonial legacy.[2] Applied to the Garifuna, this framework allows us to see what privations they've survived *and* how they've persisted.

After exploring intersectionality in greater detail and coloniality/decoloniality as well, the chapter concludes with three interrelated strategies that the Garifuna employ in their persistence. Articulation, performance, and translation are three practical ways the Garifuna (re)make/(re)create cultural practices and nurture their relationships/vincularidad with their communities, nature, and their ancestors.[3]

Intersectionality in a Decolonial Context

Given the multiple forms of exclusion that the Garifuna encounter, it is useful to have a concept that explains the mutually constructing effects of exclusion and discrimination as well as persistence and resistance. Intersectionality "attempts to capture the structural and dynamic consequences of the interaction between two or more axes of subordination."[4] Intersectionality is a useful analytical tool because it is "(1) an approach to understanding human life and behavior rooted in the experiences and struggles of disenfranchised people; and (2) an important tool linking theory with practice that can aid in the empowerment of communities and individuals."[5] As a sociological theory, intersectionality first appeared in the research and writing of Kimberlé Crenshaw, a Black feminist legal scholar, and was then further developed by Crenshaw herself to apply intersectionality in a global context, as well as by Patricia Hill Collins and others.[6] Initially, Black feminist scholars used the term to describe the challenges that Black women face in the United States due to the combined and mutually reinforcing effects of racism and sexism, arguing that Black women faced a set of challenges that was distinct from the sexism faced by white women or the racism that affects Black men due to the "interactive effects of race and gender discrimination."[7] Black women face greater challenges than either white women or Black men because their exclusion is due to multiple forms of discrimination that "interact with preexisting vulnerabilities to create a distinct dimension of disempowerment."[8] Exclusion isn't a simple additive process, rather multiple forms of difference can combine to create dangerous intersections for people facing mutually reinforcing and compounding barriers to equality. "Major axes of social divisions in a given society at a given time, for example, race, class, gender, sexuality, dis/ability, and age operate not as discrete and mutually exclusive entities, but build on each other and work together" to exacerbate exclusion, poverty, discrimination, domination, and the impact of genocidal practices.[9] The concept of intersectionality explains this phenomenon of multilayered or interconnected forms of difference that create and perpetuate exclusion, discrimination, and poverty. The major implication here is that poverty and exclusion are seldom caused by one form of difference, rather they are "intertwined and mutually constructed" by multiple forms of difference.[10]

Intersectionality is not only a useful tool for understanding inequality in society. In fact, it is a useful analytical tool for researchers when interpreting data, because it is important to not let single-issue commitments—described in other words by Collins and Bilge as "elevating one category of analysis [i.e., gender or ethnicity or social class] and action above others"—lead to biased data analysis, especially when examining the exclusion and persistence of Indigenous peoples.[11] Today intersectionality is used consistently by many activists and engaged scholars around the world trying to understand the compounding effects of multiple forms of social difference on marginalized groups.[12]

As mentioned above, Crenshaw applied intersectionality globally advocating for increased attention by United Nations agencies to how "the conjoining of multiple systems of subordination has been described as compound discrimination, multiple burdens, or double or triple discrimination" around the world.[13] Small societies like the Garifuna have been systematically excluded and marginalized due to multiple aspects of their identity that include race and ethnicity but also involve place and location: place as rural and isolated; place as context and setting; and place as a tool to observe the effects of exclusion.[14] This type of exclusion is often "obscured. . . because it tends to happen to those who are marginal even within subordinate groups."[15] In Nicaragua, the inhabitants of the entire Caribbean coast, a part of the country seen primarily as a source of raw materials, are excluded from national politics and subject to the impacts of overfishing and resource extraction by national and international companies. They are simultaneously ignored by Nicaraguan elites and most historians of Nicaraguan history: Nicaragua faces the Pacific, political and economic power is located on the Pacific side, Nicaragua turns its back on the Caribbean. It is groups like the Garifuna and other Indigenous groups on the Caribbean coast who are the most isolated and discriminated against in an already excluded region. This analysis applies to the Garifuna: the Garifuna were often treated like backward country bumpkins and looked down on by (Afro-descendent) Creole elites when they arrived in Bluefields, the de facto capital of the southern Caribbean coast of Nicaragua. This discrimination has its historical roots and present-day manifestations as well.

As the Garifuna arrived to Nicaragua in the late nineteenth and early twentieth centuries, they came speaking their own Garifuna language. However, in order to find paid work on the Nicaraguan coast, they began to speak English Creole, which is the language spoken by Creoles. Aware that they didn't want their children to grow up and be discriminated against, many elders did not teach their children the Garifuna language. In other words, they were pressured economically to assimilate, and they began to lose their language while learning Spanish and English.[16] In addition to these pressures, they faced discrimination from coastal elites for not having British facial characteristics associated with the Creoles who are descended from British colonial subjects and Afro-descendant peoples on the Caribbean coast. There were racist comments about their noses, for example. In the early to mid-twentieth century, the Garifuna were still looked down on, even as the Nicaraguan government from the Pacific side of the country extended its control over the coast. Slowly, U.S. investment replaced the British. Even with these changes, the Garifuna remained on the bottom of the social hierarchy, behind the mestizos, Creoles, and other Indigenous peoples.

The coastal peoples of Nicaragua were discriminated against by the mestizos on the Pacific coast, but on the southern shores of the Caribbean coast of Nicaragua, there were racial hierarchies as well. The primarily Creole coastal city of Bluefields treated the Garifuna as inferior. The Garifuna were assigned to a lower status by people in Bluefields. The manifestations of this discrimination have been repeatedly corroborated in our interviews. Orson is a young man in his mid-twenties who was born in Orinoco and spent a number of years going back and forth between Orinoco and Bluefields. After completing his bachelor's degree in Bluefields, he went to Spain to study for a master's degree. Now back in Bluefields, he describes how he experienced this discrimination during his travels and studies:

> A lot of young people are ashamed of being Garifuna, and so they are afraid of leaving the community and going to university. . . I tell them, you don't risk, you don't gain. But when someone from [Orinoco] goes to the university, we're often seen as "special cases," and even if we are just as good as the kids from Bluefields, we feel inferior. Sometimes we get special attention, and for me, even though you're not directly telling me I'm a fool, you feel that way when you're seen as special and the other kids feel as though it's normal to be there.

He grabbed a sheet of nearby paper, and drew two lines, one near the top of the page and the other at the bottom. Pointing to the lower line, he noted how "People see us as down here, below the kids from the city. And so we tell ourselves we have to work five times harder to overcome this gap. My first two weeks in Spain were hell. I shut down. But I knew I needed to work harder to catch up. We will never overcome that gap unless we work five times harder."[17]

Older community members in Orinoco remember feeling excluded at each stopping-point along the journey to sell fish or pineapples in the cities: just crossing Pearl Lagoon to the town of Pearl Lagoon meant being treated as yokels. This treatment intensified upon reaching the Caribbean coastal city of Bluefields. In Bluefields, the Garifuna were discriminated against for coming from the bush and not being descended from the British like many Creoles. If a Garifuna made it to Managua, the capital of the country located on the Pacific side, they were discriminated against for being from the countryside, for being Black, for being Indigenous, and for being from the Caribbean coast, which was seen as a backward part of the country. The Garifuna are discriminated against for being rural, Indigenous, and Afro-descendant.

Intersectionality is a dual-purpose concept that simultaneously explains how unequal structures disempower and marginalize, referred to as "structural intersectionality," and how experiences of compounded difference can ignite agency, leadership, and resistance, referred to as "political intersectionality."[18] On the one hand, structural intersectionality explains the oppression and exclusion that accompanies multiple forms of social difference or division. Political intersectionality, on the other hand, explains why oppressed and discriminated groups often use what Collins repeatedly calls their "oppositional knowledge" to resist the forces aligned against them, or, as Crenshaw says, "to challenge the conditions of their lives."[19] When it is clear that one has been left out of the social contract of the broader society, the contradiction between societal values versus the treatment of one's own people becomes evident. In my research about women's civil society leadership in Argentina, Chile, and El Salvador, I entitled my book *Leadership from the Margins* precisely because those who had the most reasons to despair and do nothing—mothers with disappeared children, Indigenous women in Chile after generations of genocidal state practices, militant feminists in neoliberal El Salvador, working-class women in peri-urban Buenos Aires—were, in fact, the most active.[20] They turned hard experiences into motivation, solidarity, and action so others wouldn't have to face the repression and exclusion that they had experienced. People on the margins often use the meanings, beliefs, and practices they have to fight back whether it's simply making it through the day, renewing a cultural practice that might have been abandoned, or destroying a private property sign that settlers have put up on communal land. Examples of this persistence and resistance from Orinoco are many. For example, the Garifuna call the mestizos Pañas or Spaniards because they see them as colonizers; they dedicate time to recover cultural practices such as making bami (large yucca tortillas that serve as their main starch); they persist in the face of resource depletion and identify other income sources; they build community organizations; and they regularly commute home from the city, a looping back which brings them home for holidays, for days of community celebration, and to participate in cultural gatherings through dance, drumming, food, and communication with family, living and dead. This cultural persistence, this cultural agency, this (re)claiming of Garifuna knowledge are all signs of agency and what political intersectionality attempts to describe: *a pesar de todo*—with everything they've had to face—Garifuna culture persists.

Intersectionality helps us to understand the marginalization "or mutually constructing nature of systems of oppression, as well as the social locations created by such mutual constructions,"[21] and it also allows us to see how adversity can engender persistence and resistance. In the case of the Garifuna, political intersectionality or the resistance of excluded peoples can be best visualized when a postcolonial or decolonial lens is used. "Bringing together intersectionality with a postcolonial framework seeks to more rigorously theorize intersectional hierarchies in relation to the dynamics of power associated with colonialism and postcolonial statehood and development," posits Sarah Radcliffe in her research about Indigenous Andean women in Ecuador.[22] Her research invites additions that build on her original contributions. Given our focus on persistence as a decolonial response to a postcolonial world, we will ground our usage of intersectionality using these two qualifiers, applying both "post" (read "still in it") and "de" (read "creating something new") to coloniality as we explain Garifuna survival and persistence.

Though still enmeshed in colonial and neocolonial power relations and histories, we use the term "decolonial" because it simultaneously acknowledges the colonial past, the decolonization of independence movements throughout Latin America and the Caribbean in the 1800s, and ongoing resistance, intimating the (im)possibility of Indigenous autonomy. We began conceiving our theoretical framing using the concept of postcoloniality but added decoloniality because of our dissatisfaction with the "post" of postcoloniality and how it hampered a full celebration of our theme of persistence. Clifford, himself, warns us that "the term 'postcolonial' is controversial. I use it with hesitation, lacking a better name for the. . . resolution of conquest's unfinished business."[23] Alongside postcoloniality (not in comparison), we include decoloniality because in the "de-" is persistence. Furthermore, the "de-" makes it critical and political because decoloniality is about action, unlearning, and relearning. This also fits well with our decolonial commitment in our research methods described in the last chapter. The dizzying use of so many versions of coloniality is necessary to track the effects of different epochs of colonization from the 1500s to today as well as the tactics of different colonizers (Spanish, British, and French), internal colonization practices of modern nation states, and neocolonial, extractive policies and interventions by countries like the United States.

As the resistance and persistence of Indigenous peoples and other excluded groups draw more attention and interest, new terms are emerging to describe these movements. Until recently, many theorists have used and continue to use *decolonization* to refer to the processes undergone by countries seeking to free themselves from colonial powers as well as present-day examples of Indigenous persistence. "Decolonization is, of course, not an all-or-nothing, once-and-for-all transition; and long, ongoing histories of resistance and accommodation, of unlinking and relinking with imperial forces, need to be kept in view."[24] As a concept, decoloniality includes the processes of decolonization in which countries formed under colonization gained independence, which in Latin America occurred mainly in the early 1800s. "What do decoloniality and decolonization

mean. . . ? (D)ecolonization during the Cold War meant the struggle for liber-
ations of the Third World and, when successful, the formation of nation-states
claiming sovereignty. By the 1990s, decolonization's failure in most nations had
become clear; with state in the hands of minority elites, the patterns of colonial
power continued both internally (i.e., internal colonialism) and with relation to
global structures."[25]

Decoloniality describes efforts to think outside of coloniality, to persist
outside of coloniality, to connect to nature outside of Western concepts that pit
humans against the natural world. "Decoloniality. . . is a form of struggle and survival, an epistemic and existence-based response and practice—most especially
by colonized and racialized subjects—against the colonial matrix of power in all
of its dimensions, and for the possibilities of an otherwise."[26] The possibility—the
challenge, risk, and discomfort that something "impossible" such as Indigenous
thriving[27]—as exemplified by Indigenous peoples' persistence is the heart of
decoloniality. The context for Garifuna persistence is created by a colonial history, neocolonial relations, a postcolonial present, and a decolonial future. Considering the implications of colonial legacies, neocolonial extractive processes by
world powers, and postcolonial frameworks and decolonial responses facilitates
understanding the context or what Mignolo and Walsh call the "colonial matrix of
power" against which the Garifuna persist today.[28]

This is the set of power relations, or colonial matrix of power, that perpetu-
ates the structural inequality that affects groups like the Garifuna. The colonial
matrix of power was "created by a minority of the human species (to) rule the life
of the majority of human species."[29] We see how the "extractivism, possession,
and dispossession" of Latin America and the Caribbean "have a long history in
the formation and transformation of the colonial matrix of power."[30] This context,
often obscured by "common or widespread (assumptions) that it appears to simply constitute a natural. . . fact of life," is comprised of power relations that inform
the opportunities and limitations of the present moment.[31] When you sit down in
an auditorium to watch a play, it's easy to stay so focused on the actors in front of
you that you don't even notice the background or setting or what Crenshaw refers
to as the "structural backdrop."[32] The analogy holds: just as every play will have
its own backdrop, the phenomena of exclusion and poverty will have their own
set of power relations that give impetus to and sustain the situation and the structural and institutionalized relations that validate and normalize unequal access
and simultaneously engender resistance. These matrices of power are "structural, disciplinary, cultural, and interpersonal" and foreground the everyday
actions and experiences of particular people in specific places.[33] Throughout this
book, examples show how the Garifuna persist in the face of a global, neoliberal

economy and a national political project with uneven and contradictory policies and services as well as repressive actions against groups that speak out or make demands. This is the complexity of today's decolonial moment in the Americas, in which colonial logics from the 1500s are utilized to sustain today's exclusions and resistances.

It is important to keep in mind that in many Latin American and Caribbean countries, governing elites promote a limited, neoliberal, multiculturalism. They have become "reluctant arbiters of rights grounded in cultural difference. . . [T]hey find that cultural rights, when carefully delimited, not only pose little challenge to the forward march of the neoliberal project but also induce the bearers of these rights to join in the march."[34] Nicaragua is a particularly representative example of this trend in which the state "pursue[s] superficial diversity to escape critiques of their actual agendas."[35] The populist Sandinista government of Daniel Ortega agreed to respect Indigenous autonomy and land rights in the late 1980s and simultaneously has turned a blind eye to settler incursion as evidenced by the ongoing struggles of coastal communities with settlers and land grabs and in the case of Garifuna communities, the growing encroachment of settlers (farmers, cattle ranchers, and homesteaders) on Garifuna land. Language, education, identity, and spirituality are often not seen as "subversive" rights—these can be granted by the neoliberal, multicultural state—but land and resources are another matter.

On one hand, extractive fishing practices by national and international fishing companies have destroyed fish and lobster stocks, and settler incursion from the Pacific side of the country has increased the tensions over land ownership. But on the other hand, education policy has opened up higher education for Indigenous communities preparing Indigenous youth for employment as professionals in the cities in jobs such as teachers, laboratory technicians, and call center employees. When youth leave the community to pursue educational opportunities, they seldom return to live full-time in the community. Whether deemed positive or negative, these uneven forces all bring profound changes to Garifuna communities. For example, decreased fishing opportunities create profound gendered changes in how men and women contribute to their families. The reluctance of the state to enforce autonomy laws and protect communal lands leads to illegal land sales of communal land; more fences, no trespassing signs, and private property; and decreased land for community farming. These tensions are the result of institutional and structural constraints within and against which the Garifuna survive; it is against this set of interrelated power relations that Garifuna cultural practices and identity have surprisingly persisted, even thrived. This power context—an ambivalent, neoliberal (and increasingly repressive) state, extractive business models, and settler incursion—provides the setting for the decolonial actors and themes of this book: Garifuna connection to nature; spirituality, ancestor worship, and intergenerational practices; and labor and youth. These themes all include gendered and intergenerational trajectories in which changes in the reproduction and production of livelihoods mean new and different roles for adults and youth.

This is the backdrop: the complex set of power relations that shapes exclusion, divides groups, and simultaneously stokes persistence and resistance. When this set of power relations is combined with intersectionality, we are able to see both the exclusion *and* the agency of the Garifuna as well as the aesthetic, epistemic, educational, political, economic, and environmental set of power relations or what Crenshaw calls "structures of domination" and Mignolo and Walsh call "the colonial matrix of power" that inform, create, and sustain neocolonization and internal colonization today.[36] In this way decolonial intersectionality helps explain both how the Garifuna are marginalized and serves to reveal how they are persisting.

Articulation/Performance/Translation

The actual lived strategies the Garifuna are using for their survivance (see chapter 1 for a definition of this term) can be explained by the interconnected tactics of articulation, performance, and translation. Survivance, persistence, and resistance are interrelated concepts that serve to illuminate how communities like the Garifuna flourish today even after centuries of genocidal, extractive, assimilationist, and discriminatory policies have been thrown at them. "People are improvising new ways to be native [through] articulations, performances, and translations of old and new cultures and projects."[37] Using this conceptual toolkit helps us to see agency, survivance, and persistence through the daily reproduction of shared meanings. Culture, according to Clifford, is "articulated, performed, and translated, with varying degrees of power, in specific relational situations. Economic pressures and changing governmental policies are very much part of the process, and so are changing ideological contexts."[38]

The first term, articulation, is the political, social, and economic connectedness between the Garifuna community, nearby cities, the nation-state, and the world; it is "the form of the connection that can make a unity of two different elements. . . It is linkage which is not necessary, determined, absolute and essential for all time."[39] Articulation is political action. It is about peoples on the margins who leverage contacts, friendships, organizations, leaders, laws, frameworks for the survival of their communities. It occurs at the global and local levels and everywhere in between. "In articulation theory, the whole question of authenticity is secondary, and the process of social and cultural persistence is political all the way back. It's assumed that cultural forms will always be made, unmade, and remade. Communities can and must reconfigure themselves, drawing selectively on remembered pasts."[40] Especially for the Garifuna, life on the northern edge of Pearl Lagoon on the Caribbean coast of Nicaragua and routed across the country, Central America, and even the United States, creates a multitude of opportunities and locations to create meaning: "(e)dges and borders crosscut the region, defining different conjunctures: local, national, and regional; urban, rural, and in between; colonial, neocolonial, postcolonial."[41] Articulation is inherently political because it is about relationships and connections that enable Garifuna communities to envision and construct a Garifuna future. Walsh and Mignolo refer to this strategy as "go[ing] beyond binaries, transgress[ing] and travers[ing] power domains, struggl[ing] against the dominant order."[42] Articulation is a tool for the oppressed, a dialectical negotiation and tactical assessment of the forces at play with the goal of persisting another day. Hale raises the questions "will the subjugated knowledge and practices be articulated with the dominant, and neutralised? Or will they occupy the space opened from above while resisting its built-in logic, connect with others, toward 'transformative' cultural-political alternatives that still cannot even be fully imagined?" as he analyzed the menace of multiculturalism for the Indigenous Maya of Guatemala.[43] Equally inspired by Hale's work, Clifford argues that articulation "indicates, not a necessary assimilation or loss of social or cultural identity, but rather an alliance of popular aspirations for recognition and autonomy with the agendas of state and transnational institutions."[44] Articulation is leadership from the margins. It is marginalized groups using social media, the internet, and new forms of communication to share lessons learned, find common ground, and replicate strategies. It's about transnational social movements, alliances, and collaboration. It can be observed in how Indigenous communities today negotiate their roots using globalized routes that connect them to the broader world. It's how the Garifuna use the cities for higher education, negotiate political space with the Sandinista party, get state funding to visit Honduras to recover their language and build networks with other Garifuna communities, and still come home for holidays to celebrate family and culture. Articulation is persisting through the use of the very forces that conspire against you.

Performance—the second strategy—is (re)making cultural beliefs and practices tangible and explicit through activity and display. Cultural performance can involve (re)producing or (re)enacting culture for the state and institutions that hold power, but this type of performance also involves (re)creation and (re)surgence of cultural practices that support a shared sense of "group-ness" that unites a community. "Cultural subjects 'play themselves,'" argues Clifford, "for multiple audiences: the police, state agencies, churches, NGOs, tourists; they also perform for family, friends, generations, ancestors, the tribe, animals, and a personal God."[45] In the case of the Garifuna, this performance includes dancing, drumming, making bami, making and wearing traditional clothing, language recovery, and folk art. Tracking these performances keeps us aware of "acts" and "audience." Performance is the Garifuna youth on Little Corn Island off the coast of Nicaragua performing Garifuna drumming and dancing or the performances during Garifuna Week in Orinoco or the Garifuna celebration in Seattle, Washington. This is the Garifuna grandmother in the Bronx who consults with her ancestors about her niece's new boyfriend. These are the Garifuna families who gather on Sundays to eat traditional dishes in the Bronx. The (re)production of cultural practices—the performance of cultural meanings, beliefs, and values for oneself, one's family or community, and even for outsiders—comprises this arena of persistence and thriving. Cultural performance is action that often builds on the translation of cultural messages from one generation to another, from one era to another, from one world to another. Mateo takes his grandson out to the family's land, and the grandson will take this knowledge and combine it with his own experience of life in twenty-first-century Orinoco. Performance is a key piece of the survivance of Indigenous peoples, "unmistakable in native songs, stories, natural reason, remembrance, traditions, customs, and clearly observable in narrative sentiments of resistance."[46] It is often evidenced by "the inescapable ironies of tribal survivance in and through simulations—performances both coerced and playful."[47]

The third and final strategy is translation: the process by which the Garifuna make sense of, adapt, and interpret concepts, cultural processes, religious beliefs, and political ideologies in order to survive, persist, and resist. Translation connects the past to the present. It takes old concepts and (re)vitalizes and (re)creates them. "Translation is not transmission"; it is finding new ways of making sense of the world today.[48] There are gains and losses. For the Garifuna, the youth aren't present to help the elders cut back the weeds from the tombstones of their ancestors in the cemetery because they are studying or working in Bluefields or Managua, but they're sending money home to the elders and come home for Garifuna holidays. Translation is intergenerational, and it is cross-cultural. It is adaptive. It is conversation across difference so localized cultures like the Garifuna survive. "The concept of 'translation,' better than transmission, communication, or mediation, brings out the bumps, losses, and makeshift solutions of social life. The theory-metaphor of translation keeps us focused on cultural truths that are continuously 'carried across,' transformed and reinvented in practice."[49]

Translation is the (re)membering of practices so they make sense in today's inter-connected, globalized world. Mateo is an agile translator: he uses his knowledge of medicinal plants gained from his grandparents and strengthened by his daily conversations with their spirits, which, in turn, help him better serve the community as their healer. Yet, he also takes this knowledge to Bluefields and works in the hospital, moving from patient to patient complementing Western medicine with his herbs and plants. Mateo knows that there is Western science research that shows his treatments work; he knows that buy-in from the medical establishment of Bluefields provides safety for his bush medicine practice; he also knows that the potency of his treatments is recognized by elderly patients in the hospital and the family members who visit them.

Multiple examples of cultural persistence that involve articulation, performance, and translation can be found in the documentary, *Lubaraun*, a word which means *return* or *encounter* in Garifuna. María José Álvarez, the director, is a mestizo woman with deep roots on the Nicaraguan Caribbean coast. Her documentary emerges from a close collaboration with the Garifuna community of Orinoco and the Honduran Garifuna communities from where the founders of the Garifuna communities in Nicaragua emigrated and is intended for use by Garifuna communities themselves and to help a wider audience get to know the Garifuna. Our research team watched the community of Orinoco as they viewed the documentary in which they recognized themselves and yet also realized that this was one version, not a complete version. The use of technology and media to make this documentary is an example of articulation. The strategic deployment of narrative, place, and image to reveal a vibrant and thriving culture is an example of articulation. The dances, songs, crafts, and food are performance. It is not a memory or a photograph, rather it is alive; it flourishes. When the meals that are served in Orinoco are obviously the same ones served in Honduras, the viewer sees that there is something "Garifuna" that connects these groups. The documentary serves to articulate a Garifuna being-ness that is persistent and diasporic. The documentary itself is a translation, a message: we exist. Translation isn't just about the Nicaraguan Garifuna reconnecting with their Honduran relatives; it's also about the viewer understanding that Garifuna culture is vital.

Conclusion

Out of colonizing forces—unfolding over centuries—the Garifuna have been born, continue persisting, sometimes thriving, and often resisting as they respond to an ongoing diaspora that has taken them from Africa to the Caribbean, to Honduras, across Central America, and some even to the United States. These different

historical junctures and displacements have created situations of peril and exclusion for the Garifuna on many levels best explained by intertwined and mutually
reinforcing forms of social difference that exacerbate exclusion: intersectionality.
Decolonial intersectionality helps us see the forces arrayed against the Garifuna
as well as understand how they persist in their enactments of articulation, performance, and translation.

CHAPTER THREE

Rooting: *Garifuna Connection to Nature*

Serena Cosgrove, José Idiáquez, Leonard Joseph Bent, and Andrew Gorvetzian

"We only survived because we had ancestral medicine from our
African and Indigenous ancestors. . . They were looking for where the
river meets the sea like where they had lived on San Vicente which had
been shown them by their ancestors. Nature, the sea, and land are the
face of God for us."[1]

— Focus group, facilitated by Serena Cosgrove in March 2018

Introduction

The above quote sums up how the forces of nature—the sea, the river, and the
land—lie at the heart of Garifuna beliefs; it introduces the vital importance of
nature for Garifuna culture and livelihoods. The ocean is considered a savior, a
healer, and a place to seek peace. Land—particularly where ancestors have lived,
worked, farmed, fished, and are buried—is a particularly important part of community, and land (both for homes in the village and family farms in the bush) is
held communally and worked by households along kinship lines. Nature as a site
for kin and livelihood is what we call freedom-in-place: "We still have to decolonize our minds and empower people to stop being slaves. We do this when we
proteger las tierras [protect the land]."[2] These insights are important and relevant
for today because exogenous economic interests coincide either to force the Garifuna to leave their land or to remain on some land but without access to communal
plots for gardens, what Mollett calls "displacement-in-place."[3]

Today, many Garifuna from Central America to the United States have developed a powerful critique of national development and autonomy policies based on
present-day events and the lessons they've learned from their history as a people:
"Because we started off in West Africa. . . and then we came to St. Vincent, we lost
St. Vincent, came to Central America, and right now, people's not paying much
mind to this, but we're losing Central America as well because of the land. People
[outside interests] are buying the land, and if we go back to Honduras, go back to
Belize, go back to Guatemala, Nicaragua, we have to pay more than $1,000 just
to get back to our villages, so we're losing that *and* then imagine from there. We

can only ask our ancestors: what can we do?"[4] Andy, whose comments precede this sentence, is a young Garifuna musician and the son of a prominent Garifuna leader and musician in the Bronx; his words acknowledge that diaspora—forced movement—pursues his people due to a set of colonial, neocolonial, and internal colonial power relations whose beneficiaries have never had Garifuna best interests at heart. Andy is describing how today's situation creates very real challenges for Garifuna persistence both culturally and in terms of livelihoods, both of which depend on Garifuna connection to nature.

As of the writing of this book, Nicaragua has gone from being one of the safest countries in Central America to being torn apart by state repression and protests against corruption and President Ortega's government more broadly, which means that Sandinista leaders in communities like Orinoco have even more power that can be abused. All of this while commitments to land titling for Indigenous and Afro-descendant communities remains incomplete. In Honduras, state agendas for regional development target Garifuna beaches as future tourist centers with large hotels. Furthermore, in both countries, the effects of climate change exacerbate resource depletion and increase Garifuna communities' vulnerability to hurricanes and other climate-related phenomena such as drought, tropical storms, and cold fronts.

In this chapter, we start with Garifuna responses to land titling problems and settler incursion in Nicaragua and then look at how state actions have exacerbated the land issues confronting the communities where we've been working. Then we examine similar dynamics in Honduras building on our short fieldwork stint there with the research of Chris Loperena, Keri Vacanti Brondo, and Sharlene Mollett, among others.[5] We conclude with how connection to nature informs Garifuna spirituality in preparation for the next chapter on spirituality.

Garifuna Land in Nicaragua: Signs of Tension, Signs of Persistence

As described by Leonard in the introduction to this book, the Garifuna communities of Pearl Lagoon enjoyed immense natural diversity of land and sea in his childhood. In the mid-twentieth century, the trip from Bluefields to Orinoco was one of immediate immersion in natural abundance and tropical diversity. The assortment of flora—*yolillos*, pines, mangroves, multiple types of hard woods, lilies, and orchids—and the variety of the fauna—herons, pelicans, albatross, crocodiles, lizards, screamer monkeys, squirrels, and a variety of tropical birds—were embraced by the crystal waters of the rivers, waterways, and the Pearl Lagoon itself. The water was so clear that Leonard remembers seeing the white sand sea floor and fish and manatees feeding below him. "Through our land we maintain a good relationship with our Creator, and we honor and respect the memory of our ancestors, which means to live a life of unity, in love, in justice, in liberty, in solidarity, in dignity, in joy, in patience, in faith, in benevolence, with gentleness, with temperance, and in peace with oneself and others, demonstrating model conduct for the community."[6] Corroborating Leonard's sentiments, Mateo, Orinoco's bush doctor, explains how important his daily work on the farm is to him: "I go out and hear the birds singing and praying and I pray with them."[7] Today, you do see the verdant green of palms and mangroves as you make the panga trip from Bluefields to Orinoco, but there are less birds and animals, and most of the rivers and the lagoon are brown or sludgy green because of the mud brought down river by the erosion of land inland due to the deforesting and clearing of land for settlers' cattle ranching and agricultural production.

A present-day visit with Charles, Mateo's brother, gives us all a shared experience of what Orinoco used to look like. His family lives surrounded by palm trees, pineapple plants, chickens, and a breadfruit tree. He offered us coconuts as he shared: "We have all we need. We have family to support each other, take care of each other, provide support for each other. No one is alone, we all look out for each other."[8] This scene captures what many of our research participants refer to nostalgically as the former spirit of Orinoco and reflects the principles of what Martinez, Godoy, and Garcia describe as "good living" for residents of Pearl Lagoon: family unity, reciprocity, and familial economy (in which the family can use land and natural resources to provide for themselves).[9] However, this scene is becoming less frequent in Orinoco; the Orinoco of Leonard's childhood has begun to change.

It's interesting that one of the indicators of change described by our research participants in Orinoco involves starting to see the village less as a communal space and more as a patchwork of individual houses.[10] Orinoco began to change when people put up the fences. Once the fences went up, people only cared about what happened within their own fenced area, as opposed to earlier times when neighbors helped neighbors as they all struggled with what little they had. Miss Rebecca, the owner of the hostel where we stayed in Orinoco, put fences up herself so people don't come in "disrespecting things, because it happens more and more."[11] These fences, and the threat they pose against conceptions of communally owned land and cooperative practices, are connected to broader trends that involve state promotion of internal colonization by farmers from the Pacific side of the country and state collusion with large private landowners who force residents either to join in the spoils or fall into greater poverty.

From Fences to Displacement and "Displacement-in-Place"

With the socialist Sandinista revolution of 1979, the Caribbean coast also came to be seen as a place that needed to be incorporated into the nation; it needed to become mestizo like the Pacific coast, as discussed in chapter 1. Lenin, a former director of the school in Orinoco, recalls how the revolution and ensuing coun-terrevolution brought a lot of change, especially for folks who lived out in the countryside surrounding the villages: "After the Sandinista Revolution, all the people what was in the bush came running to the community. I had a farm when I was 16 years old, now the young people don't work the land. But what they gonna do? Now there's more Spaniards owning land than all the Black people combined. And what we gonna do with the lagoon? It's empty [of fish]."[12]

The Sandinista revolutionary period (1979–1990) initially presented possi-bilities to communities like Orinoco. Forging alliances has always been a strat-egy the Garifuna have employed to survive and adapt, and there was optimism that the Nicaraguan government would fulfill their initial promises. However, Sandinista governance mistakes on the Caribbean coast, the ensuing counter-revolutionary war, in which many coastal groups formed their own rebel groups to fight against the Sandinistas, the neoliberal governments of the 1990s, and the return of Sandinistas in 2007 meant that the Garifuna have had multiple opportunities for disillusionment with government promises of autonomy and communal land titling. Autonomy Law 28 for the southern and northern regions of the Caribbean coast was incorporated into the new Nicaraguan constitution in 1987 when the Sandinista government signed a peace accord with coastal groups who had fought against the revolution.[13] Envisioned as an important opportunity for the coast, autonomy has not unfolded as it was intended. "During the next twenty-eight years the promises which their hard-won autonomy appeared to offer indigenous and afro-descendant Costeños soon came to resemble a divisive quagmire of legal disputes, patrimonial politics, and voter apathy which, while achieving a number of advances in Costeños' rights, has also seen the frustration of those aspirations which underpinned the process of autonomy on Nicaragua's Caribbean coast."[14]

The Caribbean coast has also witnessed foot dragging by the government on the implementation of 2002 Law 445 for Communal Land Titling and its five phases, which were supposed to lead to the demarcation, legalization, and clear-ing of outside settlers from Indigenous, Afro-Indigenous, and Afro-descendant communal lands on the Caribbean coast of Nicaragua. Though there has been progress regarding land titling for some of the coastal communities, the final stage of Law 445's phases—clearing or *saneamiento*—has not occurred. Sylvander describes the importance of this final phase: "While almost all communities already possess land titles, the fifth and last stage of the process—*saneamiento*—remains incomplete. *Saneamiento* refers to the clarification of land titles and is in practice typically understood as the eviction of unlawful mestizo claimants from indigenous territories."[15] It is important for communities to have legal title to their land, and it is also important to be able to use the land. This is not possible with all the settlers who have been moving onto communally held land over the past decades. This is a particularly thorny issue given the importance of land in their culture and livelihoods to all Indigenous and Afro-descendant groups on the Nicaraguan Caribbean coast, but it is especially important for Garifuna communities given their practice of household farms on communally owned land outside of the villages where they live. Today, these lands are being invaded by the Pañas or colonos or settlers from other parts of the country. Bryan explains how the government's refusal to respond to the influx of settlers or third parties is happening: "Under Law 445, Nicaraguan state officials are required to prohibit settlement of community territories by *terceros* or 'third parties' who come from outside the community. In practice, titling and demarcation have coincided with an unprecedented influx of terceros, many of whom see Black and Indigenous territories as frontier lands free for the taking. The terceros have benefitted from the state's lack of enforcement of the law, pushing settlement and deforestation deeper into Black and Indigenous territories."[16]

Though we've said settlers are comprised of peasants, farmers, and land investors and defined settler colonialism as the dispossession and replacement of Indigenous peoples earlier in the book, the preceding paragraph exemplifies why it's important to unpack who settlers are in the Nicaraguan context because we're using multiple terms—settlers, *colonos* (settlers or colonizers), *terceros* (outsiders)—and though these terms refer to the same problem, there are many people and interests involved in this process of "settling" land that is held communally by Indigenous, Afro-Indigenous, and Afro-descendant communities with a long-term connection to the land in question. Furthermore, the issue has a long history. On the Caribbean coast of Nicaragua, British colonos or settlers took land away from Indigenous peoples in the seventeenth century.[17] In the nineteenth century, coastal communities asked the British to advocate on their behalf as the Nicaraguan government attempted to "incorporate" the Caribbean coast. Then, in the early twentieth century, the Nicaraguan government gave U.S. companies concessions to Caribbean coastal lands that effectively dispossessed and displaced many communities. Since then, the Nicaraguan government has used the Caribbean coast for extraction, often taking lands away from communities, and giving it to political cronies as well as encouraging land-poor farmers on the Pacific side of the country to claim "empty" land on the Caribbean coast. In this case, land-poor farmers were displaced by the Somoza dynasty in the mid-twentieth century and then by the Sandinistas and other Nicaraguan governments pursuing similar strategies expanding the agricultural frontier from the Pacific coast into the communally held lands of the Caribbean. Even in the case of mestizo, poor farmers who claim to have legally purchased land on the Caribbean coast, they often have different concepts of the land, in which land is to be subdued, cleared, and used, which exists in opposition to many of the communities on the Caribbean coast who attribute different cultural meanings to the land as well as utilize different practices for cultivating the land.

There are many signs of a lack of faith in the Sandinista government and responses from communities as a result. In a community near Orinoco, a community member corroborated the tensions by saying, "Something I do know and even though we're isolated here, I do read books and magazines and newspapers when I can get them. Here we're far away from the Pañas on the Pacific coast. But every day they are taking over the Caribbean coast more and more. This stealing of land is not something that Somoza did. He stole fish and wood and did investments with the Creoles, but he didn't involve himself with our land. This is a new move by Ortega [current president of the country] that looks like he wants to outdo Somoza and that thief Alemán [neoliberal president of Nicaragua in the late 1990s to early 2000s]."[18] When the Garifuna have limited access to communally owned lands to raise crops for consumption, they are faced with the conundrum of "displacement-in-place": unable to live as they have, they must join the national economy or emigrate and seek ways to earn money so they can buy food.[19]

As one Orinoco community member put it: "The Pañas are coming in and cutting down the trees and cattle ranching, they are not people from here, land is holy, land is the mother, land is for everyone and the Spaniards don't get this."[20] Leonard describes it this way: "Due to the current threats against demarcation and titles, Indigenous claims to their lands are at risk"[21] as outsiders move in and there's no way to stop the flow. Miss Blanca told us that there is ongoing trouble with the demarcation and how it keeps changing and no one really knows what belongs to the community and what doesn't.[22] Again, this creates local conflict in which coastal communities are at a standstill with settlers and the government does nothing because the dispossession of Indigenous, Afro-Indigenous, and Creole lands is in the state's economic interests.

According to Dolene Miller, the Creole representative on the committee for the implementation of Demarcation Law 445,[23] many costeños feel that Central America should not have been split into countries north to south but east to west. In the case of Nicaragua, in fact, the tension between the Pacific coast and the Caribbean coast can be likened to "water and oil that never blend."[24] Government commitments to autonomy for the Caribbean coast and commitments to respect Indigenous, communally held lands created hope for some because "Nicaragua cannot be two countries" as Miss Patricia of Orinoco tells us,[25] but the state continues to put obstacles in the path of providing deeds for communally held land, creates alternative power structures that undermine the Caribbean coast's regional governments, and does nothing to stave off the influx of illegal settlers.

Signs of Tensions

Present-day tensions over land are visible when one visits the Garifuna communities around the Pearl Lagoon basin. A path connects Orinoco to a neighboring Garifuna community a few kilometers north called Marshall Point. The elevated path runs parallel to the lagoon, cutting through swampy terrain that often floods the path that has been under construction for years. As we walk with Mateo along this path, the group is shocked to pass by a large section of fenced-off land with a sign at the entrance that reads "PROPIEDAD PRIVADA: PROHIBIDO LA ENTRADA" (Private Property: Entry Prohibited). Such a sign in earlier decades would have been unimaginable due to its direct contradiction of community values. While one is still able to pass freely through this "private" land by taking a path that cuts through fields of swaying Taiwan grass, the sentiment is that the sign violates the idea of community land and is an indicator of the emerging tension over land rights present throughout the Pearl Lagoon region. Once we get to Marshall Point, another hand-painted sign highlights the importance of land and current tensions. Nailed to a post carrying electric wires that reach above the Moravian Church, the sign reads: "Welcome to Marshall Point. If my people, who are called by my name, will humble them self and pray and seek my face and turn from their wicked ways, then I will hear from Heaven and will forgive they sin, and will heal their land. 2 Chronicles 7:14." We ask ourselves if this sign is an early indicator of community organization around land, or trust that a higher power will deal with the tensions.

Not all interactions with settlers, or Pañas as they're called, start out negatively. Multiple times we've seen Miss Rebecca amicably greet mestizo farmers, who've come to visit her from their homes in the bush inland from Orinoco so she can purchase chickens and vegetables from them. However, even in these cases where coexistence seems possible, there are now signs of tension. For example, initial observations from visits to the small Garifuna community of San Vicente of Pearl Lagoon in March of 2016 showed a similar, mutually beneficial relationship between San Vicente and Nueva Esperanza, a primarily mestizo community further inland. San Vicente is the smallest of the five Garifuna communities that surround Pearl Lagoon, with a population of less than five hundred. There is no cell phone tower, no electricity, and the dock is in bad repair and difficult to access. It is also the only Garifuna community with visible tread marks of vehicles, which lead east to Nueva Esperanza and the Nicaraguan mainland. On a return visit with Mateo in 2017 during Holy Week, however, he commented how he is particularly worried about this community, fearing that "they are abandoned, it could be easier to take advantage of the land, the people, and the resources."[26] During this visit, a new hand-painted sign, dated September 24, 2016, stated the following:

> Welcome to the community of San Vicente in the municipality of Pearl Lagoon. The communal government together with the general community are notifying all mestizos that the law of our community of San Vicente is that no one has the right to sell titled land nor buy such land without our approval, and we also give notice that all of the mestizos on our communal land must pay taxes and he who does not pay taxes must leave the land by order of communal leaders and the national police. Thank you.

Requiring payment of taxes is technically illegal, but shows how communities are having to negotiate to get something out of the deal with the settlers, a process that has been observed elsewhere on the Nicaraguan Caribbean coast as well: "Residents of other titled Indigenous and Black communities have attempted to deal directly with the settlers, often entering into rental and even sale agreements with less than favorable terms."[27] What do these signs mean for Garifuna identity in the face of outside incursion, especially given the legacy of exploitation and violence during the revolution and counterrevolution and the current strategies of the government to divide and usurp the lands of coastal communities? The appearance of signs are manifestations of Garifuna push-back against these invasive forces or at least indicators of what James Mittleman describes as "infrared politics [that] one must dig deep to excavate the everyday individual and collective activities that fall short of open opposition."[28]

Community-Level Problems and Lack of State Response

According to Orinoco community leader, Kelsey, "territory is a big issue for the Garifuna. Land means so many things: ocean, rivers, water, forest, creeks, mountain. Land gives us food and what we need to survive. It gives us security. Now there is a cultural clash regarding different views of the land. The Spaniards see our land and see future *potreros* [fields to run cattle on]. The government sees our land and sees a way of making money by putting in the canal."[29] Kelsey is critiquing the Sandinistas' unrealized plan to push a canal through the country, which would mean that many coastal communities in the southern part of the Nicaraguan Caribbean would lose land for the project. Furthermore, community members have an explicit critique of the current Sandinista government and the president Daniel Ortega as described by one of our research participants:

> I am very bothered with the regional government and Ortega's people on the Pacific [side of the country]. They are the ones who are making

problems with Indigenous lands. They are Ortega's people and the sad thing is that the same Sandinistas who are Garifuna or Miskitu have joined these Managua politicians who never have cared about us. And the Garifuna, Miskitu, and Creoles receive money for the communal land and then the problems start. They receive money from those who run drugs and those who are with Ortega, but those who die are never from Managua. Rather, it's us the folks from autonomous Indigenous groups. And they say we Indigenous people have rights, but this is a lie. They only think about us when the elections are coming up.[30]

The Sandinistas use a divide and conquer strategy that means offering a couple of community members access to some resources in exchange for loyalty to government policies. Those few get benefits, leaving the rest of the community fighting over clientelist scraps that often aren't even relevant or appropriate, like sending pigs or cows to people who fish. Then loyalty to the party becomes more important than loyalty to your community. Multiple conversations with community members in which they repeatedly requested anonymity speak to this pattern, in which certain elected community leaders take advantage of their positions to sell community land to outsiders. According to one former communal government leader, in fact, "the community stops being involved (in community politics) because they see the discrepancy between word and action. The coordinator of the communal government is measuring off land and selling it."[31] In resonance with the above reflections, we heard the following in Bluefields from a professional committed to work in the communities: "the government party is putting the Indigenous and Afro communities in harm's way. We Garifuna, Miskitu, Rama, and coastal population are people who have been excluded and the government is willing to do anything to take away our lands. They're doing it in the dirtiest way by having campesinos fight with Indigenous people over land. And the big landowners and politicians who are behind it all don't show their faces because they are cowards. We are the poor people who die."[32] Other scholars have witnessed these trends on the Caribbean coast of Nicaragua.[33] Bryan summarizes it in the following way: "In fact, supporting the illegal settlement of Black and Indigenous lands appears to be one way that Sandinista officials have managed newly dispossessed populations while adding to their electoral support. Interviews I've conducted in several Indigenous communities in the RACCN [Caribbean north] suggest that settlers receive preferential access to Sandinista-sponsored rural assistance programs that offer credit for small-scale agriculture. Both efforts demonstrate the Ortega administration's commitment to a national economic growth model that relies extensively on dispossession as means of accumulating wealth."[34]

Gendered Effects of Land and Livelihood Pressures

The land grabs by mestizos from the Pacific coast side of the country put pressure on the communal lands of the Garifuna, but this is made even worse by the pressures that community members are under to sell their own land, even though legally it is prohibited to sell communally held land. Waiting on the dock in Orinoco for a panga ride to a nearby community, we spoke with six men there who were talking about selling their land, needing money more than they need the land. They felt they didn't have a choice. They're up against a wall: if they sell their land, they receive some money, but they produce less food for themselves, meaning their costs go up. They live here in Orinoco, where many products are more expensive due to its distance from urban centers. Also, there are fewer jobs here, but because they are forced to sell land, they can no longer produce what they need for themselves. Before there was subsistence and some form of sustainability, but at least people could get by. Now they find themselves with little choice and in a different form of poverty, because they have even less ability to produce their own food, having become dependent on food and other consumer goods produced on the Pacific side of the country.

This situation, in which community members themselves consider selling land, is connected to the fact that there are not as much fish. According to Mateo, some community members have sold land to the mestizos because they don't want to farm the land anymore: "they think the Black man shouldn't be a farmer, should be fishing."[35] The difficult part of this is that fishing has been so depleted in the Pearl Lagoon and out on the sea due to overfishing by the commercial fleets that many are unable to earn a living fishing. One of the school teachers in Orinoco told us: "We don't work. The fish is bajo, bajo, bajo. A lot of people live hand to mouth. In fact, the whole country needs work."[36] So, they sell the land because they don't want to be farmers, but then have to fish to survive and there are fewer and fewer fish.

These economic changes have gendered effects at the community level as we've seen in Orinoco. Miss Heidy—who works closely with Kelsey in the women's collective that brings women together to prepare traditional Garifuna foods for sale—sees that these changes are creating more work for women. When men stop fishing and farming, women have to take on more responsibilities: "women are doing the farming now."[37] Interestingly, the point here isn't that women are doing the farming. Garifuna women are hard workers, and they have always farmed, which is corroborated by the historical record. Multiple mentions in British records from the eighteenth century describe women working the fields on the island of St. Vincent. One such account indicates that women "sustained every species of drudgery: they ground the maize, prepared the cassava [manioc], gathered in the cotton and wove the hamack."[38] Contemporary researchers also come to similar conclusions. Keri Brondo describes Honduran Garifuna women's active role in farming, both for past generations of women as well as present-day farmers. Moreover, the selling of land affects women more than men: "Stories of land loss center around women, because land loss, whether to a mestizo or to another Garifuna. . . is a process by which women have lost resources to men."[39] The point that Miss Heidy is making is that the men aren't helping. When men can't fish, some of them are not able to find other sources of income; she says "Mostly men doing fishing, though now there is less and less [fish] all the time."[40] This dynamic can create an identity crisis for men (meaning they can no longer consider themselves providers), and it ends up putting more responsibility on women to cover unpaid reproductive work at home, farming, and other forms of income generation.

Miss Magda has a little store near the Orinoco pier. She has a couple of businesses, including a panga that takes people into Bluefields and back. She's also been on the community council, but left disillusioned when a male colleague used his position to sell communal land. A frank conversation with Miss Magda elicited the following analysis: "The biggest problems for women are lack of jobs, no money anyway, domestic violence happens a lot and not just to me. My husband used to drink too much. He would say that I was jealous. That's when I decided to let him do what he wanted to do and I was going to dedicate myself to my kids and move on. I would take the kids out to have fun and not pay any attention to him. Then he stopped drinking. I think it had something to do with my attitude. Now he dedicates himself to the farm and natural medicines."[41] In fact, since her husband stopped drinking, he's now treated as a leader in the community. We could tell that she is proud of her decisions, his changes, and how respected he is today. This story resonates with other stories we heard from strong women in the community who seem to have more agency and power over their lives than their counterparts on the other side of the country. Gender expectations for women, particularly mothers, in Garifuna communities include a lot of hard work, but they also include more freedom and independence. Virginia Kern's formative work on gender and the Garifuna in Belize sustains our observations. She writes, "Female sexuality and labor are not treated as the property of men, nor are women subject to the authority or direct control of men in their daily lives. They choose their own spouses and leave unsatisfactory unions at will. They control the products of their labor and can acquire and hold property in their own right."[42] In today's Orinoco, the independence that Garifuna women, particularly older women with children, have is accompanied by a lot of responsibility and hard work, so much so that in many cases they are the only sources of income for their families. Women's employment is not just in the informal sector, outside of the formal economy.

Correspondingly, although there are few paid positions in Orinoco, most of them are held by women (for example, teachers, nurses, and doctors). It was common to hear the following comments: "We ladies are powerful. We depend on ourselves for self-support. . . Everything here is ladies."[43] As women carry the responsibility of income earners, this can increase the respect they receive in their families and the community. But it also means, in some cases, that men haven't found new things to do and are at a loss.

And while some women have been able to access the available jobs in the community, young women are vulnerable to early pregnancy and sexually transmitted diseases, exacerbated by the fact that "Nicaragua has the highest adolescent birth rate in Latin America and the Caribbean."[44] Kerns describes how Garifuna women in Belize, even young women, have sexual freedom, but this is constrained by "[t]he prospect of being left literally holding the baby [which] troubles many young women."[45] Miss Rebecca, who worked as a nurse in the Orinoco health clinic for decades, repeatedly mentioned the need for increased sex education and public campaigns to fight pregnancy in young women as early pregnancy limits their opportunities. Because girls and women have primary responsibility for caring for children, having children at a young age means you either have to stay home to take care of your child, or hope you have another woman family member to care for your child if you want to keep studying or leave to find work. Either way having children too young means women get more work and often fewer opportunities.

Many of the community leaders of Orinoco express their concern about the younger generation. For example, Mateo's shepherding of the communal land he cultivates is for the future. His connection to the land is inspired by the past and the present; Mateo simultaneously seeks advice from and receives guidance from his ancestors on what plants and herbs to use through his dreams, and says the cultivation is "also for those who come afterwards," meaning the next generation.[46] In this case it is Mateo's grandson because his children don't want to work the land. The issue that the younger generation doesn't want to take on the same tasks as the older generation comes up repeatedly in our fieldnotes. Explored more thoroughly in chapter 5, the point is "no paddle, no dory"—you need oars to get your rowboat somewhere, the sage advice Kelsey has for young people.[47]

Garifuna Land in Honduras: Signs of Tension, Signs of Persistence

As a research team, we have spent a lot less time in Honduras carrying out research with Garifuna communities than in Nicaragua. Initially we visited Honduras to understand Nicaragua better because this is where Central American Garifuna communities have come from and this is where the largest population of Garifuna can be found. From simply trying to understand Nicaragua better, we came to see that this is a story of the Americas. There are Garifuna in Nicaragua, Honduras, and the other Central American countries with access to the Caribbean, and also, many of them have left Central America for the United States. They are still Garifuna; they are surviving the Americas. Many Garifuna in Honduras still speak the Garifuna language and relevant to this chapter, the struggle over communally held land is just as serious there as it is in Nicaragua.

The natural world—the sea, the beach, the land where the village lies, and the surrounding bush where many community members farm the land—is an integral part of what it means to be Garifuna. In a focus group with Garifuna community members in the village of San Antonio on the Caribbean coast of Honduras, we were told, "We Garifuna are more outside than inside. Seventy-five percent of our reality is headed outside of Honduras. And now they want to take away our land by law. They want our beaches. Our spirituality is connected to the sea. Healing takes place on the beach. After one's family, the most beautiful thing is the beach. If you were to see us throwing garbage on the beach, that would make us pigs."[48] There were nods of agreement around the circle as focus group participants complemented each other's comments. Another community member added "going to the beach is feeling healing for us. Here is where I find my Black God who I know. I am grounded here facing this water and I feel the air of our ancestors and this gives us solutions to our problems."[49] These comments reveal the contradiction that the Garifuna face today: their connection to the natural world is their spirituality, and it is their natural world that the state and private investors want to develop for tourism and housing for elites. Because the natural world, including the sea, forests, the land where villages sit, and the surrounding land farmed by the community, is sacred, anything that puts their natural world at risk puts their very existence at risk. The three top risks to Garifuna culture in Honduras are acculturation, illegal sales of communal land, and loss of the language according to three different focus groups we facilitated. "If we lose our language and the land, we lose everything that is ours. The good thing, though, is that there are leaders emerging who are aware of this."[50]

In Honduras, land titling programs in the 1990s focused on "settled, 'urban,' residential land, excluding traditional harvest and agricultural lands."[51] So many Garifuna communities are having to fight for the land outside of the villages where they've grown their food for centuries. Many Garifuna communities are thinking about strategies they can pursue to safeguard their communal lands through such actions—examples of articulation—as organizing, training, and leveraging outside expertise. As one community member put it, "We are also suffering from a lack of creativity when it comes to the sustainable use of the land. We need to strengthen the link between our ideas and our land; we need to be thinking about how we can develop activities and get technical assistance to work the land."[52] Another community member chimed in: "Good use of the land requires training and community organizing. A lot of people get depressed; they don't have anything to do, and they get involved with drugs and alcohol and related vices. It's not easy with fishing. Yes, we have the right to fish, but there is so little fish."[53]

And again, similar to Nicaragua, Garifuna elders in Honduras are realizing that though their children come and visit them regularly, many of the younger generation don't want to be farmers in the bush. Community elders ask themselves: Who will take over the land that we still have? Ernesto relaxes against the warm wood wall of the family kitchen after a long day in the bush. He too is worried about what will happen to the land he's been farming all these years. He says, "None of my children will work the land. Does it make sense to hire someone to work it? I understand the temptation to think about selling it."[54] Ernesto's reflections evoke Mateo's confession that none of his children will take over the farm in the bush outside of Orinoco: Mateo's only hope is his young grandson.

The Honduran government and investors are developing coastal lands as tourist destinations, what Keri Vacanti Brondo calls "the onslaught of coastal tourism and housing development."[55] One of Loperena's research participants describes these policies by saying "they use development to enslave us."[56] Not only do the development projects include false promises for local communities, they use the local cultural attributes of Garifuna communities to sell the resorts. "Nonetheless the luxury amenities available at Indura [a tourist resort] are inaccessible to local Garifuna communities."[57] Multiple comments during our focus groups expressed people's concerns about what this means for their villages and farms. "Tourism is a threat to our ancestors' land and [even worse] it's sad that young, trained professionals are those who betray the most by selling land for money."[58]

Given the weakness of the Honduran state and disillusionment with its promises, Dr. González, a Honduran Garifuna medical doctor and leader in the Bronx, discusses the lack of progress in Honduras over the last generation. She says, "We are worse off than before because of these [government policy] processes. The privatization of Honduran beaches has created a situation in which one runs the risk of being shot if they walk through a private beach."[59] Yet, similar to the Garifuna communities of Pearl Lagoon, community members are being convinced to sell their land even if it is illegal. "Many times it is the Garifuna themselves who sell their land. Poverty creates problems that make people have to sell their terrain. Land is not for sale; land can't be sold. People have to make a real effort to sell the land. But because there's someone who will buy it and becomes the owner, then they want to take over everything. Lands held in trust—communal lands—means we have to take care of the land."[60]

Conclusion

The importance of land for the Garifuna and the challenges to Garifuna liveli-hoods related to land are not solely because their connection to land is what sus-tains their spirituality. Nor is it just because the government of Honduras pursues the strategy of "neoliberal governance put in place to advance megatourism and [luxury] housing projects that favor a select few investors" and the government of Nicaragua continues "to strengthen its control over all branches of government, including the national police force, [so] Black and Indigenous communities face increasingly desperate conditions."[61] These are all contributing factors, but it's also that for centuries the Western-driven project of coloniality—colonial, neo-colonial, and now internal colonization processes—have treated the Garifuna and their ancestors as less-than-human, in other words not white and not of European descent. This is what justified the enslavement project of the sixteenth, seven-teenth, and eighteenth centuries; the denial of citizenship of the late eighteenth and nineteenth centuries; and the megadevelopment projects of the twentieth and twenty-first centuries. In Nicaragua, this tendency is exemplified by state author-ities who repeatedly referred to Indigenous activists protesting the inter-oceanic canal project as uneducated and uncivilized. In both countries, this means that more and more folks have to participate in diasporic journeying that takes them away from communities in order to support themselves and their families. How-ever, this does not mean the end of Garifuna culture; it means that *a pesar de* (even at this high cost) the Garifuna persist.

We see this persistence in their communities of origin in both Nicaragua and Honduras where elders continue to communicate with ancestors in the gathering of medicinal plants and the daily movement to and fro between villages and farms in the bush. We see this persistence in commitments to community organizing and community efforts to preserve their language, as in Honduras, and in efforts to preserve traditional food dishes by the women's collective, as in Orinoco. And at the heart of it all is a visceral knowledge that they are connected to those who have come before them, their ancestors, and that their ancestors continue to inter-cede on their behalf. This happens in communication with the ancestors through dreams and through daily interactions with the natural world, be it walking along the beach in Central America or New York City, or by taking care of the natural world through not littering and acting sustainably, wherever they are located.

This twenty-first-century commitment to the natural world resounds through-out all of our fieldnotes. There is Mateo in Orinoco who dreams with his ancestors at night so he can find and harvest the medicinal plants the next day to heal this com-munity. There is Kelsey in Orinoco who has helped organize a women's collective to turn produce from the farms into traditional Garifuna dishes like the yucca tortilla known as bami, a generations-old form of carbohydrate that predates corn tortillas and bread for the Garifuna. There is Cora in San Vicente who says she'll raise her family there subsisting off of fish and trading with the mestizo farmers inland; she never wants to leave. In Honduras, it's Sister Soyapa who self-identifies as Garifuna and organizes the religious celebrations so they happen on the beach under the full moon. And in New York City, it's Central American Garifuna who keep the connections alive by saving up to visit communities of origin on a yearly basis and who still know that walking down to the beach—be it the Hudson River or Long Island Sound—is part of what it means to persist as Garifuna. In New York, the Garifuna, there, also persist, continuing to translate the old into new forms of being Garifuna. For example, Milton, a Garifuna language teacher living in the Bronx, articulates this aspect of today's challenge/opportunity: "[The flow of Garifuna people to the U.S.] has been a highway of growth. This is because of the exodus of Garifuna from Honduras, the harassment about our land, the lack of employment. Now we find ourselves in a situation in which we have to create something new to survive."[62] The growing number of Garifuna in the United States means that they are creating new ways of worshipping the ancestors and connecting to the natural world there. As Kenia tells us, "In New York, we can do some of the rituals but for some, we have to go back to Honduras."[63] Only some parts of Garifuna cultural practices can be translated across the Americas, and so the seasonal routing back to communities of origin in Central America is sustained: "Yes, I'll be going back for Easter. You know, I want to go back and visit home, go back to the routes, to the coconut trees, to the beach, to the ocean breeze drumming outside in my village, you know, it's a beautiful feeling, so I'm definitely looking forward to going back."[64]

The relationship of the Garifuna to the land carries a strong spiritual component. Leonard describes it this way: "The Garifuna spirituality has to do with our relationship with our Creator, our relationship with our ancestors, and our relationship with nature, with the understanding that this is the center of our persistence."[65] Broken promises through the centuries with national governments about land ownership have led to fences and troubles with Pañas in Nicaragua and the struggle to maintain communal lands as the government allows foreign investment concessions to ancestral beaches in Honduras. We can't forget that the struggle for the defense of communal lands and natural resource conservation are part of an ethic and sociopolitical approach of Indigenous and Afro-Indigenous peoples that responds to a different connection to the earth and human relations than that of the mestizo. And yet, the Garifuna persist, and yes, there are signs of resistance, but the gravity of the situation weighs heavily on them, given how the land is intimately tied to the worship of the ancestors, the root of Garifuna identity.

CHAPTER FOUR

Believing: *Garifuna Spirituality*

José Idiáquez

"The important thing for the Garifuna is that what affects one of us affects all of us. There are still people who don't understand this. Ancestor religion—the presence of our ancestors in our daily lives and the struggle for nature, land, and sea—we can't separate it from our spirituality. It's a spirituality of combat. Not because we want to be conflictive, rather because all of our history has been a struggle; it's been dispossession; and it has been fleeing to survive. Our spirituality is ecological. We have to defend our natural resources."[1]

—SISTER SOYAPA, interviewed by Serena Cosgrove in March 2018

"Love, it comes with a fire, and that fire comes from the ancestors. *Unitement* is strength, loving one another is culture. We're leaving that foundation of people looking to help people. People tell me, let's go make money, but no, I just love my Garifuna people, and my ancestors. . . We can do things here, we are made in His image, and His image is love, just pure love, and we can do things in that image!"[2]

—MATEO, interviewed by Andrew Gorvetzian and Leonard Joseph in January 2018

Introduction

When I arrived in Orinoco in January 1992 after thirty-three hours of travel from Managua, I found a small town without electricity and whose inhabitants drew water from wells or carried it from springs. I arrived around 6:30 in the evening, as candle light illuminated the altars in the homes. It was common to see Christian saints interspersed with photographs of deceased relatives. After months of living with the Garifuna people, I realized that these altars were not mere images from a photo album. These representations of who have come before were a source of struggle, identity, persistence, joy, and resistance because Garifuna ancestors, who are with God, continue to support them in their struggles against oppression, poverty, and injustice. This is the heart of Garifuna spirituality.

I found a festive town where dance, drumming, singing, and poetry were practiced on a daily basis. The spiritual celebrations inspired by the ancestors permeated all aspects of life. Even in the face of challenges such as war or natural disaster, what prevailed was the organization of dances to celebrate birth, healing, the harvest, fishing, illness, and even death or some other request of the ancestors. "We endure all the cries and struggles through song. That is why the drum is very important in our life," commented Agustín.[3] Drums celebrate life and protect against death for a people whose celebrations are a way to maintain the cultural and natural wealth inherited from their ancestors. In the 1990s, life was precarious due to poverty and post-conflict isolation, but there was a palpable sense of communal unity in the face of these challenges. There was a respect for leaders. At the same time, these were a people who had suffered hardship for centuries, and the weight of oppression and colonialism was present, but through evoking God and their ancestors, seeking their wisdom and advice, and taking care of their elders, disease was healed. It was a town of interfamily solidarity: "When a Garifuna suffers, we all suffer and we all cheer up."[4]

While the Orinoco of 1992 may seem simpler and more peaceful in my recollections, I know that persistence, resistance, survival, and struggle in the face of threats remain constant qualities for the Garifuna. However, the fast pace of globalization and economic integration means the difficulties the Garifuna have confronted in the past decade are multifaceted, complex, and oppressive. The Garifuna communities of Nicaragua are changing as they are incorporated into cell phone networks and gain access to satellite television; these new developments affect how community members spend their time and think about themselves and their world. Nonetheless, ancestral spirituality is key for understanding how the Garifuna view the world and face adversity. When I speak of spirituality, I refer to it as the connection the Garifuna have with what is sacred, and it cannot be separated from their relationship to nature, from the defense of their land, from the persistence inherent in their beliefs and traditions, and from their abilities to create alliances, to survive war, and to overcome government exploitation and repression. By exploring these themes central to today's manifestations of survivance and persistence, I hope to reveal the complexities of the effects of modernizing processes under a neoliberal, capitalist system and how the Garifuna use spiritual practices to resist these ambivalent developments.

In this chapter, I open with an introduction to Garifuna ancestral spirituality in Orinoco and Pearl Lagoon in Nicaragua, followed by a review of the historical events that explains how the Garifuna came to incorporate Christian elements into their spiritual practices even as far back as when they lived on St. Vincent in the Caribbean. This is followed by a present-day exploration of Garifuna spirituality in conversation with other religions. I close the chapter by exploring Garifuna spirituality in the diaspora of New York City.

Ancestral Garifuna Spirituality

Isidro says, "Garifuna carry our ancestors in our blood. The spirit of John Sambola [the founder of Orinoco] and our deceased relatives are among us. John was a community leader, both spiritually and religiously. When we listen to the drums, the living dance with our ancestors. When we are grieving and in trouble we are with our ancestors who never leave us. We all go together."[5] With this comment, Isidro explains ancestral Garifuna spirituality to me and how it is a way of living, feeling, thinking, acting, seeing the world, people, nature, all of which is inspired by the spirits of the ancestors. The ancestors give meaning to the lives of the living as they confront personal and collective struggles. The ancestral spirituality and the struggle to defend the earth, to preserve the culture, and to protect its traditions are inextricably linked. Spirituality is not the exclusive property of the religious, but rather an inherent part of human culture. Spirituality belongs to all human beings.[6] There are non-Christian spiritualities and spiritual non-believers. To seek the meaning derived from human suffering, injustice, death, and sorrow touches the depths of the human condition and does not necessarily have to be framed in a religious context.[7] For the Garifuna, the important experiences of personal and community life are celebrated with rituals, dances, drums, and other activities, often with multicolored costumes. Positive and negative energies can be present in these activities, and ancestral wisdom is the guide to overcome negative energies. The rituals seek protection from negative energy (meaning from chaos) and the summoning of ancestors and their victories to the collective consciousness. In these ways, the ancestors are present in the daily life of the Garifuna, serving as guides for families and contributing to the unity of the community with an authority bestowed by their death. In order to understand this relationship, it is important to explore the most significant moments of Garifuna spirituality: birth, illness, and death.

In these transcendental moments, we can see how the Garifuna reconstruct their relations and reinforce ethnic cohesion through ritual. "The rite is a set of actions that, precisely because of its recurrent and methodical character, evokes and reproduces the internal experience in which a community expresses itself objectively and recognizes itself socially as a whole, as a body."[8] The symbolic value of Garifuna rites explains their capacity to remember events, acts, or behaviors carried out by the ancestors in another time and in another space, and to apply that knowledge to solving the challenges in the present moment. In Garifuna rites, there is a combination of ancestral presence and Catholic ritual. Kerns, the author of the foundational ethnography about the Garifuna in Belize, argues that the Garifuna don't distinguish between Indigenous or Christian ceremonies because the point is to honor the ancestors: "(t)he rituals form a whole, all intended to satisfy the dead, protect the living, and express the 'gratitude' of living kin to the deceased. Shamans, who conduct some of the rites, are pious, usually practicing Roman Catholics, as are the older women who organize most rituals."[9]

Religious syncretism—the fusion of elements that leads to a new production or a new reality—emerged when the colonial powers imposed their religion through violence on the Indigenous peoples of Latin America and the Caribbean. In the case of the Garifuna, who suffered this imposition, they knit Catholic belief with their own beliefs in order to survive and persist as a people. Kerns described this syncretism as well: "'Christian' and 'indigenous' (Arawak, Carib, African) elements are nearly inseparable. [The Garifuna] have been directly acquainted with Roman Catholicism for over 250 years, since their emergence as a distinct cultural group. On that basis alone, Christian elements are nearly as 'traditional' to. . . ritual as those derived from Amerindian and African sources."[10]

Since the ninth century, Christianity has been synonymous with the culture of Western Europe, and the colonial projects of those countries facilitated the rapid expansion of Christianity. In Latin America, Christianity carries the responsibility for this historical atrocity. Christianity remains the religion of the dominant powers, and as long as colonial and neocolonial imperialisms and interests exist, the imposition of religions whether Catholic, Protestant, Moravian, or Anglican, to mention a few, must reflect deeply on this charged historical and political heritage. Religion becomes an instrument of subjugation, and there is a long Christian tradition of using the anti-idolatrous struggle to justify the oppression of Indigenous peoples and people of African descent arguing that they are beings without civilization or rights. Within this paradigm, they are called "satanic" and "pagan" and are ridiculed for still following their own spiritual practices. This set of beliefs bred the destructive results and the domination inherent to the colonial strategy. The Garifuna were not immune to these devastating consequences of colonization. Johnson describes how theologians and sociologists continued to perpetuate this discrimination against Garifuna beliefs due, in great part, to the limitations of their own worldviews and prejudices. These researchers used the fact that the Garifuna didn't have churches and worshipped their ancestors to justify ethnocentric conclusions about a lack of religion simply because the Garifuna didn't fit into orthodox definitions of what it means to be religious.[11]

The Garifuna ancestors on the island of St. Vincent encountered the Protestantism of the English, the Methodist missionaries, and the Catholicism of the French. In order to preserve their ancestral spirituality, the Garifuna had to undertake heroic struggles, in which there were many martyrs. Catholicism ended up becoming the system most amenable to negotiation, thus allowing for the continued practice of ancestral worship. In fact, ancestral worship was seen as similar to the worship of the saints in Catholicism. Through a syncretic accommodation with Catholicism, the Garifuna built relationships with the French Catholics. From Catholicism, they practiced what was useful to them, and disregarded what did not align with their beliefs. It is the ancestors who give the believer the strength to resist the powers attempting to dominate, enslave, exile, or kill them. A clear example is that they baptized the children as they deemed it a way to obtain the protection of the ancestors; however, they were not interested in marriage and other Catholic rites that did not take the ancestors into account.

Syncretism as revision takes place when a religious worldview is opened, assimilating it, reinterpreting it, and, ultimately, recasting itself in its own identity. The fact that the dominant religion has the capacity to rewrite new elements into the contested (Garifuna) religion does not necessarily mean that the Garifuna religious worldview loses its validity; rather, it recreates elements of itself within a new framework. Garifuna spirituality can be understood in this form of syncretism as revision, as the ancestors are not negotiable and have remained present throughout their history. The ancestors have resisted all the various sociopolitical conflicts that the Garifuna have faced, and Garifuna spirituality involves the leadership and participation of men and women, with vital roles for all.[12]

In order to better understand the persistence of ancestral worship, an examination of the rites of birth, healing, and death is important. For Garifuna midwives, there are two key moments to ensure the reception and integration of a newborn child in the community. One is the rite of invocation to the spirits of the ancestors for the protection of the child. The second is the rite of Catholic baptism as an offering of the child to God, in thanks for that new life and for the child to be a member of the community. These rites allow us to understand how Garifuna spirituality carries ethical values, reinforces ethnic identity, and serves as a motivation for the sociopolitical struggle in defense of its natural resources. Dominga, a Garifuna midwife, explains, "This is a belief only for us Garifuna. Before healing or doing a labor, you have to ask for help from the ancestor spirits. What would become of us Garifuna without the strength that our ancestors give us? That is our secret. The placenta is never left lying. It has to be buried because the earth protects it. This is how midwives taught me when I was learning this work."[13]

In the burial of the placenta the child is linked to the earth as well as to their community. The ancestors offer access to a new mode of existence through the ritual associated with birth. The Garifuna who moves away from the ancestral practice is not an *idehati*, or collaborator of the community, but rather a *wuribati,* or cursed person who can betray and destroy the community. The rejection of this bad behavior puts the emphasis on the danger of breaking the harmony that must exist between the Garifuna and their natural and historical worlds. This ritual also connects to baptism, which serves as the divine legitimization of the protection of the ancestors. Faith in God as the source of all power is a fundamental part of the inheritance of the ancestors and corroborated by Clara, another midwife serving Orinoco:

> The midwife cannot do anything without the power of God. Our relatives who are with God communicate in many ways, and also in dreams. My grandmother who was a midwife told me never to forget that God is the one who does everything and protects us. He made the sea, the plants to make medicines. This prayer was taught to me by my grandmother when she was at the births and told her, "May God receive you and live in your spirit. So be it." I never forget to say this when I am in a birth or a baptism because it is God who gives us life and protects us from diseases and evil.[14]

In this way the Catholic, Anglican, or Moravian ritual of baptism becomes a means of accessing the ancestors. The ancestors have their home in Heaven and by participating in the baptism they become a bridge to receive the protection of God.

The protection of the ancestors remains present when the Garifuna become ill and the rites that exist in a time of sickness serve as an extension of the rite of birth. When the disease is extreme and the Garifuna have exhausted all means to achieve healing, a single community of living and deceased who fight to save the sick person's life is formed. It is at that moment that the *walagallo*—or dance of the roosters and known as *dügü* in Honduras—is performed. This comes from the conviction that the person has become seriously ill because he has chosen wrong behavior and it is up to the spirit of a family member to protect the individual from their own mistakes by causing an illness that leads to a change in the life of the ill person. This way of understanding the disease implies the conviction that the ancestors, even after death, have authority over their children and grandchildren to correct wrong behavior. "It is the spirits of the sick relatives who tell me how to proceed," said Isidro, the *sukia*, or healer, of Orinoco. In this ritual, for three days, they dance to the rhythm of the drums, sing ancestral songs, and cook the meals that the ancestors request. The sacrifice of the roosters is key to the ritual because the blood and the earth are a source of life and unity between the living and the dead. The blood is fertilizer of the earth, which symbolizes fertility. Through the earth, the requests made by the ancestors can be satisfied symbolically. The sacrifice of the rooster erases the faults committed by the patient.

There are other means besides the walagallo to pursue healing for someone who is ill. The experience of Mateo, Isidro's grandson, who saved his uncle is an example:

My uncle was poisoned because he had not defecated and urinated for 33 days. The doctors told me they could not do anything. I urged the doctors to operate on my uncle. I received through dreams with my ancestors that the herbs to cure my uncle were in the hospital courtyard. It was a lot of bad smell, and I told the doctors that if they opened my uncle's stomach I would clean it and get the dirt out of the stomach. The doctors let me do my job with the help of my ancestors and my uncle was saved. The herbs made him go to the bathroom normally.[15]

The alliance with the God of the ancestors generates an active resistance, in the sense that it drives individuals to perform actions with security, strength, and optimism as Mateo did to save the life of his uncle. With that same security and optimism, Mateo performs deliveries of newborns and cures people from snake-bites and other diseases: "I communicate with my grandfather and my deceased (relatives). That gives me strength and confidence I need to heal the sick. I teach my grandson about the plants that heal. That's how I learned."[16]

With this same confidence and optimism, the Garifuna bid farewell to the dead in the ritual of death. When the child is born, the midwife offers the newborn child to God and the ancestors. When a person dies, the community enacts the rite of death, in which they act as a collective midwife. The community gives the dead body to God, invoking the ancestors so that the deceased can be received by the mother earth. In the vigil, the drums and the sound of the shell, blown as a horn, represent the community as comprised of the living and the dead. This singular entity becomes responsible for delivering the deceased into the hands of God with the assurance that they will experience a fuller life. In Garifuna spirituality, there is no contradiction between body and spirit. The body of the deceased is not something to discard, as antagonizing the relationship between the body and the soul would prevent the deceased from becoming an ancestor, a deceased entity who nonetheless lives and dwells within the community of the living. The value of the bath-purification ritual is analogous to the baptism of the child. This rite consists of obtaining a good death from God, a death that allows for the transformation of the deceased into an ancestor. "My great-grandmother taught me," recalls Esperanza, "a very old Garifuna prayer, to help the one who is in agony. 'My God, look out for me' (*Arijabanon Bungiu Nuguchi*). And this is said in the name of the person who is dying and in the name of the child that is born. The deceased is like a child that needs to be cleaned."[17]

Despite the social and political complexity that exists today, the persistence of the Garifuna continues, and it is primarily due to Garifuna women who pass on the protection they receive from God and their Garifuna ancestors. Kerns argues that women, even more than men, remember the ancestors more actively, stating that "women [don't] forget their parents after death. [Garifuna] ritual centers on the remembrance of deceased lineal kin; and older women—mothers of the living and daughters of the dead—organize the requisite rituals, collect the funds needed to perform them, and take most prominent part in them. In doing so, they protect and represent their children, grandchildren, and other lineal kin to the ancestors."[18] The concept that God provides them with community, solidarity, justice, ethical values, and the capacity to struggle against evil and death comes from their parents and grandparents. Garifuna hospitality, family values, obedience, respect for ancestors and parents, concern for sick family members, being discreet and cautious (*duari* in Garifuna), surviving challenges and illness, and prayers of praise and prayers for faith (petition) to God who gives life and forgives are all values that lead to the survivance of practices and Garifuna unity.

To sum up, Garifuna rituals are the expression of a spirituality that arises from a syncretism that has the hallmark of resistance and involves the leadership of elders, women and men, and the participation of other community members, including youth, in dances and drumming. Garifuna spirituality has a sociopolitical dimension that varies according to different contexts and times. The history of the Garifuna, in general, and those of Nicaragua, in particular, is marked by constant struggles with colonial powers in the past and neocolonial powers today, and by a commitment to the preservation of ancestral teachings and the defense of the land. The community rediscovers its sense of unity and becomes aware of how to respond to each new political situation by leveraging ancestral wisdom.

Ancestral Spirituality and Defense of Natural Resources

As we pointed out in chapter 3, we cannot forget that the struggle for the defense of the land, natural resources, and the cultures of Indigenous and Afro-descendant peoples is sustained by an ethical and sociopolitical approach that understands justice as a response to both the needs of Mother Earth and the oppression of marginalized peoples. This means that Garifuna spirituality has political implications and emphasizes the importance of the sacred relationship between human beings and nature. It is this sacred connection that is fundamental for mitigating the adverse consequences of the environmental and ecological effects of climate change and resource extraction.

The fight for land and the right to use natural resources have been the constant struggle of the Garifuna people, as for many of the Indigenous and Afro-descendant peoples throughout Latin America and the Caribbean. Currently, in both Honduras and Nicaragua, Garifuna communities continue to be stripped of their lands, a situation summed up by the words of Jacinto, "We arrived in Trujillo deported from San Vicente. In Trujillo we had problems and we are fleeing to Nicaragua. Here it was not easy either and we had the same problems as in Trujillo. Always fighting for the land left by our ancestors. . . And now, they want to take that land away from us. And we will continue fighting because that is the land left by our ancestors."[19] The Garifuna express their deep conviction that not only have they been made of the earth, but that it is the place where they die and are born, where they join the family of the living and then the family of the dead. I was witness to this in the 1990s, and I continue to see it in the twenty-first century. As Vernan, a Garifuna musician and teacher in Bluefields explains, "Being Garifuna is a gift from the Almighty God. . . From our cosmovision, we know when there will be rain, when there will be tides, fish or no fish, whether or not to trust strangers. Nature gave us that understanding, and God created nature."[20] This profound spiritual connection that Garifuna communities have with nature reveals the significance of the threat that environmental destruction represents for the Garifuna in spiritual terms. Threats to communal land ownership manifest themselves when large landowners hold thousands of hectares: according to data analyzed by the Universidad Centroamericana-Managua (UCA), 57 percent of the land of Nicaragua is held by 7 percent of the population, while 40 percent of rural families (some 170,000 families) have no legal title to land.

In Nicaragua, while the government speaks of love for Mother Earth, it prevents the Indigenous and Afro-descendent communities of the southern and northern Caribbean regions from self-governance due to state economic interests in the natural resources of the coast. In recent years the peoples of the Caribbean have suffered invasions of land by colonos (settlers from the Pacific), who level the forests to raise cattle, extract precious wood, and pollute watersheds with mining and farming. This situation generates violence and instability on the coast and is exacerbated by the threat of megadevelopment projects such as mining concessions and the Interoceanic Canal. Mr. Cecil, ninety-two years old and a lifelong resident in Brownbank, a small Garifuna community on Pearl Lagoon, explains that "in Orinoco the Spaniards of the Sandinista Government are already damaging the land. As it is happening in the north Caribbean. They use the land for cattle, and they put in a lot of chemicals. The invaders destroy the earth and leave us in misery. It has always been like this."[21] In the collective memory of the Garifuna people in Central America, land and resources are cultural and spiritual elements necessary for physical, cultural, and spiritual survival. The threats of megaprojects, overfishing, pollution from mining, and deforestation are not only physical threats, but also profoundly spiritual ones.

When I began to visit the Garifuna communities of Honduras, such as Limón, Santa Fe, Sangrelaya, Barrio Cristales, and Río Negro in 1993, I saw how Garifuna communities confront a state whose actions represent an attempt to divide the communities. Doña Ana affirmed this, "We Garifuna cannot bow our heads. That land belongs to us, and the military and the landowners have to know that we Garifuna will not allow them to steal what is ours. Those lands are sacred, but we know that these people do not rest because they want to steal land for livestock. These people who have the power want to divide us and take advantage of our riches. That is how it has always been."[22] Doña Ana is expressing an experience that she has lived as a Garifuna and speaks to the great task of avoiding divisions and the possible weakening of the community in the face of the threats and actions by people who want to take away their lands and natural resources. "Do not bend your head as you defend sacred lands" is a common motto that springs from the spirituality that has been forged through oral transmission and through rites for many Garifuna.

In Nicaragua, this new threat comes from state politicians and Sandinista party leaders who have the political and economic control of the country in general, and the Caribbean coast in particular. Sandinista leaders, whose power emanates from faraway Managua, exert their power in ways that evoke the colonial past. Control by national and regional governments prevents the territorial governments of Indigenous groups from exercising their rights. It is a strategy to fracture organizational structure, on the one hand; and on the other, it is creating struggles with colonos (settlers) who occupy the land. "Political parties come in, and people join them because they can get rich, and they only care about the benefits of the party and they do not care about the people. They trying to divide us."[23]

Current state policies inflict an especially sharp pain on the Garifuna given the promises that were originally made in the 1980s. The promise to legalize the lands where Garifuna communities had historically lived and the promised political participation of ethnic groups in economic, political, cultural, and social matters was what motivated the Garifuna of Nicaragua to support the Sandinista revolution. Consistent with their historic tradition of making alliances as they had done in San Vicente and in Trujillo, the Garifuna found in the Sandinistas the allies of this new phase. Sandinista support was a key factor in facing the domination of the Creoles and the constant pressure of the Miskitu. Freddy Estrada, a friend of mine during the 1990s, said, "Because I believe in the strength of the spirits of my ancestors, I grabbed the weapons to defend my people from that unjust war. I do not like war, but someone who does not defend the lands that our parents and grandparents left us is not Garifuna. That's what the Garifuna did in this war. Our ancestors in San Vicente and in Trujillo also died to defend their lands and their people."[24] For the Garifuna, neither the interests of the Sandinista political party nor the defense of a socialist political ideology was their priority. Rather, it was their community interests that conditioned their "support" for the Sandinista revolutionary project in the 1980s. In other words, it was a way to exercise persistence in a situation of adversity. Unfortunately, none of those promises were fulfilled and nowadays the situation is worse and Garifuna are vulnerable to the repression of the Nicaraguan state as described in the previous chapter.

Garifuna Spirituality and the Navigation of New Churches

The nature of Garifuna spirituality must resist threats to the land from outside political and economic forces, but another challenge is the proliferation of different Christian churches in Garifuna communities and their varying degrees of hostility to Garifuna ancestral worship. In this section, I explore the relationship between Garifuna spirituality and these different Christian churches.

It is nothing new that many religious denominations visit the Caribbean coast of Nicaragua to seek new followers. These groups, mostly Pentecostals, Jehovah's Witnesses, and Assemblies of God, came to the Pearl Lagoon basin to preach the Gospel. While I lived in Orinoco, I witnessed four groups that arrived in search of converts, and I continued to meet them in Trujillo and in various Garifuna communities of Honduras in 1993. In many cases, the Garifuna population of the various communities came because these churches offered cans of meat, food, and clothes; in other cases, they arrived and provided dental work and other medical services. Many of these groups came from the United States and other countries in Latin America, such as Brazil, Mexico, and Guatemala. Agustín explained this phenomenon to me and how it occurred both during and after the Sandinista revolution (in 1980 and again in the beginning of the 1990s): "The people were present because there had been a terrible war and the shortage was strong throughout the country. And for the Garifuna, receiving a free treatment of his teeth or of another type was a privilege. But that did not mean that people were converted. Besides, those visits were isolated."[25]

What has changed at present is that these new religions have built churches in the communities, and conflicts and divisions are generated among the Garifuna as a result. The strengthening of Evangelicals and other denominations is due, in the case of the Garifuna communities, to several factors. One of them is a lack of leadership by the local Delegates of the Word (lay representatives of the Catholic Church) and the absence of Catholic priests and nuns in the communities. This has created a religious vacuum that Evangelical groups have occupied. "The evangelicals have been strengthened, and because there are Garifunas who have renounced their culture. This situation is causing many divisions and conflicts."[26] This creates conflict because though these groups do offer services and resources that communities need, they frequently do not stand up when injustices are committed against the Garifuna. Furthermore, many of these groups demonize ancestral worship in the same way the first Catholic missionaries did.

In some cases, this process has allowed for new iterations of Garifuna spirituality to emerge, and this articulation of something "new" has already happened and is a dynamic process. The experience of Martin, brother of the deceased drummer, Absalón, is very significant in this regard: "I am a saved person and I believe in the drum and in the walagallo (dügü). I believe that the ancestors are present and have power. They can manifest. The drums allow the spirits of our ancestors to dance and enjoy. The body dies, but the spirit remains alive. And they are the spirits with whom we speak. We must be in proper communion with the spirits of our ancestors, serving God, doing good to people, speaking well of people and helping. And I am from the Pentecostal Church."[27] Martin's experience shows us that a Garifuna can be both Evangelical and still worship the ancestors. In this case, both in his adherence to the Pentecostal Church and his fidelity to the ancestors, he manages to feel the presence of God in his life. It is a matrix of elements that do not merge, but rather exist separately according to the moment that is needed.

What we have observed in our ethnographic work is that current religiosity does not tend toward pure types, but rather the tendency is to combine new forms with the traditional beliefs of people and groups. Religious options are abundant and out of the abundance emerges new forms of syncretism. Martin's experience demonstrates this syncretism as an aggregation, an adding on of new practices that support his survivance. Pentecostalism has diverse branches and this group of churches is known for speaking in tongues inspired by the power of the Holy Spirit. Another significant feature of why Pentecostals are successful on the Caribbean coast is singing and dancing. When people go into "trance" and speak "other languages" the sound of the songs is raised and the dance intensifies. This is something very familiar to Martin as a member of the Garifuna community and brother of a drummer.

Another factor influencing Garifuna spirituality is that some believers also use a political calculus when deciding which religious group they will join.[28] In the current Nicaraguan context, this political calculus has become critical. In Nicaragua many Evangelical and Pentecostal churches are suffering relatively little repression even as the Nicaraguan government unleashes death threats against priests and bishops of the Catholic Church. There are few Evangelical, Pentecostal, or other denominations that have denounced the assassinations and the repression of the dictatorship since the political crisis of April 2018 began. Moreover, many non-Catholic churches are receiving economic support and a series of privileges from the government. If talk is focused on heaven and eternal life, there will be no conflict with the oppressors of the people. The struggle against unjust powers can result in the loss of life.[29] Given this complex web of religious affiliations, political alliances, and the resultant new syncretic forms of Garifuna spirituality, the task of clearly defining Garifuna spirituality today has become increasingly ambiguous and thus challenging to articulate.

Given the ambiguity inherent to this task of defining modern Garifuna spirituality, it is crucial to focus on the key elements common to Garifuna ancestral worship and Christianity in general: Jesus Christ and the ancestors. In the Garifuna ancestral worship view, Jesus is the model ancestor, one who was obedient to his parents and who opted for solidarity with the oppressed. A community member during a focus group in Honduras describes how "the Lord chose me to be part of this community to continue in this spiritual practice. Despite my Catholic identity, the *chugu* (dügü) remains my ancestral religion."[30] When Christianity and ancestral worship meld, a new syncretic interpretation emerges. Jesus is interpreted by the Garifuna as the bearer of a set of values who exemplifies the love of God for humanity: obedience to God, obedience to his parents, fidelity, justice, and solidarity. From this fusion of God and ancestors, the Garifuna experience the protection of those superior beings that guide them. This is how the courage of Freddy, who spoke earlier about taking up arms in defense of his community during the 1980s, is understood. During the war, Freddy felt on the one hand the responsibility of taking up arms so that they would not continue to kill young people who were forced to participate in military service; on the other, he felt obliged to defend the ancestral lands. Freddy saw danger if the war continued.

It is this communal spirituality that gives strength to Garifuna commitment to the land, rivers, sea, and their ancestors, as these are a vital part of their culture and have supported their survivance. Don Isidro was in charge, along with Esperanza, of performing the ritual of the walagallo or dügü, and he said, "The Garifuna cannot forget that we will not survive in our struggle for life without our ancestors. They are our strength because they are with God and they want to see us united. If we are divided, the powerful take advantage of our lands, of the wood, of all that God has given us."[31] Don Isidro's explanation is echoed when twenty-six years later his grandson Mateo comments, "We have to trust in God, that's all. . . We need to think about those who are dead, because we will be dead soon, so love your people now. Tomorrow may never come, the time is now for a clean, loving Orinoco. With a Church, a clinic, and a school. Building, producing, that is love. Life is one."[32]

Both Mateo and his grandfather Isidro, from two different generations, are convinced of the importance of keeping God and ancestors in mind. The presence of diverse religions in a community does not mean the loss of a belief as strong as the ancestral one. As Eric, a young man who plays the drum in the walagallo ritual, explains: "The spirituality of the Garifuna people is a very deep and powerful belief. Our ancestors are with us in our diseases. They communicate to us in our dreams."[33] This is a process that obliges us to listen respectfully and pay attention to how community members weave different religions and practices together in order to stay in conversation with their ancestors in daily life. In this process we have to emphasize the political implications of a deep and sustained spiritual commitment. No matter the religion, the fundamental issue is the spirit of struggle and commitment to their ancestors.

Garifuna Spirituality in Diaspora

In the unity and force of the community is where the spirits of the ancestors manifest themselves. Today's globalized world threatens this cohesion. We have heard testimonies of the loneliness and struggles faced by young people when they leave their families and decide to emigrate; on the cruise ships when the young single mothers leave their children with grandmothers; and when young people leave Garifuna communities for Bluefields, Managua, or Costa Rica. "Cultivating spirituality does not aim to flee the world; on the contrary, it is a way of feeling integrated within it and more in solidarity with everything that lives and suffers, more fully linked to the center of reality."[34]

The worshipping of ancestors is typical of a spirituality that believes in the afterlife and the relationship of the living and dead as a community that persists. Garifuna ancestral spirituality has been present in the diaspora from Africa to the Caribbean, from St. Vincent, to Honduras, and from there to Belize, Nicaragua, the United States, and other countries to which they have migrated. It is an inner strength that empowers and strengthens them to overcome obstacles on a personal and community level. Without that strength there is no resistance. The past of the ancestors, which is present in the here and now, is what makes it possible to integrate all aspects of the life of the Garifuna: fishing, agriculture, life, sickness, death, love, and adversities. All of them are linked to that ancestral spirituality. As the Jesuit priest, Father Tomás, a Garifuna of Honduras, points out: "If we lose that ancestral force, we will lose our capacity for resistance. The ancestral spirituality, our obedience to them is not negotiable for the survival of the Garifuna anywhere in the world they live."[35]

It is vital to trace the effects of the diasporic present on Garifuna spirituality outside of Central America. As Luz, a Garifuna professor in New York City, states: "What causes the most division in the Garifuna community? It is definitely religion, no doubt about that. It divides us the most, it shows our colonized mentality, and when you have a colonized mentality how do you get out of that?"[36] This issue is important because an inherent trait of a diaspora is dispersion, and dispersion can be a weakening factor in that it is the opposite of cohesion. This challenge of dispersion comes from the shock that Garifunas experience when they leave their communities of origin for a city like New York. If it is traumatic for a Garifuna to move from Orinoco to Pearl Lagoon, Bluefields, or Managua, or for a Garifuna from Sangrelaya to live in Tegucigalpa or in regions where there is little population that speaks their language, how much bigger will the shock be in a country like the United States with another language or working on a cruise ship serving people of many nationalities and diverse languages? If we add that often immigrants are blamed by dominant groups for violence, disease, and lack of employment, the experience of alienation and suffering can be even greater.

For many Garifuna, there are feelings of fragility, abandonment, and uncertainty that force them to make decisions that, in many cases, are not desirable but don't seem to have any alternatives. The following example was shared with us by two Garifuna sisters in the Bronx:

> Margarita has three children (one daughter and two children) in the Bronx. They have had to change religion out of necessity. The Pastor of her church gave them food and got a job for one of her children. Understand the difficulties for people who leave their ancestral land and go to the United States. Know that it is a mistake to renounce the ancestors, but also understand that there are people who have given up alcohol and drugs because they are in those churches. It is good that women unite as Garifuna because we are the ones who spend more time with our children.[37]

From these experiences arise many questions, doubts, and feelings found in the Garifuna community of the diaspora. It is not strange that with so much complexity, discrimination, and conflicts (even between families), there are questions such as: "Who clarifies what is the difference between religion and tradition? I know that many Christian Garifunas are against the idea of bathing and feeding our ancestors. But a true Garifuna has to balance her beliefs and faith between the religious and the traditional."[38] The Latin word from which tradition derives is *tradere*, and it is no coincidence that the same word can be translated as "to transmit" or as "betray." In the creative process of transmitting what we receive, it is possible to betray what has been transmitted to us. Traditions are fundamental in the process of adapting Garifuna identity to modernity. This identity is strengthened when the family plays a role as producer and reproducer of inherited cultural behaviors. One of the most important resources is oral transmission, through which the elderly, who are usually grandmothers and mothers, transmit their knowledge, legends, and beliefs. If we analyze the example that was shared with us about Margarita, we can understand that she was seeking community and access to resources for her children's survival. We cannot generalize and say that that every Garifuna who changes his religion is a traitor. We have already seen that Garifunas can be Pentecostal and continue to maintain ancestral spirituality, as Martin explained earlier.

We also have examples of Garifunas in New York who are still Catholics and believe in the strength of their ancestors, and they become a bridge between the ancestral land and the diaspora. And often, it is women who are responsible for transmitting and defending the traditions. In Santa Fe, a small beachside community in Honduras, our host was a Garifuna woman who had lived in New York for thirty years. We stayed in her home built over the course of decades, and we documented in our field notes: "People did not leave here and forget about it. I'm sitting here in a house that is literally New York transplanted here in Santa Fe. It is a beautiful house, with furniture and appliances from another country. Yet in 1984 she went to New York. For years and years they always maintained this big dream to build this house here. Thirty-four years later, it is here. A successful story of return. Successful in that there was a vision, a plan, and a persistence. And a connection to this place that was always there."[39] This transfer of a New York lifestyle to a remote Garifuna community in Honduras is an example of the complexity of the diaspora. This elderly couple made the decision to build the house, but it was the wife who insisted on returning to the ancestral land. She hopes that her grandchildren will visit the place where their great-grandparents were born. As Johnson points out: "the homeland is conceived both as a geographic backwater compared with the city, and as a hallowed place: hallowed because it mediates the past in some way that resist[s] transience, even though the homeland village may be fully engaged with processes of modernity."[40] The owners of the house in Santa Fe worked very hard for many years, but never lost contact with the ancestral land. That sacred land is a haven of peace for a person who has worked day and night in adverse situations. This couple chose to return to the community of their ancestors because the sea is a sacred spectacle that God gives them. The countryside, the rivers, the mountains, and the moon illuminating the sea make them feel fully realized. "When you have a problem, sit here in front of the sea air. Spirituality is here where our spirits summon us."[41]

As we have seen, religion is a factor that can contribute to the union or disintegration of a community. Despite all of this complexity, there are so many signs that Garifuna ancestral spirituality persists. However, it is important to not judge a Garifuna person who decides to belong to another church that does not preach ancestral teachings. In the Bronx we have witnessed that deep longing and sadness exist for the land they were forced to abandon. In several testimonies we heard about the challenges of redefining or recreating the ancestral force in a strange land, and, in chapter 6, we will describe these challenges in greater detail.

Garifuna Spirituality in Orinoco Today: Many Branches on a Firmly Rooted Tree

We inhabit a world in crisis and the Garifuna are no exception. We have examples of the persistence of the Garifuna through an ancestral spirituality that has sociopolitical implications. Political problems and community divisions cannot be separated from the destruction of the natural environment. "Spirituality, the worldview always has to be with reality, because every day we live spirituality in nature. We always stay by the sea, we always look for the river and the sea because they are those resources without surviving."[42] Ancestral spirituality is a way of living, thinking, and feeling, and it has its source in the testimony transmitted by Garifuna grandparents, parents, uncles, and others, who are now converted into ancestors.

It is not easy for Garifuna youth to stand firm in their ancestral beliefs because of the bombardment they receive from other cultures and worldviews, especially those young people who have to leave their communities to study or find work. Younger generations experience the religious phenomenon in new ways. Various studies in the sociology of religion indicate that young people born in the 1980s are more likely to practice new religious forms.[43] Today's youth, through social networks and smartphones, live the contradictions of communicating with others while in physical solitude. This contradiction also presents a distance between how they experience religion and how their parents experience it. Despite these contradictions, it cannot be said that Garifuna youth are forgetting their ancestors; rather they are finding new ways of living ancestral spirituality.

When we study religion critically, we encounter ambiguous and conflicting situations, with historical complicity in today's forms of violence. What we perceive is that violence today has multiple causes and unfortunately many of them are linked to injustice and the loss of the dignity of the human beings. Unfortunately, there are religions that claim to be instruments of peace, but in practice they contribute to fomenting violence, wars, and terror. As we have seen in Martin's experience in Orinoco, one can belong to a religion (in his case, Pentecostal) and maintain his ancestral spirituality. What matters is the spirituality of freedom, the one that seeks the truth and has sociopolitical consequences as lived by their ancestors. That spirituality is what generates the resistance and survivance that creates strong bonds and helps the humanization of groups and people. And it is what allows the Garifuna to support the defense of land, culture, and natural resources. From the perspective of Garifuna spirituality, the earth is the place where the ancestors' remains rest. The earth becomes the closest point of contact and communication. As Mateo explains, "Garifuna spirituality remains strong, as a tree, rooted firmly, only now with more branches."[44]

During Holy Week in 2017, our visit to Orinoco and the other Garifuna communities culminated in a memorial service for a recently deceased drummer on the Saturday afternoon before Easter, a day on which Catholics typically celebrate one of the most important masses of the year. Around two in the afternoon, we joined the community members ambling to the drummer's home tucked into a small cluster of homes by the sea; the women wore bright flower print dresses and headscarves, and the men were in crisp button-up shirts. In front, the Moravian pastors from nearby Marshall Point and the elders of Orinoco presided over a wooden table against the bright orange façade of the house, under a strewn-up tarp that covered the path where the mourners sat, while women labored in the kitchen preparing a meal for dozens of people and huge speakers blared gospel music. The service summoned a considerable number of people, among them young people, girls, boys, and adults (though without a doubt, there were more women than men), who joked and gossiped before the ceremony began.

The activity took almost two and a half hours in stifling heat, with only the occasional whiffs of sea breeze leaping from the sea and inflating the tarp gently like a sailboat on the open lagoon. Everyone listened with respect to the preaching from the pastor, the testimonies from close friends, and a solo sung by the drummer's daughter. At the end, the audience sang in unison; but though we sang the same songs, they came from two different sources, as the Catholics sang dutifully from their Catholic song books and the Moravians from the leaflets their pastor had distributed. At one moment, the pastor spoke of faith as a visa, a means of getting you from one place to somewhere else, and finished by declaring, "religion doesn't matter, but Jesus Christ does," which received a rousing "Amen."

After the service we rested on the dock as the sun descended across the lagoon, and soon made our way to the Catholic church to prepare for the Saturday mass. Even as we rang the bell, few people came to the church, and even fewer community members went to the cemetery to visit the graves of their ancestors. The absence of people in the church suddenly made sense, because for the Garifuna to support and accompany the family of the deceased drummer in a multifaith ceremony for the death of her brother is a way to fulfill belief in God and the ancestors. The ancestral worship persists, but it happens in a multifaith service under a tarp beside the sea instead of in a particular church.

Another branch on that tree of Garifuna spirituality has a digital dimension. During Holy Week of 2018, we were in Santa Fe, Honduras, and we were exhausted, looking through our phones while taking a break in the afternoon. Our morning consisted of marching beside the sea in a procession that moved to the beat of relentless drums, on the way to mass in which the powerful energy of the songs made the idea of sitting down to rest almost impossible. After dozens of offerings were danced up the aisle to be placed on the altar, choruses rang out in the exultant Garifuna language that resounded throughout the lofty curves of the church's high ceiling. Those choruses echoed in the backs of our minds when we received some tragic news from Orinoco: Absalón, the lead drummer of Orinoco since the time I was there in the 1990s, had passed away. The livestream of the funeral service, which we were able to watch on Facebook, instantly brought us back to Orinoco, where it was remarkable to see that most of those who played the drums and sang were young. Eric (whom we will meet in chapter 5) and other young people were present, and prominently so, proudly accompanying Absalón's body with their own drums, stepping into their role as the new generation of drummers for Orinoco.

Conclusion

Both of the examples above are a sign of the importance that the ancestors have and the solidarity they generate in the Garifuna communities, and while we were geographically isolated from Absalón's funeral, we were also connected to it through our smart phones. Thus we were able to participate in this rite from far away, as so many Garifuna migrants must do.

When I write about the persistence that rests at the heart of Garifuna spirituality, the faces of Garifuna ancestors with whom I had the privilege of living come to my mind. The ability to incorporate new practices without losing identity remains a characteristic of the Garifuna people. We can't predict what will happen tomorrow, but as long as there are photographs (and now videos on social media platforms) and small altars, like the ones I saw when I arrived to Orinoco for the first time almost thirty years ago, the presence of the ancestors will be alive.

CHAPTER FIVE

Routing: *Youth Persistence*

Andrew Gorvetzian

"Let us dream big. Orinoco is connected to the bigger world, but afraid of the bigger world. . . Don't be afraid, the limit is the sky. Good things come by the hard way. People say, why study if there's no work. But we can't be waiting for the jobs to come, we need to be prepared ahead of time."[1]

—ORSON, interviewed by Andrew Gorvetzian and Leonard Joseph in January 2018

Introduction: The Weight that Garifuna Youth Carry

We gathered at the door of the church to process through the community to the graveyard as part of the Holy Saturday vigil in Orinoco. We began to sing as our small group of ten people exited the building into the courtyard, twilight falling over the town. In 1992, the church used to be so full that there was standing room only. Now in 2016, our research team of five comprised half of the congregation. As we traversed the path to the graveyard to bless the ancestors, we heard other voices, young voices, singing the same songs quietly through the darkness. A group of young men had stopped to sing, and while they did not join the procession to the graveyard, their brief contribution served as a reminder that while they may not be in the church, they had not forgotten the songs. The small congregation may show how much has changed in Orinoco, but those voices of young people ask that we look beyond initial appearances to try to understand the challenges that Garifuna youth face and the choices they make for survivance in the modern world. The land, the churches, the families, and other societal forces have seen sharp fragmentation, and the pressures that have increased contact between Orinoco and the outside world fall disproportionately onto the shoulders of the young.

This ethnographic chapter elucidates how Garifuna youth of Nicaragua confront these challenges today by assuming new roles as translators of inherited strategies of Garifuna resistance while also creating new strategies by appropriating tools of globalization and turning them into opportunities for cultural articulation and community building. Crucially, they do this in a postwar context that largely separated the Garifuna from the land in the early 1990s at the same time that neoliberal market forces increasingly inundated Garifuna communities, two historical factors whose impact informs young people's current context. Despite the magnitude of challenges that Garifuna youth confront today, there is hope that Garifuna youth can adapt to these circumstances on their traditional lands, in their communities, and by migrating and living in diasporic communities where they reassert and recreate Garifuna identity to adapt to present circumstances.

Shipping Out and Hearing the Ancestors' Call: Eric's Story

The primary means of migration out of Garifuna communities begins with a panga ride across the Pearl Lagoon, and as the journey continues farther away from home, Garifuna youth face increasingly strong forces of acculturation that can obscure their Garifuna identity. After three hours bouncing on the waves by panga, a young person from Orinoco will arrive in Bluefields. As shown in chapter 1, Bluefields has long been dominated by primarily English-speaking Creoles and, more recently, by growing numbers of mestizos. Many young people arrive to study at the Bluefields Indian and Caribbean University (BICU) as well as at the University of the Autonomous Regions of the Nicaraguan Caribbean Coast (URACCAN). Other youth in pursuit of education and opportunity may leave the Caribbean coast entirely, boarding a bus for seven to eight hours to cross the country to go to Managua, the mestizo-dominated capital city that is the country's political and economic hub and home to the largest universities: the Universidad Centroamericana (UCA) and the Universidad Nacional Autonoma de Nicaragua (UNAN), among others. The farther they get from the mostly homogenous Garifuna communities surrounding the Pearl Lagoon, the more their minority status as Afro-Indigenous amplifies. In Bluefields, the Garifuna are an Afro-Indigenous minority among the majority Black Creoles, and in Managua, the Garifuna/Creole distinction blurs even further as they become Black minorities among the majority of mestizos. Furthermore, the Garifuna identity is essentially unknown by most on the Pacific coast. Due to the division between the Caribbean and Pacific sides of the country, the Garifuna become part of an invisibilized "Caribbean coast" identity that becomes a primary means of identification in Managua.[2]

This conflation of identities from the Caribbean coast results in blanket discrimination and stereotyping on the Pacific coast that Garifuna youth must learn to navigate. During the initial meeting of a student group at the Universidad Centroamericana (UCA) called "La Juventud de la Costa Caribe en la UCA" (UCA Caribbean Youth), I conducted a focus group with students from all parts of the Caribbean coast who were studying at the UCA. I asked if they ever felt discrimination for being from the Caribbean, and thirty hands went up immediately, as one Creole student told the story of how "a professor told me it is normal for people like us to have academic struggles, because we are from the Caribbean coast." Raising both hands to his chest, and then lowering one to his waist, the student continued, "People from the Pacific are way up here, and people from the Caribbean are down here, according to some professors."[3] Garifuna share this stereotype with all people from the Caribbean coast, even as every stop of their migratory journey reinforces their minority status within that group. As a result, they must confront multiple levels of discrimination that pose a significant challenge to embodying a distinct Garifuna identity under the weight of acculturating forces that determine ethnic identification within Nicaragua. When Garifuna youth leave their communities, they find a country largely unaware that this ethnic group exists, and a world that demands complex negotiations of what it means to be Garifuna in the twenty-first century.

Those substantial obstacles of acculturation and discrimination that occur when young people migrate are compounded by questions and contradictions at home. These questions result from a modernizing process that has pushed their communities from a subsistence-based economy to an increasingly market-based economy. This change has happened furthermore in an emerging milieu that has since "annihilated space through time" via technology and economic policies and brought with it increased volatility that severely interrupted values and established practices.[4] Martinez, Godfrey, and Garcia note that these interruptions "Have implied a reduction in quality of life, with the need for consumer goods that weren't necessary before, commercial relations that exploit the community, a degradation of natural resources, and less economic autonomy for families, all of which are typical challenges of development models of extractive capitalist nation-states."[5] In some ways, this is a new iteration of the same story. The history of the Garifuna has been inseparably linked to the very colonial forces pushing them out of their homes, thus demanding a resistance in order to survive and hold onto their identity and culture.[6] It is well documented how Garifuna youth from across Central America, both men and women, have migrated in search of supplemental income, education, and other opportunities for decades in the face of such threats.[7] However, the volatility of today's context requires that we look deeper at how this long-held practice manifests today. Eric's story captures much of these challenges and opportunities.

Eric, Leonard, and I walked to a little bar in Orinoco alongside the shore of the Pearl Lagoon on a warm and sunny afternoon. Eric, a father and drummer in his early thirties, is taking on a larger leadership role within the community, a role he is assuming after having left Orinoco for a time. We began talking about what brought Eric back to Orinoco after he had left to work on a cruise ship. Sipping on bottles of Coca-Cola beside the lagoon, he explained:

> One night I had a dream telling me I needed to go back, and later that morning Kelsey called me and told me that an older woman was sick, that she needed a walagallo. I knew then that I needed to go back. So we went back and we did the walagallo. She had been to the doctor in Bluefields and they couldn't do anything for her. And so we did the walagallo, and when we hit the drum she sat up, and she started talking, and now she's better. Things move backward if I'm not here. I stay here for the love of my community.[8]

Eric represents what Orinoco may look like going forward, now that he has been called back by belief in the ancestors through the walagallo. He left Orinoco, and his work on a cruise ship brought him as far north as Alaska. He explored a world far beyond Orinoco only to return and put down roots in Orinoco. Now that Eric is back in his community and is a young leader dedicated to his community's future, he faces contradictions and challenges with new strategies that celebrate and allow his culture to persist in the face of numerous obstacles.

Eric exemplifies the give and take of negotiation of a new cultural identity in the current moment. One of the ways in which Eric pursues this negotiation is through his drum making and drum performances. At his home, while Eric stretched deer skin taut over hollowed out tree trunks and meticulously used a razor to shave away fur, revealing the skin beneath that would eventually, when dried, reverberate with the ancestral beat, Eric lamented how this long-held practice has been repurposed to generate income: "I don't like to sell my culture, but I need to. But you can't really pay for handmade culture."[9] The use of old techniques and tools repurposed for the current context shows us that "cultural forms will always be made, unmade, and remade."[10] The need to generate an income through selling drums is a result of Orinoco being a tourist destination in a national market economy, while the crafting of the drum is an inheritance of the techniques that the ancestors have used for generations. The resulting product provokes intergenerational tension, as some from older generations view the sale of cultural items such as drums to tourists as a betrayal of the community. However, the infusion of imported foods and loss of land means fewer people work the land or fish at subsistence levels, and those that do still need to generate income to buy food they once produced themselves.

Eric has recognized the impact of this reality on his community and has envisioned another way to create community in today's world through performance of Garifuna culture. He is the leader of a youth group of dancers, with three different groups of youth varying in age from five to twenty. They travel around

Nicaragua and beyond to share Garifuna dance and culture, and perform for the tourists who arrive at the guesthouses in Orinoco. For young people, this is how they make community, by practicing their cultural dances and performing it to a wider audience. Through these performances, Eric is answering a call to the "larger Garifuna nation" within a "smaller Garifuna world."[11] Eric's travels with this group have brought him into contact with other Garifuna throughout Central America, both physically and digitally. During travels with the group, he found himself with a group of Guatemalan Garifuna drummers, and "though we played with slightly different rhythms, the connection was clear as we played."[12] Eric also shares the importance of drumming for Nicaraguan Garifuna in the documentary *Lubaraun,* depicting the travels of Garifuna in Nicaragua to Honduras in hopes of reigniting Garifuna language and culture in Pearl Lagoon.

Youth Garifuna persistence requires complex negotiation and compromise, yet it also has moments of resistance that reveal the limits of what can and cannot be negotiated. As Leonard, Eric, and I finished the last drops of our sodas to the gentle cadence of the waves, we watched four kids, none more than seven years old, grab some paddles and push out into the lagoon on a dory, creating a striking silhouette as their little bodies sailed further out against the huge horizon of the lagoon. "Every kid from Orinoco knows how to manage a dory—if they can't manage one, they aren't from here," Eric commented. Watching these kids expertly navigate the boat on Pearl Lagoon, I asked, "Is Garifuna culture going away anytime soon?" Eric responded, "No, it's strong. But there are people here, the [evangelical] churches say the walagallo is a sin, say drumming is a sin, but how can drumming be a sin? But the Pentecostal (it's the Tabernacle, Go King, and Adventist) churches that are trying to discourage walagallo and the drumming."[13] However, the rejection of the walagallo did not stop some of these churches from asking Eric to make them drums, which Eric refuses to do. Though many choices represent compromise, there are some aspects of Garifuna culture that cannot be sold. It's one thing to sell a drum to a tourist; it's another to sell it to a group that says drumming is a sin. I mentioned the work we were doing in New York with Casa Yurumein, and he began to sing the Yurumein, the song that meant always looking back for a home, which they sang on the ships coming from St. Vincent to Honduras. To be Garifuna is to sing yourself home, and that strength carries on through the generations in the lyrics of Yurumein that carried over the lagoon as we sat in a thoughtful silence.

Eric's story reveals an intergenerational tension between those who view the concerts as a sin or as a profane act against what was once sacred, while the younger generation sees them as an adaptation that creates community in a new way. These tensions are similar, perhaps, to the voyages and movements Garifuna ancestors had to choose to survive. Eric is critical of the structural forces that ask him to commodify his culture in order to survive, as it is a decision he has been forced to make in order to survive and maintain his commitment to being a young leader in Orinoco. And yet, despite these constraints, the beat of the Garifuna drum continues proudly when Eric plays in ceremonies that honor the elder wal-agallo drummers who have gone on to join the ancestors. These videos are shared among Garifuna via smartphones and social media as we saw in chapter 4, when a Facebook post appeared on our phones in Honduras, showing Eric proudly playing the drum at the funeral of Absalón Velasquez, one of the three main drummers in the Orinoco community. We shared that video with our friends in Honduras, and felt the connection of the drum across the digital airwaves, shrinking space and time, and allowing for a connection with Garifuna hundreds of miles away. It is in this context that Garifuna culture finds itself today, choosing routes out of the community, while finding strength and strategies for preserving their roots. In order to understand the depth of these new forms of survivance, we must understand the historical roots that created this setting within which youth must fight so hard to maintain Garifuna culture in Nicaragua.

Historical Context:
Interpreting Modern Tensions in Response to Past Conflicts

"What seems eminent is the demise of Garifuna culture [in eastern Nicaragua]. The national influences from interior Nicaragua are being felt more strongly each year. Spanish-speaking farmers are entering land traditionally farmed by the Garifuna. . . With the increased pressure of foreign ways around the lagoon. . . Garifuna ways are being lost by the younger generations, no one under 34 converses in the language, and no more Garifuna dances are held."[14]

"The migration of Garifuna out of eastern Nicaragua is now greater than ever. The majority of migrants are young people going to Bluefields, and in lesser numbers to Managua, San Jose in Costa Rica, and the United States. However, even though migration may continue, the prognosis for the survival of the Garifuna culture is good. . . The way of life in many Garifuna villages has changed very little in the last thirty years."[15]

The first quote, a dire one, comes from Davidson's fieldwork in Pearl Lagoon in the mid-1970s before the revolution in the 1980s, and the second, more hopeful one, comes from Coe and Anderson's work in postwar Pearl Lagoon in 1996. Both describe phenomena that could encompass much of the current state of affairs of the Garifuna in Nicaragua: threat of cultural loss, Spanish-speaking farmers or colonos invading communally held land, and rates of emigration that are higher than ever. However, they present markedly different prognoses for the Garifuna going forward: Davidson sees an imminent disappearance, while Coe and Anderson see a largely uninterrupted and adaptive persistence. What could explain these different conclusions, and what does that mean for the situation that young Garifuna face today?

In order to answer the question and understand how Garifuna youth survive today, it is necessary to briefly review the interceding decade between the two quotes, as the Garifuna experience of the conflict of the 1980s in Nicaragua and the aftermath of the 1990s paradoxically planted seeds of hope for cultural revitalization, while also setting in motion processes of acculturation and increased extractivism that affect young people so severely. The triumph of the Sandinista Revolution in 1979 brought with it cautious optimism on the part of the Garifuna for two reasons: the potential for legal recognition of their communal lands, and the possibility of increased participation in political and economic affairs at the national level.[16] This hope inspired the participation of Garifuna in the war against the Counterrevolution or Contras, which marked the years from 1984 to 1990. Orinoco served as a critical military base for the Sandinista forces in the Caribbean as young Garifuna saw their military duties as a means of serving their community, thus uniting the Garifuna in defense of their land together with the Sandinistas.[17] The 1980s gave hope that the Sandinista government could lead to a brighter future for the Garifuna, and likely served as a hopeful source of unity in the face of the imminent demise that Davidson observed prior to the 1980s.

When Sandinista rule abruptly ended in the 1990 presidential election won by Violeta Chamorro, the subsequent neoliberal, postwar context presented a challenging panorama for the Garifuna. While the Garifuna participated alongside the Sandinistas during the conflict, Martinez, Godfrey, and Garcia stress that the conflict "turned the forest into a dangerous zone" in which the Sandinista army feared any collaboration with the Contra forces, and as such, "agricultural practices and their transmission from one generation to the next were affected by these restrictions."[18] An elder resident of Orinoco describes how "after the Sandinista Revolution, all the people that was in the bush came running for the communities. I had a farm when I was sixteen years old, but because of the war, now young people don't know how to work the land."[19] This removal of many Garifuna from their communally held land occurred precisely as new technological and economic forces would lead to the significant increase of extractive practices that would devastate local ecosystems, and Garifuna communities and ways of life, over the course of the following decades.[20]

As such, in the immediate aftermath of the conflict that saw increased Garifuna unity, the seeds that were planted by this convergence of factors were not immediately visible, and this may explain why Coe's tone in 1996 remained optimistic despite the mass emigration. Father Chepe documented how many values of the Garifuna in the early 1990s remained strong, churches were full during Holy Week, and the spirit of subsistence-based economics and strong communal ties still kept the Garifuna communities of Pearl Lagoon united.[21] Furthermore, despite the failures of the Sandinista Revolution, autonomy for the Caribbean north and south regions still offered the chance of cultural revitalization through education, as the Bluefields Indian and Caribbean University (BICU) and the University of the Autonomous Region of the Nicaraguan Caribbean Coast (URACCAN in Spanish) opened their doors in 1991 and 1993, respectively, in the hopes of providing culturally relevant education for the ethnic groups of the autonomous regions.[22]

Today, we are seeing the contradictory results of these processes in the postwar context in Nicaragua. For decades before the war, the Garifuna of Pearl Lagoon adhered primarily to values such as *abu amurno* (hand go, hand come), a value steeped in ethnic unity that ensured that even if one woke up with nothing one morning, they could depend on neighbors to ensure basic needs were met.[23] A meeting with a male elder in Orinoco on a visit in 2017 showed that this value still survives: surrounded by coconut trees, chickens, pineapple, and his family, he asked us, "What else do we need? No one here is alone, we all look out for one another."[24] As we walked away, Father Chepe recalled that, despite the lingering trauma of the war, this scene was a much more common sight in 1992. Today, this has begun to feel like the exception instead of the rule. The scene served as a poignant reminder that while the early 1990s did bring with it new sources of hope, the ensuing decades have proved that the combination of removal from the land, the broken promises of the Sandinista Revolution, and the rapidly spreading market and technological forces have led to a context described by a woman elder in this way: "I lived through the war and saw many things. And today it is worse."[25] This is the landscape that young Garifuna face.

Roots of Conflict in a Present-Day Context

The war forced many Garifuna from their land at the same time that global markets increased the speed and efficiency of their penetration into the isolated Pearl Lagoon region in the 1990s, separating many from their source of self-sufficiency while creating increased dependence on imported goods. This demanded more sources of income, both to cover purchases of products that were once produced in situ as well as more imported goods. That need has led to further fragmentation, as dissolving communal ties were replaced by an increasing need for income to purchase the brand name shoes that communal ties could not provide. And so, while there have always been complex effects of globalization on the Garifuna of Nicaragua, the 1990s were a particularly challenging context. "It started with the [Air] Jordan [shoes]," said Miss Rebecca, who operates the guesthouse we stay at in Orinoco.[26] For Rebecca, the omnipresence of the Air Jordan shoes in the community brought with them the desire for disposable income to buy them, a phenomenon familiar to other Garifuna communities along the Caribbean coast of Central America in the 1990s as well.[27] This desire for money to pay for shoes, watches, clothes, and other goods that people see in Bluefields or on the television comes as more services such as electricity, processed food, cooking oil, televisions, and cell phones become increasingly available and seen as necessary in order to go about living daily life. These forces have severely disrupted subsistence living and its inherent reliance on communal ties. As we accompanied our friend Mateo on his farm one day, he grieved the old ways: "Everyone together, that's culture. I take care of you, you take care of me, I give you something to eat, you give me something to eat. But now people are talking about fish for the [commercial fishing] company!"[28]

The increased presence of global market forces such as commercial fisheries that have overfished the lagoon has frayed old communal dynamics and makes young people feel pressure to join the market economy and the consumer goods that comprise it. As a young Garifuna woman expressed, "I have friends who work in Managua or Honduras or Guatemala, and I don't know if it's true, but they have good watches and expensive shoes."[29] Whereas before one could generally rely on one's neighbor for basic needs in the spirit of *abu amurnu*, the needs and desires require more than a good neighbor—they also require a steady income that is hard to find in Orinoco, as there are only a few *chambas* (odd jobs) in Orinoco. Like Eric, many youth leave to get an education or look for a job, often on cruise ships that employ hundreds of Nicaraguan workers from the Caribbean coast.[30] A young Garifuna woman explains: "Sometimes I want to go to Costa Rica because they say there's work, and so I can have money to pay for my studies. But then I need to work because there's just no money."[31]

This sentiment of having to get out of Orinoco is internalized from a young age and has affected many young Garifuna in the Pearl Lagoon region. After a long day of fieldwork, I sat down to join Miss Rebecca's grandchildren watching the Disney Channel. Her four-year-old grandson looked up at me when I told him I was leaving for Bluefields the next day and he shouted joyfully: "Bluefields is where

I go to make money!"[32] The perceived need to migrate to survive is planted early, and due to the sheer quantity of young people who leave, there is a fear among the older generations that they will never come back after having joined the modern world. In the mid-1990s, it was described in the following way: "The migration of Garifuna out of eastern Nicaragua is now greater than ever. The majority of migrants are young people going to Bluefields, and in lesser numbers to Managua, San Jose in Costa Rica, and the United States."[33] Today, the pressures to leave communities for access to higher education and employment remain very high.

This migration takes place alongside technological growth that has brought more images from outside to Orinoco and Pearl Lagoon. A Movistar cell phone tower has joined the Claro tower as more people connect to the wider world on their smart phones, in addition to the increasing channels available on TV. The growing availability of cell phones, television, and consumer goods allows windows into different worlds, and this contact exerts pressure on young people to join a world where shoes, sunglasses, clothing, and a job in a call center represent an escape from perceived poverty and lack of opportunity. In La Fe, one of the Garifuna settlements on the Pearl Lagoon that sits in a wide, flat, green field dotted with palm trees that capture the sea breeze from the lagoon surrounding the community on three sides, we watched the "Sorry" music video by Justin Bieber with a group of young Garifuna before entering church for a mass during Holy Week. One mother lamented "Now that they have the 3G, they live in their phones."[34] These technological forces have entered Garifuna communities at increasing speeds, and we have seen these changes throughout our fieldwork visits as we watched the construction of the cell phone tower and the connectivity that came with it. The lure of migration to urban areas to achieve the lives presented in music videos and social media exerts a subtle but powerful pull away from rural communities with a force that weak signals from transistor radios in the 1990s (Father Chepe's means of connection to the outside world in Orinoco in 1992) simply could not generate. As one young Garifuna man put it: "I have no hope of doing anything. I have to get out of Orinoco."[35]

More violent incoming forces exacerbate these more subtle pulls of the world beyond the communities and challenging economic circumstances, namely the international drug trade. Orinoco's geographic location along maritime smuggling routes of the Caribbean coast has led to an increased presence of drugs in the community, and a subsequent increase in violence as shipments of heroin and cocaine from South America pass directly along the Caribbean coast of Nicaragua. Isolated and rural coastal communities like Orinoco are left particularly vulnerable to the adverse effects of the drug trade that has grown substantially since the 1990s, as exemplified by the death of a fourteen-year-old boy who many community members believed fell in with the drug runners and was found with his throat slit in a river.[36] That violence accompanies new ways of making money that were not as present before. As we sat by the dock in Orinoco, watching the pangas bounce along the waves of the lagoon, a community member described how one day a friend was fishing and came across a package of cocaine in the sea, and decided to sell it because it had much higher profit margins than fish did.[37]

These volatile forces of removal from the land, economic and technological development, and violence related to drug trafficking force many young women into compromising circumstances. Antonia, a sociologist at URACCAN, one of the two main universities on the Caribbean coast of Nicaragua, describes this phenomenon as "abandoned communities."[38] The stress of the abandoned communities falls primarily onto young women, as teen pregnancy rates remain high in Orinoco, decreasing mobility for young women who often remain in the communities to raise these children. As England notes, it is typical for men to migrate in search of economic opportunity, leaving the women behind to take care of the children in addition to maintaining many of the family structures.[39] Male migration out of the communities, combined with the influx of violence from the drug trade that consumes some of the men who stay behind, means that many young women are left to care for children as single mothers whose partners are either absent or alcoholics in a community that has felt the effects of eroding communal ties. Kenia, who works for the Youth and Violence program of the Nicaraguan nongovernmental organization, Foundation for the Autonomy and Development of the Atlantic Coast (FADCANIC), describes a common situation in which alcoholic partners abuse single mothers in front of young children. Thus, these kids leave home early not only to look for economic and educational opportunities but also to get away from the violence, further fueling breakdowns in family structures.[40] As one young Garifuna woman explained, "I prefer to live alone as a single mother, I don't want to have anything to do with my son's dad, because he beat me."[41]

Gender-based violence and drug-related violence are threats to many Garifuna, but both past traumas of the 1980s and today's current political crisis often aggravate the situation. Some Garifuna support the Sandinistas, resulting from historical commitments as well as the present-day benefits of party membership. They recognize that President Ortega's initiatives to increase tourism and government funding for "Garifuna Heritage Day" in November represent concrete means of maintaining Garifuna culture. However, others live in constant fear that anything they say against the Sandinista party will lead to dangerous consequences. After a long morning of fieldwork in Orinoco one day, an impending thunderstorm forced us into a community member's home. As we took shelter during the heavy downpour, the trill of the drops on the tin roof provided a protected environment within which our friend's anxieties spilled out: "The [Sandinista] political party comes in, and they come in and they divide. They join the party because they can get rich, they only get benefits from the party, but they don't care about the people. They are trying to divide us, but some of us lost family in the Battle of Orinoco [during the 1980s] for the Sandinistas, and now they come in and put someone in charge who doesn't have the respect, the love. And so we're divided, and we can't do anything if we're divided."[42] This sentiment informed many of our conversations, many of which were prefaced by the phrase "tengo miedo" (I'm afraid). This trauma goes deep in the community, and makes the environment within which young Nicaraguan Garifuna navigate even thornier.

As a result of this confluence of forces in Orinoco's modernization process and historical factors that emerged from the postwar context, today's youth migration out of the community, long a practice of Garifuna communities, presents significant challenges to the Garifuna in terms of maintaining connection to the land, to the ancestors, and to one another within the community. Given this, signs that Garifuna culture is re-emerging through the action of young people in Nicaragua is truly remarkable; of course, it may be *because* of this volatile panorama that young people seek to root themselves in an identity that transcends the challenges of current circumstances.

Maintaining Roots through Looping Routes: Youth Strategies for Persistence

The context described above, and its connection to historical factors that have affected Garifuna communities in Nicaragua from the 1990s until now, gives us a deeper understanding of how Garifuna youth have confronted these obstacles with strategies that evoke ancestral ways of survival with modern adaptations. In Orinoco, the roots of Garifuna identity live in medicinal herbs, in the lagoon, in the beat of the drum, and in the stories told by the elders. But Garifuna culture also exists far beyond Orinoco because it is necessary for many to leave in order to be able to support family members and realize vocational goals. These routes can too often carry young people out of the community entirely, as many elders fear. However, the looping nature of these migration patterns, or "a lot of coming and going" as Clifford calls it, represents opportunities for new means of articulating Garifuna identity.[43]

Though this return to Orinoco may or may not be permanent, it connects Orinoco to the wider world and allows for ideas and opportunities to come into the community. During a conversation on the top deck of her hostel in Orinoco, Kelsey explained to us, "I don't know if I want them to come back to Orinoco because they can't reach their fullest potential here."[44] Later, when we wanted his perspective, her son Orson told us, "That's true. I would only consider living there permanently if I had a business."⁴⁵ Though Orson hesitates to commit to a full return, his mother exemplifies this routing nature as she has established a hostel in Orinoco that serves traditional food and organizes performances of Garifuna dance and drumming for tourists, even as she splits her time between Orinoco and a second home in Bluefields. The new realities mean young people may never permanently return to Orinoco, but Kelsey emphasizes that no matter where they end up, the connection to Orinoco and Garifuna culture will endure if parents can instill it in their children. Orson offers an example of this enduring connection, which remains even if he does not return permanently to Orinoco, "It means everything to me to be Garifuna, even though I left Orinoco at a young age to come live here in Bluefields. I get goosebumps when I hear the music, and at night we offer prayers not only to God but also to the ancestors. I go back to the community and try to talk to the young people, telling them that if they don't risk, they don't get, so don't be afraid [to leave and try something new]."⁴⁶

While these young people have left Orinoco, Orinoco hasn't left them, a trait of a diasporic society in which relations with the homeland are maintained through projects, remittances, or frequent visits.⁴⁷ As more young people leave Pearl Lagoon in search of education and jobs, these types of relationships will increase in scale and importance, pointing to ways in which Garifuna identity persists among young people who no longer live on the land where their ancestors rest. Though young people may continue to ship out, Leonard points out that it is "in land that we find our great home, the land that our Creator has given us. The place where life is born and where our ancestors rest, who always intervene on our behalf."⁴⁸ The land still holds a powerful spiritual significance for young people. As Ray, a young Garifuna musician and teacher from Orinoco, who now lives in Bluefields explains, "Our mind always has to go back to the land. . . Especially because of the increase in globalization and how this is invading our minds."⁴⁹ Youth migration out of Orinoco has meant radical change for those who remain behind, but it also changes the way those who have left perceive Orinoco. In some respects, Orinoco takes on a "spirit geography," becoming an ancestral place of origin like St. Vincent, the place where the ancestors rest and from whence they can still intervene.⁵⁰ Youth still go back to Orinoco for holidays, for funerals, and for celebrations. Indeed, there are even moments when ancestors' calls do bring a young person permanently back to the community even after shipping out in search of economic opportunity elsewhere; Eric's story of shipping out as a young man and then routing back is a critical means of understanding that looping strategy. Garifuna youth in Nicaragua negotiate new strategies of persistence through roots that connect them to long-practiced traditions, routes that bring in new tools, and intergenerational dialogue that facilitates how these new tactics may contribute to the survival of Garifuna identity into the future.

Roots: Mateo and His Grandson on the Farm

We wake up early to accompany Mateo along a marshy path that leads from Orinoco out into the bush where he farms communal land with techniques he learned from his grandfather, Isidro. That morning, we would learn that on the land, the intergenerational transmission of values continues. As he dipped his bucket into the well and carried it to fill a trough for a group of anxious pigs and ducks, he explained that it is here that he can do the work that is so important for him to keep connection with God, the ancestors, his community, and the next generation. He learned about ancestral medicine from his grandfather on this farm, and it is here that he is passing his knowledge on to his grandson. Father Chepe knew Mateo's grandfather in 1992 when Mateo was a teenager, and now Mateo's own grandson ran around the farm asking to smash up the herbs to make the medicines. As he guided us around the farm, Mateo prayed while collecting herbs to make the medicines that his ancestors show him, often in dreams. These medicines will be shared with the community, and this is a task that he is passing on to his grandson. Mateo insists that his work is for those who come "behind"; he is not an isolated individual, but rather a key connection between the ancestors who help him to remember or rediscover old herbal remedies on his farm, give that medicine to the community, and then preserve the memory and pass it on to his grandson. Mateo's long deceased mother told him that this little grandson would take care of him, and Mateo explains, "My little grandson, he always tells me 'I'm gonna make you.' That means that he's gonna take care of me, learn from me, and carry the traditional medicine onward."[51] Mateo, his grandson, his grandfather, and his mother live in communion with one another, carrying the seed Father Chepe saw in Mateo's grandfather's hands in 1992.

As we rested in the wooden cabin raised high on stilts in the middle of a grove of banana and palm trees, Mateo prepared a tea with herbs he has just harvested and asserted that Garifuna identity is "firme" (strong), as long as this relationship to the ancestors and the land is maintained. If people start to become lazy and stop giving thanks for what they have, that's when the relationship with the ancestors sours. He feels the effects of the erosion of family structures though, and sees how absent fathers and mothers are making it difficult to instill values in young kids. The changes have threatened this ethic, and as Mateo tells it, "I always gotta bring people up."[52] People like Mateo are crucial in ensuring that traditions survive in the midst of these challenges and that people feel connected to them, and his grandson suggests that this work will continue. As such, there are signs that despite the removal from the land, this knowledge that is grounded in the land will persist. While this is a means of survival that uses old wisdom, there are new ways in which Garifuna youth are using the routes of globalization and the opportunities it presents to suit their own ends.

Routes: Esther and the Garifuna Nation

During a fieldwork trip to Honduras for Holy Week of 2018, we traveled to Sangrelaya, one of the first communities founded by Garifuna on the Honduran coast after they were forced from St. Vincent. Under a ferocious tropical sun, we walked through the streets made of soft sand to the gentle sound of the waves crashing on the nearby beach, grateful for the occasional hints of sea breeze that managed to push their way through the trees. We were on our way to meet with a family whose daughter, Esther, had migrated from the community to study in Nicaragua. She left her home in Sangrelaya, however, with a very defined mission in mind: to travel from Honduras to Nicaragua in order to continue the cultural revitalization work that has been occurring in recent years through frequent exchanges between Garifuna people in the two countries. In order to do so, she has begun giving Garifuna language classes at her new school, the Bluefields Indian and Caribbean University in Nicaragua, where she also studies political science thanks to a scholarship that Kelsey helped her obtain from Orinoco in order to come and do this work. Esther's case is an example of how technology and the ease of communication it provides allows for young Garifuna to contribute to cultural revitalization in Nicaragua. As she explains in a video that the BICU produced about her work:

> I like to share my knowledge with others, and as a Garifuna, I feel very proud of my roots, and I love my culture. I also choose an enculturated evangelization, and by this I mean that we should thank God from where we truly are, from our roots. . . Here in Nicaragua, they have lost part of their culture, of their identity as Garifuna. The fundamental piece that they lost was the language, and this is something that has really caught my attention and is one of the reasons why I'm here, to support the recovery of the language for the Garifuna of Nicaragua. We need to understand who we are, where our roots are, and recognize the importance of recovering our mother language, because according to our cosmovision, it identifies us wherever we are, and with whomever we meet. To be away from home, away from my country isn't easy, but the truth is, with a faith in God, and in our ancestors, I've learned to persevere.[53]

In addition to the facilitation of Esther's arrival to Nicaragua, technology has also allowed her to spread her work much further through producing this video about her efforts to revitalize Garifuna culture via social media and other online platforms. Garifuna scholars, activists, and bloggers now occupy a growing digital realm in which they share documentaries, stories, and history of the Garifuna people online. One of the most prominent of these Garifuna scholars and bloggers is Kenny Castillo, who noted that Esther's type of commitment can be seen as part of a larger trend of a growing connection that Nicaraguan Garifuna are building with their cultural roots. In a recent blog post, Castillo writes, "The good news is that in the past few years with the effervescence of Indigenous and Afro-Indigenous movement, the Garifuna of Nicaragua are claiming more space, yelling more loudly and powerfully that they are ready to reclaim what was lost. Esther is contributing to that."[54] A new Garifuna nation has emerged as Garifuna youth follow routes out of their communities while maintaining their roots, spurring the growth of a transnational Garifuna nation that has both been gravely threatened by modernizing paradigms and simultaneously empowered via the effects of a "smaller Garifuna world" as a result of the space-time compression that globalization has engendered.[55]

These examples of re-appropriation of the tools of globalization and modernization that have so severely impacted the Garifuna of Nicaragua are a sign of hope for the Garifuna. In Sangrelaya, we spoke to Esther's mother in their home just off that sandy road by the beach. There, she told us that because of her daughter's work, she has come to see that the ancestors are real, and that the community feels a renewed sense of hope in the work that Esther is doing, using routes out of her community to spread the roots of Garifuna identity in places where contentious histories and complex presents had threatened to rip them out entirely. Young Garifuna use tactics both old and new in resisting and recreating Garifuna culture, and there needs to be an understanding that new challenges require new ways forward.

The Role of Intergenerational Dialogue: "No Paddle, No Dory"

We come back to the lagoon and the shores of Orinoco, where the young Garifuna navigate the waves against the massive horizon, in order to understand that young Garifuna from Orinoco push out into an uncertain future, and the ways they negotiate new identities can evoke tension with the older generations who have seen so much change in the last twenty-five years. Therefore, the need for a dialogue between generations is crucial going forward. A combination of ancestral wisdom rooted in the voices of the ancestors, held in the hands of older generations, and combined with the voices of youth are crucial to understand the new means of resistance.

In the words of Kelsey, "no paddle, no dory," meaning that without the guidance of the older generation, kids won't know where to go.[56] This is a particular challenge given the "abandoned communities" effect described earlier, but in cases of intergenerational cooperation there are signs of hope. Kelsey affirms the importance of the role of the parent in the child's life in order to help children identify ways that they can use their education and experiences outside of Orinoco in conjunction with their Garifuna identities in order to bring new ideas into the Pearl Lagoon region. This is an idea by which Kelsey lives, and as her son Orson describes, "My mom encouraged me. I saw the master's degree in the house, Master Kelsey, and I wanted that."[57] Older generations serve as guides and models, and yet older generations will never be able to fully dwell in the world of young people. In balancing the importance of ancestral wisdom and young people's application to current challenges, there lies a healing power and a source of hope.

During a trip to Orinoco, we went around sunset to visit Leonard's great-aunt Marta and great-uncle Ivan, ninety-three and ninety-four years old. She's wheelchair-bound and her bright white hair was pulled back in a braided bun; he was wearing an old Target customer representative polo. Ivan was the drummer of the biggest drum, or the ancestral drum, during the walagallo, and Marta was the granddaughter of John Sambola, the founder of Orinoco. She spoke of John fondly; he was a *curandero* (healer) who died at the age of 106, and she still speaks to him in her dreams. I asked them about the walagallo, and Ivan pulled out a tattered copy of an old newspaper, which showed a grainy black and white image of a walagallo with a group of people gathered around a table full of food. He explained, "When a person got sick, and went to Bluefields and the doctor didn't have a cure, we had a walagallo. If they didn't get up on the first drum of the big drum, we knew it was too late. But it started on a Friday, and we had a feast on Saturday, a huge long table full of food. And then we had the punch on Sunday, the *kusuza* mixed with the rum. The ceremony was sacred. It's lost now. The younger people don't care, or they do concerts. But you don't do concerts, the walagallo is sacred."[58] As the sun set orange over the lagoon, they sang the song that opens the walagallo ceremony, complemented by stories of feasts and dancing at ceremonies long passed. We asked them to sing another song, one for dancing or celebration, and they couldn't remember any more, so Ivan asked to sing the walagallo once again, a request that provoked a round of laughter. Suddenly, emerging from the laughter, a soft song flowed from Marta's lips, quivering like a record on an antique phonograph, a love song that ended with her singing "Goodnight" into the last bit of twilight over the water just outside. There is no better medicine, and the moment reminded us of the need to venerate the mysterious healing power of the walagallo and its songs from the ancestors that call them back to Orinoco.

Ivan and Marta's songs evoke memories of a time in a much different Orinoco, while young people today are trying to figure out what Orinoco will look like.

That old Orinoco survives in memory and stands in contrast to the challenges that Orinoco now faces, and the volatility of the current context may tempt older generations to cling to "local history of how things once upon a time were. . . a long lost and often romanticized daily life (one from which all trace of oppressive social relations may be expunged)."[59] Young Nicaraguan Garifuna face a different world than did previous generations, presenting unprecedented challenges from the forces of globalization. As a result, young people are trying to navigate the current moment through practices both old and new, even as some older generations at times fail to recognize what is new as Garifuna.

Beyond intergenerational tension, there is tension among young people themselves. Some hear the call of educational and economic opportunities in cities, and in pursuing that call, "leave Orinoco behind like *basura* (trash)," which a young Garifuna man expressed as he looked up from his phone during a conversation in Orinoco.[60] He was about to leave for his first year of university, and he harbored conflicting feelings of wanting to stay but feeling the need to leave. He reconciled this by planning to bring what he learns outside of Orinoco back home: "I can't leave this place, here [are] my roots, people think Orinoco like any other town. But I wanna see Orinoco grow, I wanna see Orinoco go from being a town to a city! But I need to go to where there are jobs. I need to be a good professional."[61] Orson echoes sentiments of that young man of wanting more for Orinoco despite feeling the frustration, both from leaders who discourage youth from pursuing different opportunities as well as from those who passively accept the changes without trying to affect those changes. There is frustration between young people and elders who have different memories of what it meant to be Garifuna and different visions of what it will mean going forward. There are those who would leave their Garifuna identity behind "like basura" and seek only that which globalization and consumerism have to offer, and those who would see a future in which "the culture and globalization walk together."[62] Orson sums it up simply, "Let us dream big—look for a broader project, don't lock the doors to a bigger vision, because there are a thousand ways to help contribute to the community. . . Orinoco is connected to the bigger world, but is afraid of the bigger world."[63]

Conclusion

In confronting the fear that Orson refers to and embracing the many ways to help the community by going into the bigger world, new forms of resistance become possible. Garifuna youth face an immense set of identity-based barriers in a globalized world that has pushed Afro-Indigenous youth to the margins: they are young, they are Black, they are rural, and they are Indigenous, and the further away they get from their home communities around Pearl Lagoon, the more they are reminded of their minority status. The modern context has precipitated significant shifts in cultural practices and lifestyles that have left many elderly Garifuna lamenting what has been lost, and yet we see young Garifuna contribute to and use globalized networks and technology to articulate these forces in their struggles for autonomy and survival, setting their eyes on cities and digital spaces as destinations and means to finding new ways in which they can find new ways to nourish their roots. They make these decisions as previous generations have, with the hope that leaving and looping back home, be it physically, digitally, or merely holding Orinoco as a spiritual homeland, will eventually generate new ideas that allow for the continued survivance of Garifuna culture. This survivance takes place even in the face of forces of modernization that one member of the Garifuna diaspora described as "demonios desconocidos," (unknown demons) that have come into Orinoco and other Garifuna communities across the Garifuna nation.[64] However, there is hope in belief in the ancestors. When a young person like Esther is selected by the ancestors to carry the seed of Garifuna spirit forward, "there is no way that young person can escape that fate."[65]

The Garifuna have been in diaspora since their inception. They have faced grave threats before, and the ancestors have lived on to aid in current struggles. The issues today that Garifuna youth face may be uniquely nefarious in their complexity, but there are signs that through reconnecting with roots as they travel on routes through the volatile chaos of today's world, young Garifuna continue to find new ways to express what it is to be Garifuna. Indeed, this is how the Garifuna have always survived. In order to understand these strategies on a global scale, we now set out for the streets of New York City.

CHAPTER SIX

Rooting, Routing, and Believing:
Garifuna Persistence in Nicaragua, Honduras, and New York City

Serena Cosgrove, Andrew Gorvetzian, José Idiáquez,
and Leonard Joseph Bent

"This renaissance [of Garifuna culture] is resistance against the threat of acculturation. It's something very New York, where there are so many cultures and we're just one inside this monster. You want to be you in the monster, and you have to maintain your own. But I see others fighting to maintain their culture and that inspires me to maintain my own. To deny your culture is to deny yourself. . . Why live under the shadow of another culture?"[1]

—COMMUNITY MEMBER, interviewed by Andrew Gorvetzian in July 2018

Introduction

On a trip to Orinoco in January 2018, we got off the panga and awkwardly climbed onto the dock, looking ahead at Orinoco as we pulled our backpacks on and took our first wobbly steps, shaky but glad to be back on solid land after the journey from Bluefields. Looking up, we saw not one, but two cell phone towers now blinking over Orinoco, and we pulled out our phones to notice strong cell phone service. Whereas in 2015, when we started our project, our phones were useful only for their flashlight application in Orinoco, we now had stronger service here than in Managua. Orinoco, indeed, was becoming more and more connected to the wider world in front of our eyes. This connection, we would learn, brings new challenges as well as opportunities for participation in a pan-Garifuna community that extends beyond the shores of Pearl Lagoon.

Our research has shown that migration routes as well as the increasing connectivity offered by technology have paved wider transnational routes within the "Garifuna nation" that connect Garifuna in New York and Honduras to their counterparts in Nicaragua. The Garifuna in Nicaragua are experiencing a resurgence of many cultural practices; many cite their exchanges with Garifuna in Honduras and beyond as a primary cause. These routes can inspire a new sense of what it is to be Garifuna in a global context, instilling a desire to maintain one's own distinct culture while simultaneously navigating the "monster" that is the convergence of many other cultures in New York City. This chapter will describe how the Garifuna negotiate the complexities of the ethnic and racial dynamics of New York City that underscore the essence of an ethnically based "Garifuna nation" that seeks to supersede national identity and unite Garifuna peoples with a common tie to St. Vincent, their ancestral homeland. The chapter connects that negotiated identity back to Honduras and Nicaragua, where ethnographic evidence demonstrates that the articulation of the Garifuna nation has carved out a space in which the long-marginalized Nicaraguan Garifuna have been able to revitalize various elements of Garifuna culture that had been fading. Connecting the concrete path that ties uptown and downtown Orinoco to subway trains that rumble over the streets of the Bronx and Brooklyn shows how seemingly disparate places are all connected to and grounded in, sometimes gracefully and other times more disjointedly, Garifuna identity in the twenty-first century. Building on the work of other scholars who have done work on the Garifuna diaspora in New York City, we will see how the Nicaraguan Garifuna fit into, or are absent from, the Garifuna diaspora there, and what the implications are for a larger, pan-Garifuna identity today.[2]

Dilution or Difference?
Nicaraguan Garifuna and the Garifuna Nation

The night before our arrival in Orinoco, we spoke about how we were hoping to make the best use of our trip. As Leonard reflected on his experiences growing up, he brought up the apparently innocent act of importing culture from outside until "all of a sudden you find out you've been assimilated and a hundred Creoles are singing hymns in Spanish during mass [instead of in English Creole]." *Giffiti* (a traditional medicine for the Garifuna now being commercialized and sold as a rum-like liquor by some Garifuna entrepreneurs), when diluted by more and more water, ceases to be giffiti at some point. This slow, subtle, and latent assimilation has negative effects; the more elements of a cultural or ethnic identity that are not practiced, like food, games, history, spirituality, and language, the farther a community gets from its roots.

The previous night's conversation set the tone as we walked to Miss Rebecca's hostel, set down our bags, and took a quick siesta. A booming thunderstorm passed overhead, with the sound of the downpour pounding the metal roof. After the storm passed, we took the path that curves through Orinoco, connecting "uptown" to "downtown" with a stretch of concrete sidewalk a few dozen meters long. Taking in the reggae music blasting from nearby speakers and catching glimpses of Pearl Lagoon through the small alleys between homes, we came to our friend Miss Patricia's new construction project looming over the path: a two-story home, hostel, and general store stocked with eggs, packaged plantain snacks, toilet paper, and other items. She sat on the porch, straw hat on her lap, as a few grandchildren popped in and out of the store, and we spoke of the old days, when "there was a lot of discrimination for speaking Garifuna, for being Garifuna," she said with a laugh. "But now. . . all of the sudden people wanting to be Garifuna."[3] Miss Patricia's comment is about how there might be a resurgence of Garifuna identity going on, something multiple community members told us on this trip that it "means everything to be Garifuna."[4] This pride persists even as another culture comes in, sometimes innocently, other times more ambivalently, and in the resulting mixture a new product comes out. The mingling of different cultures produces new flavors of giffiti: is it just different or is it diluted? Who makes this distinction? And why is there an interest in being Garifuna now, when it has been a source of discrimination for so long?

As our travels to New York would teach us, this "wanting to be Garifuna" is a sign of cautious hope for the strength of the root system of Garifuna identity and practices. A conversation with Luz, a Garifuna professor at Boricua College in New York City, is instructive here: "Tenemos muchos jóvenes que dicen que son orgullosos. [We have a lot of youth who say they're proud of being Garifuna.] I'm a proud Garifuna. That's not enough. But it's hard, the forces against us are so big."[5] Those forces have pushed many Garifuna out of their homes and into a larger diaspora community, where Garifuna face complex negotiations about what it means to be Garifuna in a global context. England describes how the Garifuna in diaspora face a multitude of contradictions as a result of their ability to fit into multiple diasporic spaces: "Garifuna do not find an easy fit in the racial categories of the United States or in Honduras. They do not easily identify with the indigenous categories of Central America or with the racial categories of African American and Hispanic in the United States. Nor do they completely identify with their nation-states of origin."[6] As a result of these tensions, some Garifuna speak of an ethnically based Garifuna Nation, which seeks to synthesize the contradictions and complexities that Garifuna identity undergoes in the diaspora. They do so by positioning St. Vincent as a spiritual and ancestral homeland, giving all Garifuna a common place of ethnic origin that resolves the questions of Garifuna identity as based on national or racial origin. The articulation of the Garifuna Nation began in earnest in the 1990s with the formation of various networks and federations led by Garifuna activists from Belize, Guatemala, and Honduras. Through the work of transnational migration networks as well as the increasing connectivity offered by the internet and smartphones, the Garifuna Nation has grown to occupy a digital space online.[7]

However, the Nicaraguan Garifuna have in some ways been forgotten in the forging of this pan-Garifuna identity. Perhaps the most striking feature of many conversations that we had in New York City came at the very beginning, when we mentioned that we were working with the Garifuna in Nicaragua. This elicited looks of surprise followed by exclamations of "I didn't know there were Garifuna in Nicaragua" or "I recently found out about the Garifuna in Nicaragua," usually due to a documentary they saw on YouTube. Though some research participants knew Nicaraguan Garifuna from their work in Garifuna networks and recognized the important work that was happening in Pearl Lagoon, the Nicaraguan Garifuna were largely absent from conversations, with most mentioning the Garifuna of Belize, Honduras, and Guatemala. For decades, migration has been forging transnational routes between the Garifuna in Central America and New York City. However, our work in the Garifuna communities of Nicaragua show that while some Garifuna migrate to the United States, it is more common for Nicaraguan Garifuna to migrate to urban areas within Nicaragua (Bluefields or Managua), to Costa Rica, or to Grand Cayman island in the Caribbean. As such, the Nicaraguan Garifuna have formed only a small part of the diaspora in New York City. Nevertheless, they are forming a part of the larger Garifuna Nation in important ways that demonstrate the resilience of Garifuna culture in today's convoluted cultural contexts.

Routing in Pursuit of Opportunity: Costs, Benefits, and Complex Negotiations

We arrived in New York for another round of fieldwork on April 20, 2018. Father Chepe was supposed to be with us, but he had to return to Nicaragua early to face the eruption of the crisis in Nicaragua, which as of this writing has claimed over five hundred lives due to violent repression by the Sandinista government. All four authors were together in Seattle beforehand, enjoying a weekend retreat for the drafting of the ethnographic chapters of this book. But the following week it was Leonard and Andy together in New York, Serena in Seattle, and all worried about Father Chepe's safety as a member of the Civic Alliance in Nicaragua. The Civic Alliance brings together various sectors from across Nicaraguan civil society, including church leaders, women's organizations, university students and presidents, and rural campesino movements trying to negotiate a resolution to the violent response of the government to civilian protest. The crisis revealed that the tensions we had been witnessing on the Caribbean coast had finally exploded in Managua, the capital. Historically, tensions in Nicaragua begin in the rural and more isolated areas, and Managua wakes up at the end. Looking back at our field notes from our years of working together, we realized we had been witnessing a repetition of this historical pattern through our work on the Caribbean coast.

Father Chepe publicly condemned the Sandinista government's repression of the massive civic demonstrations against Daniel Ortega. As a result, Father Chepe received death threats from government allies, threats that provoked widespread denunciation from international observers. These death threats resonated particularly loudly for us, as the fear and violence we had witnessed on the Caribbean coast now struck one of us.

We were glued to our phones in the evening at the hotel, trying to get WhatsApp messages through to loved ones in Nicaragua. Leonard knew Ángel Gahona, the journalist in Bluefields whose gruesome murder had been caught on Facebook Live while he was filming the violence.[8] We felt pain from what we saw on that screen in a second home thousands of miles away while being in the cacophony of the Bronx, where so many who have fled the difficult contexts of Central America have landed. In the United States, we could turn off our phones and stop the gunshots that our friends in Nicaragua were hearing. We were safe, while also feeling some of what many here in the Bronx must feel as they maintain their links with loved ones facing challenges in their countries of origin. In moments of immense difficulty, witnessing conflict back home through a screen even as you are far away from it instills a bifurcated consciousness. You are safe because you are far away from home, yet all you want is to be home.

For many Garifuna living in New York, this bifurcated consciousness is a constant reality, fueled in part by a desire to return to Central America, to return home to their roots. This longing is partly a result of never wanting to leave in the first place, but being forced to do so by a matrix of national and global interests that have made subsistence impossible and compelled new generations of Garifuna into diasporic journeying in search of new opportunities and ideas. Migrating to the United States is one of these survival strategies, and for many New York is a stop along the way of a trip that will eventually loop back home. Interviews with Garifuna in New York capture the nature of this idea of looping transmigration, seeking economic or educational goals in New York and grappling with the mixed feelings that emerge as a result of the sacrifices necessary in order to achieve those goals:

> I want to go back to Honduras. There's so much to do there with all that I've learned here. . . I go crazy here. A majority of people want to go back to avoid all the shit here.[9]

> I'm tired of the system here, I've been here for thirty years and I'm tired. As soon as I got my legal status and was able to go back, I went back home as often as I could. But I'm not ready to go back permanently yet. I still have economic goals I need to achieve first."[10]

There are a lot of challenges that the Garifuna face here. That economic question is difficult. People have to work so much that they can't get involved in the associations that there are here that promote culture, and this is due to a lack of money. So I stay here because of the opportunities there are, but I'm planning on going back. In New York there are so many opportunities, so we have to take advantage.[11]

Leaving in search of opportunity with an eye on eventual return is a common migration strategy that can yield fruitful results. In Honduras, we were able to see the outcome of this routing and looping migration strategy as we were received into the beautiful seaside homes of Garifuna returnees who built their homes slowly over the years, working as public school teachers, city government employees, and hotel workers in New York City, organizing within the Garifuna communities there even as they always had their eyes set on a return to their roots. Karla, a retired public school teacher, returned to a large beachside home and is active as a church leader and political organizer in her community of Santa Fe, Honduras. She is an example of how the Garifuna use migration as a survival mechanism, paving transnational routes that allow for the looping between the global north and home communities to achieve economic and educational goals. While this strategy has proved successful in economic and educational terms for many Garifuna, it has also come with another task of negotiating what it means to be Garifuna in a global context, where connections to the African and Latino diasporas while simultaneously confronting discrimination as a result of being Black Spanish speakers in the United States provide challenges and opportunities for defining what it is to be Garifuna in diaspora.

Garifuna as African: Dancing at Ghana Fest in Crotona Park

Crucial in the creation of a distinct cultural identity in this globalized context is the use of music, and in New York City there are multiple examples of this work. One example is Bodoma Cultural Band, a family of musicians who perform throughout the New York area and beyond. We connected with Bodoma Cultural Band and their leader, Bodoma, when they performed at Summer Stage in Crotona Park in New York. They would be returning to Crotona Park a few days later to participate in Ghana Fest, a celebration of the Ghanaian and wider African diaspora. We were looking forward to feeling the energy of their drumming and dancing again soon.

At the event a few days later, an emcee welcomed the crowd in English and a Ghanaian dialect, as many people wearing brightly patterned wraps and headscarves milled about under a tent, and a Ghanaian group sang and danced in the shade of a huge umbrella. They invited the Queen of the Ghana association to come and give a speech surrounded by her compatriots as representatives from the offices of Mayor Bill de Blasio, New York State Assemblyman Michael Blake, and a New York City Council member looked on. Each office offered a variation of the same speech: it is important to be present for the government to recognize the Ghana diaspora, to recognize cultural diversity in the era of Trump, and to make sure people felt welcomed. They finished with a declaration saying today was Ghana Heritage Day.

It soon came time for Bodoma Cultural Band to start singing. The emcee introduced the Garifuna performers, and Linda, a member of the committee that planned the event and represented the Garifuna, got on stage and said, "We are Afrodescendants, our race, our culture was a mixture between Arawak Indians and West Africans. We were actually exiled from St. Vincent. A lot of Garifuna people have survived in Central America. You will find us in four countries: Belize, Guatemala, Honduras, and Nicaragua. So anytime you see someone who says it's a Garifuna, it's a fellow brother and sister from the African diaspora. So I hope you enjoy this cultural band, it's called Bodoma Cultural Band!" They began to play, though Bodoma, the father and leader of the band, couldn't be there, and so his eldest son, Andy, took up the leading role with the band of mostly young teenagers rocking their drums. As they played, out came *wanaragua* dancers in rainbow skirts and white masks with exaggerated facial features mocking the British invaders of St. Vincent. As they leaped and spread their legs wide in the air to the beat of the drums, a magnetic energy attracted a much larger crowd. Onlookers approached the stage even as one of the young singers, another of Bodoma's sons, stumbled slightly, but the drummers kept going as he regained his composure. LeRuz, a young Garifuna hip-hop artist in New York, hopped onto the stage and danced to lyrics sung in Garifuna, English, and Spanish. Andy's Congolese girlfriend joined LeRuz, Andy shouted mid-beat "We are part of the African Diaspora!" and the drums roared as people danced under a hot July sun.

Afterward, we spoke to Andy and to the young band members. The late afternoon sun behind the trees hit us directly, reminiscent of our time in Honduras. After the show, we were hot and sweaty, and the band members drank cold water and sat on the top seat of the amphitheater. Some were born in the United States, others in Honduras; some answered in English, others in Spanish, but for them, those national distinctions weren't so defined. A young women noted, "I feel like Garifuna doesn't have any borders, it doesn't matter where I am, I am just Garifuna, if I'm here or if I'm in Honduras, I'm just Garifuna and I'm proud to be that way."[12] Andy elaborated:

To be Garifuna, is a special privilege, it's a huge privilege, because like I said during the performance, we are the only African descendants to have never been enslaved, and you know, in two hundred-plus years, six hundred-plus years, to still maintain our culture, is a huge accomplishment as a nation. So being Garifuna is really special especially as an artist, to inspire the youth and also have them join and perform as part of the band, you know, it's a huge motivation for everyone else who wants to be a part of this experience. So being Garifuna is really special. It's important for us to be here at Ghana Fest because those that don't understand our culture, being here they can actually connect because they can understand more. Even if you're not Garifuna, we still are a whole Africa, that's where it all started, so to be here is really special, we're here, we're back, we came back to our roots, we came back to our roots. Our roots are in Africa, they're in St. Vincent, they're in Central America. It's all of it. Because we started off in West Africa, before West Africa we started off in Mali, and we moved all over Africa, and then we came to St. Vincent, we lost St. Vincent, came to Central America, and right now, people's not paying much mind to this but we're losing Central America as well, because of the land."[13]

Afterward, as we carried some of their equipment to the car, the young band members waited on the sidewalk and started playing, again with a frenetic energy that attracted dozens of people over to watch and film them as they danced and sang alongside the road. When Andy showed up with the car, they all shouted, "We gotta do this! Let's go to Manhattan and do this! We can put out the hats and people will give us money!" As we enjoyed the impromptu show, Andy's girlfriend explained: "I'm Congolese, but when I met Andy he invited me over for dinner, and it was crazy because the mashed plantains and the other foods, I felt just like I was in a Congolese home. Then they started sharing more about the history of the Garifuna and I became interested and just started learning more and more."[14]

The Garifuna can find many aspects of themselves within the African diaspora. Andy, a Garifuna musician in the Bronx, teaches a Congolese girlfriend about Garifuna culture, food, and history, and she begins to learn the language through song as they realize they eat much of the same food. To migrate means to risk losing a connection to roots, yet it can also represent an opportunity to rediscover old roots in the diaspora. The looping nature of migration means that these new experiences loop back to home communities, bringing in new ideas and perspectives that foment pride in Garifuna identity. As a young woman in the band shared:

What I like about being in the band is that every day I learn something new. When I used to live in Honduras, I knew I was Garifuna, but I didn't care about it that much. So when I got to the U.S. and got into Bodoma Garifuna Band I was surprised, I was like wow, I really like this, there was so much love for me. So every day I learn new things, we go to places, I explore, and it's something nice for me because being Garifuna is something that you have to be proud of yourself, you cannot forget that you are Garifuna.[15]

The diaspora experience presents an opportunity to forge new paths for what it means to be Garifuna. The Garifuna in New York are able to move in this African diasporic space, finding similarities within it while also carving out space for Garifuna identity. Much of what Andy said in the descriptions above capture the elements of the Garifuna Nation, a connection to the wider African diaspora, placing St. Vincent as the birthplace of the Garifuna but the roots extend to Central America and Africa as well. It took a trip across Manhattan to Brooklyn to see how this same Garifuna prowess in navigating diasporic spaces manifested in a much different space: that of the Latino diaspora.

Garifuna as Latino: Playing Drums at Mass in Brooklyn

The subway crawled across the bridge over the East River, downtown Manhattan gleaming in the Sunday morning sunshine. The train slowly emptied as it continued toward the end of the line, and the Manhattan skyline became a hazy outline in the distance. We got off and walked along Livonia Avenue, past the towering public housing where a few men sat in the park, and saw an NYPD mobile spotlight streaming on the sidewalk under the train tracks in the middle of the hot morning. We turned on Mother Gaston Boulevard, and the public housing turned into little two-story, brick row houses sitting side-by-side, like people on a rush hour train, with red and white metal awnings over the doors and windows.

We knew we were headed in the right direction when we heard drums resounding through the open doors of the brick building ahead. Walking into the church, we saw the Garifuna drums at the front, one Garifuna man playing two at the same time, another playing the cowbell. The church pews showed few empty seats, but we squeezed in toward the back. The Spanish mass catered to a predominantly Dominican and Puerto Rican group, and the Garifuna stood out, easy to identify as they kept gesturing, waving, smiling—communicating with each other across the space, from the drummers and some of the singers at the front, to the group to my left, and then across to the other side. We turned around and saw José who smiled and waved, obviously happy we'd accepted his invitation after we had met in the Bronx at the Coalición Mexicana.

The music was in Spanish with accompaniment from the Garifuna drums, and the priest was an Irish-American priest who was visiting the church for the first time. He was there from the Diocese of Brooklyn as the head of the Annual Catholic Appeal of 2018. He spoke in Spanish about the work that the diocese provides for those in the area, such as pro-bono legal services for migration; he spoke about the exploitation of some *abogados* to whom many pay and pay and pay only to realize they're being robbed, and the importance of providing trustworthy legal services. At the end of the mass, he mentioned that the congregation sings more loudly than many others he has visited; undoubtedly, the Garifuna drums had a role in that.

After the service, we went and spoke to José, who then introduced us to Arnaldo, the president of the Garifuna association of Brooklyn, a middle-aged man in his fifties or sixties with a salt and pepper beard and hat and sunglasses. He told us that we needed to come back when the whole choir is there in the church (the association has almost twenty-two members in the choir that contributes most of the singing), as a lot were on vacation in Honduras, Guatemala, and Belize. There is a big mass in June when the Bronx and Brooklyn Garifuna communities celebrate a Garifuna mass. This is a time for unity, because the rest of the year the Garifuna masses are celebrated in different places throughout the city.

The drummer and his cowbell-playing partner stood outside the doors of the church and explained that they are both from Honduras. We told them it was hard to keep up with all the Garifuna activities in New York. We were going to try to go to mass, even though there are events in the park here in Brooklyn for Garifuna. Curious about the question of land, and thinking about the development of Brooklyn right now, we asked them if they feel the effects. Gentrification and urban development in New York have similar displacement effects to "development" in Honduras and in Nicaragua. The drummer said it got too expensive for him to live here, so he had to move to Long Island: "I have to have a lot more of a plan now to still come here, but I do it." The drummer said: "Garifuna wisdom, from the Caribbean, you gotta move, if you in the water with a shark and you don't move you gonna die!"[16] They need to move like this, because if they don't, there is a risk that the Garifuna will disappear as a minority group in a congregation that is mostly Dominican and Puerto Rican. But the mixing and resulting hybridities also allow for new, unexpected developments as well. One is married to a Dominican woman, and says that she speaks more Garifuna than he does. "She's learning to sing Garifuna. She's doing better than I am! It's good that she's trying to learn the language, because it's getting lost everywhere. In Belize no one speaks it. And here, it's worse."[17]

This sentiment reminded us of Andy and his Congolese girlfriend; we note the parallels in how a Garifuna musician in the Bronx sees how much is shared between Garifuna culture and her Congolese culture, while here in Brooklyn a Garifuna musician teaches a Dominican wife about Garifuna culture, food, and history, and she learns the language better than him through song. The ability of the Garifuna to fit into multiple spaces stood out as the drumming resounded throughout the congregation on that hot Sunday morning. As they negotiate these multiple diasporic spaces, the Garifuna reconcile their Afro-descendent, Indigenous, Spanish-speaking, and Latino roots, all of which contribute to the larger Garifuna Nation. The identification with the Garifuna Nation allows for the Garifuna to advocate for the specific needs of their ethnic group, and they do so in public spaces in New York City.

Garifuna as Garifuna: Advocating at a Town Hall in the Bronx

The previous sections have depicted how the Garifuna bring their histories and practices with them as they navigate the cultural and ethnic landscape of New York City, showing only some of the ways the Garifuna are adapting and maintaining their cultural identity against the onslaught of acculturating forces that strip the language and other aspects of culture away in today's world. Such strategies are crucial in New York City, a city that one research participant referred to as a *monstruo* (monster). A *New York Times* article from 2015 highlights this struggle, both in terms of resisting assimilation as well as defining a distinct Garifuna identity.

> "The Garifuna culture is in danger of extinction," Ms. Hermosa said. "But they are doing all they can to preserve the traditions, to inspire the young people. . . Indeed, their blend of cultures puts the Garifuna in an odd situation in this country, where authorities see them as Latino because of their country of origin. . . What do you do when you have to check a box that says you are black, Latino or other?" Ms. Hermosa said. "They are something more, Garifuna."[18]

It is challenging to define what that "something more" entails. Johnson writes that the Garifuna going to the Bronx has resulted in an "ethnic reclassification of Garifuna from 'Carib' and Amerindian to more rigidly 'Black' and 'African.'"[19] However, the fluid ethnic identity resulting from the Garifuna mixture of Latin American and African roots prevents that rigid categorization of "Black American." In an interview in the Bronx, a Garifuna man revealed how his use of Spanish can serve as a means of breaking down the perception that others have of him as a Black American. "This is important because in this country they're afraid of the Black man. But there are differences between us and Black men. That's why I speak Spanish in order to distinguish myself, so that people see I'm not a Black American."[20]

The negotiation of various, sometimes conflicting identities in the U.S. context presents challenges for the Garifuna and a subsequent need to define their needs on their terms. They exist concurrently within the African and Latino diasporas, navigating each through shared cultural elements such as food, religion, and music, while also confronting the challenges faced by being perceived as Black Americans who also speak Spanish and Garifuna. These challenges demand that the Garifuna define who they are on their own terms.

One of our research participants invited us to an event happening up the road at Lincoln Hospital, telling us it would be a good place for us to be able to see how it is that the Garifuna distinguish themselves within the New York monster. That evening, we went to the nearby Lincoln Hospital, where the Encuentro Garifuna y Centroamericano was taking place. The event was sponsored by the NYC Mayor's Office of Immigrant Affairs, and when we walked in there were a dozen tables set up with literature and representatives from many different social service organizations, universities, and government agencies offering help with housing, health needs, and immigration. As we passed through the auditorium, a woman recognized us: Azula, who was in the mass in Santa Fe back in Honduras. Azula's presence cements the interconnected nature of these two places, New York and Central America. People come and go, never really leaving. Azula is another case of the successful migrant, owning a shipping company with her husband by which many migrants ship goods back home to Honduras. It's all part of a complex network that has developed and facilitated how the circular nature of Central America and the diaspora moves and grows.

We sat and watched as the event began with the booming of drumming that burst into dancing, led by Felix Gamboa. Through beautiful costumes, drumming, dancing, and singing, they evoked a spirit that was as powerful here as it was at mass in Honduras. The event seemed to be almost, if not entirely, organized and led by women. Three women in particular, all wearing their headscarves and traditional dresses, were the main speakers and emcees. They spoke with a powerful conviction: "This is a space to discuss those things that affect us most." A Garifuna pastor prayed in Spanish as one of the women prayed in Garifuna. One of the three women who organized the event, Mirtha Colón, began to tell the history of the Garifuna people, speaking of the exile in 1797 to Roatan, how hundreds died in the journey from San Vicente to Roatan. Drawing on that history, she drew the audience into the urgency of the current moment, one in which the nature of Garifuna migration is a phenomenon that is forced upon them by larger power structures, making migration a strategy to survive. However, despite the imposed circumstances, the Garifuna resist and learn to move in order to continue onward.

We haven't had the same forced migration like that of our ancestors from St. Vincent, but our migration is forced because we are always looking for economic stability. Today, you will still hear Garifuna, we continue speaking even though we are now on our fourth generation of Garifuna born here in New York. We've been migrating for fifty years. The Garifuna community suffers as do many others in New York. We have problems with education, with economics, and we've always struggled to claim our rights. We need youth programs, and we need jobs. We will work hard when we have the opportunity. This is something positive: we want to change the lives within our community for the better—we want a racial, ethnic, and cultural earthquake to do so. It is our resistance that is our strength. In order to rescue our values, we need the support of the City of New York. Our number one priority of this space is to create public policy for the Garifuna.

At that moment, representatives from the city read that Mayor Bill de Blasio had proclaimed the day, April 21, officially "Garifuna Town Hall Day in the City of New York," part of a policy of general support for migrants in the city. We then attended breakout sessions, with representatives from many different agencies around New York, to talk about housing, migration, youth, jobs, and elderly care.

At the Youth Breakout session, they honored young people who had made paintings and drawings for the event, many with the themes of resistance and Garifuna pride. The poster for the event had one of the drawings as the background artwork. One of the main points from this meeting was the need for distinct programs that adhere to Garifuna identity and priorities. As one of the panelists noted, "If we don't create a distinct Garifuna identity, then people may just think we're Jamaican or African, and how do we create the right programs if we're all seen as just the same?" One of the representatives of a nonprofit in the Bronx commented that he had no idea that there was such a strong presence of Garifuna, and that it was a rich and distinct culture. He was open to the idea of working with Garifuna youth to create those types of programs to serve the needs of Garifuna.

Returning to the auditorium, Mirtha stood and proclaimed, "This is a people who respond when we have to. We will take one another's hand and push onward," as the stage erupted in the final event: dancing, singing, young women in bright blue dresses and young men dancing and break dancing, and finished off with another rendition of the *wanaragua* dance. One woman got out of the audience, jumped on stage, and danced to wild applause. It was a great party as the Garifuna drums roared in the presence of state structures that they leveraged to advocate for themselves and the distinct needs of their community.

As in Orinoco and Honduras, women are the ones in charge of much of the civic organizing done in New York. Mirtha and Bartolomé (Tola) Colón, who spearheaded the Garifuna Town Hall, are examples of this type of work, replicating matrifocal kinship ties that are so crucial to the maintenance of Garifuna solidarity both in the villages in Central America as well as in the diaspora.[21] As Tola explained to us later,

> We do what we can with few resources, and we're happy when the government helps us, because we are a minority. We always think about returning [to Central America]. We live with nostalgia. We work with young people here and there to try to prevent so much migration but it's hard when there aren't jobs for young people. And then with the discrimination that we face, that destroys us as a people. Us women, we worry more about this, just like Barauda did [a folk hero in Garifuna stories who took her husband's pants to fight the British]. We women push, while some men remain unconvinced. But our traditions are lost as we try to adapt and that hurts. And then when things don't work out, there's the temptation to get involved in illicit activities. We would like to be able to live on our own land but there are problems preventing us from doing so.[22]

Mirtha echoed this sentiment of the difficult process of advocating on behalf of the Garifuna in New York: "The most important thing is to know how to move within this space in order to organize and do what you have to do for your community."[23] The work of Tola and Mirtha Colón are clear examples of the matrifocal kinship structure of Garifuna culture, described in detail in Kerns's and England's work. The matrifocal kinship structure is a system in which "women, as mothers, serve as the foci of households, extended kin groups, and rituals" and is a crucial glue for Garifuna society.[24] As England describes, the matrifocal kinship ties that exist in villages in Honduras extend along transnational routes, whereby Garifuna women in diaspora play important roles in maintaining solidarity and fostering social ties. Indeed, the presence of Azula at the event and her giving us her business card for her shipping company is another sign of how women remain crucial nodes in the economic, social, and cultural ties that expand across the Garifuna diaspora.

Felix Gamboa kept the beat of the event on his drums, and it was the women who were the organizers and the emcees, keeping the Garifuna family connected. In this way, the Garifuna persist in diaspora by finding "the particular within the plural" of the cultural "monster" that is New York, filling space that allows the full expression of their distinct needs as an ethnically based community.[25] Bodoma, the leader of Bodoma Cultural Band, puts it this way: "It is very important work to maintain our culture, because if we don't do it, it'll be lost in the politics here."[26]

(Im)possibilities of a Decolonial Future: Facing Internal and External Tensions

The work of forging a unique space from which to advocate for the specific needs of the Garifuna nation represents a significant success for the Garifuna in articulating a distinct ethnic identity; nonetheless, it also unearths tensions that reveal the challenges of reconciling a colonial past with a postcolonial present in search of a decolonial future that allows full autonomy for the Garifuna across the Americas. The negotiation process of Garifuna identity is constant, involving perceived gains and losses that reveal more deeply rooted frictions. At a mass in the Bronx, two elderly women stand under the shade of a tree in bright purple dresses and white head wraps. They had come to the Bronx from Honduras for the annual gathering of Garifuna, which was to take place in New York until an emergency change was made to hold the event in Belize when so many participants were denied visas to enter the United States. We shared some photos of the youth from the Bodoma Cultural Band playing drums on the sidewalk in Crotona Park. One of the women looked and sighed, "Youth are losing the culture completely. They don't speak [Garifuna], they respond to me in Spanish. They don't come to mass, I'm sure there will be no young people at mass."[27] Glancing at the photos of the drummers under the trees, she asked: "Why aren't they in the church?"[28] Though the beat of the drum goes on, it may take place under trees blocking a hot summer sun rather than under a church's roof, with some verses in Spanish instead of Garifuna. As we endeavor to take the side of the community against forces that threaten the vitality of Garifuna and other Indigenous groups, we're sobered by the challenges of decolonial research methods and the (im)possibility of a decolonial future.

Dügü as Unity and Division: Grappling with Colonial Legacies

In overcoming strife, the Garifuna have proven to be adept in their movement through the streets of New York City. Indeed, this characteristic is a result of having existed and survived on the margins for so long. On an overcast, muggy day in the Bronx, we sat down in a Honduran diner a few blocks away from the subway with Luz Solís, a professor at Boricua College in Harlem. Sharing plantain chips and caldo, Luz explained more: "For us, we can fit in, survive, and thrive in multiple spaces because of the marginalization that we've faced, which led to our fighting to preserve our culture and Garifuna identity."[29] However, this negotiation process, while demonstrating an impressive adaptability, also exposes difficult fault lines inherited from a legacy of colonialism whereby the Catholic Church both promoted the inclusive syncretism that has allowed many elements of Garifuna spirituality to survive while also perpetuating violent oppression in the conversion process, as we saw in chapter 4. Luz continues, "They processed us, they changed our name to Spanish names so we could become Catholic. They stripped us of our names, of our history, so that we could become Catholic. Then they sent armies to contain us when we tried to fight back."[30] The Garifuna endured and resisted the imposition of religion, having to adapt and negotiate while having their names changed, hiding some aspects of their culture while combining others with those of the dominant culture in order to survive. The history of resistance to forces that have tried to assimilate or outright destroy the Garifuna demonstrates an impressive feat of survival while also resulting in tensions among the Garifuna themselves. Addressing these tensions and questions will be an integral part of understanding what it means to be Garifuna going forward.

Conflicting interpretations among Garifuna over the value of the dügü, or wal-agallo as it is referred to in Nicaragua, captures the magnitude of these challenges. The dügü is a spiritual practice through which the ancestors call for families to come together, often in response to a grave illness within the family. The members of the four families of the afflicted person, that is, the families of the maternal and paternal grandparents, must be present in Honduras or Nicaragua in order for the dügü or walagallo to be an effective treatment against illness, especially when other Western medicine fails. A table is set full of food as ceremonies take place for three days, a communion between the living and the dead as well as a celebration of the Garifuna relationship with nature, with the sea, with the mountains, and with God. However, the Garifuna confront internal and external forces antago-nistic to dügü, despite the intention to bring the Garifuna together in communion with their ancestors. This results in a fierce point of debate among Garifuna, as some believe the dügü is a ceremony that should be left in the past, and the ancestors along with it. As one community member from the Bronx explained to us in an interview, "I can't speak much about the ancestors. When I was a girl, my mother didn't bring me to the meetings with the ancestors, she said it was for adults. Sometimes I put out food for my grandparents, but my mother always felt ashamed. The ancestors chose her, and so she dedicated herself to another church where she lost her fear of the ancestors. She was able to reject them at this church. So now, my kids don't know anything about the ancestors. With so many divisions in the world, what are you going to do? Cultures get lost."[31]

Beyond internal stresses among Garifuna relating to the role of the dügü, addressing these debates represents a significant challenge for our research team engaged in a decolonial methodology. Our methodology is deeply political as we choose the side of the Garifuna against the larger neoliberal economic and geopolitical forces that would see the annihilation of the Garifuna. However, we then confront the divisions among the Garifuna themselves as a result of the colonial and neocolonial forces that the Garifuna have had to resist from the margins for generations, asserting their own autonomy as subjective participants with differing views among themselves. Christopher Loperena, another anthropologist who has engaged in activist political research with the Garifuna land defenders in Honduras writes, "alignment with land rights activists placed me in awkward tension with positivist approaches to social science research *and with members of the opposing communal faction.*"[32] Loperena takes the side of the Garifuna against the land developers who threaten to take away land, only to find himself in opposition to those Garifuna who see the development of land as an opportunity for income generation and jobs, placing him in a challenging ethical dilemma as a researcher. With the dügü, we come across a similar division among the Garifuna. Castro, a young Garifuna man in New York, shares an opinion that runs counter to our assumption as a research team: "In my humble opinion, I'm Garifuna and I love my roots, but according to the Bible it's clear that this tradition is not pleasing to God. Just today I was listening to a Catholic Priest who spoke about this. And he was clear about these points, that this [dügü] does not please God."[33] While we as co-authors view the continuation of the dügü or walagallo as a crucial practice for the Garifuna going forward, we also find ourselves making value judgments that contradict what some Garifuna say about their own culture, leading to awkward and uncomfortable positions as Loperena describes.

These tensions and contradictions are natural outcomes of the legacies of colonialism that we inherit and embody in our praxis, and will likely not dissipate anytime soon. Midway through our meal, Luz explained, "You cannot decolonize until you empower those colonized to have their own coin. Without your own coin, it will always be someone else's face on the coin, and you'll always be living in their world. It's about power. Until we can write, until we can say things in our own voices and have it be heard, and have it lead to change we will be colonized. In the meantime, we focus on our communities, on after school programs where we can teach our dance, our history. This matters. But it's all uphill until we can change the face on the coin."[34]

Much work remains for the idea of decoloniality to become a reality. The scope of the colonial legacy that we inherit and its complex manifestations on power dynamics and social relations are hurdles to be negotiated imperfectly in the present. Despite the many successes that the Garifuna have achieved through migration and navigation of the diasporic landscape in New York City, the outlook remains stubbornly rooted in ruptures of the past that require more work in order to achieve some sort of meaningful reconciliation. Luz continued in this vein, unpacking how Garifuna persistence can confront this mingling of past, present, and future that complicate aspirations for a decolonial future:

In Honduras, at the bananeras, the Black kids were only allowed to go to school until third grade, and then they went on to work. We were limited in our means of transforming our knowledge into something bigger. This became embedded into us. Then, you have this migration where we migrate from rural areas of Honduras to the U.S., to New York, and people bring all their families and extended families, and so people who have never seen a Honduran city are now in a city in the U.S. But there is a limitation still, people migrate here to work, and so they work, go home, work, go home, there's no way to interrupt this with education. My generation was able to get an education. It allowed us to transform the knowledge. But now, my kids are born here. They can't think like me. My kids can't think in Garifuna like I can because they don't have that connection to Honduras. So what happens? There is this inconsistency in the Garifuna community. We still have the songs, we teach those to our kids, and they recognize them and sing them, but they only have phrases and not fluency. We transmit histories and values in our songs, the ancestors live in the songs, the language survives in the songs. At the end of the day it comes to economic resources. We spend so much time talking about what we don't have that we don't see what we do have, and this is a part of the problem of a colonized mindset. Sin embargo, los Garífuna nos quedamos fuertes porque creemos en los ancestros. Son nuestros guías, nuestros ángeles, nuestros protectores. (Nevertheless, us Garifuna remain strong because of our belief in the ancestors. They are our guides, our angels, our protectors.) They are so prominently there. They save us through their knowledge of nature, of the cosmos, the environment, a respect for nature. This is why the dügü is so important. We offer the food to the ancestors. We offer the food to those of us who are there now. We offer the food to the land by burying it. And we offer the food to the oceans so that the fish may eat and multiply. When we give to the sea, when we give to the land, it gives back to us. Esto es lo que se aprende en las canciones, y en la lengua. Hay mensajes para otros mensajes. Los ancestros hablan en códigos (This is what we learn in the songs, and in the language. There are messages for other messages. The ancestors speak in codes). They spoke through the songs. They told us you have to give, that there is a fundamental reciprocity, and this has to be in your *heart*. It's not the food, it's what's behind the food. It's behind the food, which is the reciprocity in your heart, which comes out in your offering the food. People think too much about the people: they see it as a waste of food. But it's so much more than that. El dügü es llevarse bien, va mucho más allá de la comida. Es vivir bien, vivir sin la hipocresía. (The dügü is to live well together, it goes far beyond the food. It is to live well, without hypocrisy.) When it becomes material, it divides us. What happens now, is it becomes so expensive to buy food, to dedicate the time to organizing the dügü, to getting the families together to go to Honduras. It's such a simple act. It's to be together with the ancestors, with nature, with God, with each other. Yet it becomes so difficult.[35]

Rooting: Nicaragua Garifuna within the Garifuna Nation

Despite the role of the dügü as a focal point of tension that reveals deep frictions among the Garifuna, it remains a ceremony that fulfills the demands of the ancestors for the reunification of family that has been stretched across national borders. This idea of uniting the Garifuna family is crucial in the articulation of the Garifuna Nation. This chapter has described the context within which the Garifuna Nation emerged as a response to the contradictions and complexities that the Garifuna face in the diaspora in New York City, especially given the specter of the colonial legacy that still causes division among Garifuna today. Our interactions in the diaspora highlighted the almost invisible participation of Nicaraguan Garifuna in this nation, at least in New York City. We hope to shed light on how our time spent in Orinoco and the Pearl Lagoon region shows that the rootedness within this Garifuna Nation is having an impact in Orinoco, as it is facilitating the exchange of what it means to be Garifuna going forward.

We return to the path that brings us from Orinoco to Marshall Point, which we walked upon in earlier chapters and where we saw the "Private Property" signs nailed to fences erected on communal land. Passing by the signs and the fences, we continue on through Marshall Point, a sleepy town by the sea where a local man produces his giffiti now sold in Bluefields in a distillery made from a barrel, a hollowed-out canoe full of cool water, and a roaring fire. We pass the distillery on our way to one of our favorite spots for a Toña beer at the end of a day of fieldwork. The owner of the bar by the lagoon is Miss Peralta, who spends the year commuting from her grand red-and-yellow home by the sea to Canada, where she spends half of her time.

Miss Arlene is one of Miss Peralta's sisters who lives adjacent to Miss Peralta in a house painted bright yellow, red, and green, the same colors as the Garifuna flag. Beside her home, Miss Arlene has a little hut she built the month before, which she has called the Garifuna Museum. It is full of Garifuna artifacts such as sticks and shells from beaches in Honduras, two drums, little trinkets, hats, saws, fishing net, and little pieces of white paper with Garifuna words and their English translations. The idea for the museum came as a result of a trip to Honduras to participate in a cultural exchange with Garifuna there. She learned a lot on the trip: "We make our bami too thick here, they taught us how to do it right." But the trip proved to be the germination of a long gestating idea, whose result we were now standing in. Miss Arlene goes on, "It's been an idea in my head for a long time to do this, but after that trip I really decided it was time to do it. I'll make it better, but it's a start."[36]

In the Pearl Lagoon region, these exchanges with Honduras and the larger Garifuna Nation have given birth to language classes now taught in the primary school, allowing for the kids to get some exposure to basic Garifuna phrases. Esther's story in chapter 5 captures this type of exchange, and it is worth repeating here the words of Garifuna blogger Kenny Castillo when he says, "The good news is that in the past few years with the effervescence of indigenous and Afro-indigenous movement, the Garifuna of Nicaragua are claiming more space, yelling more loudly and powerfully that they are ready to reclaim what was lost. Esther is contributing to that."[37] There are Garifuna who negotiate this context by recognizing the Nicaraguan state's support for these types of classes and other cultural activities as well as the government's promotion of tourism, which allows for some income-generating activity in the Orinoco and the Pearl Lagoon region, even as those very same neoliberal economic forces are responsible for the depletion of natural resources in the Pearl Lagoon area and force the youth to migrate away from Orinoco in order to survive.

Here we see how the Garifuna, like other Indigenous communities today, negotiate their roots using globalized routes that connect them to the broader world. The Garifuna of Nicaragua use cities both in Nicaragua and in Costa Rica, Grand Cayman, Europe, and the United States for higher education and economic opportunity. They negotiate new economic opportunities within the often antagonistic state apparatus of the Sandinista party in Nicaragua, get state funding to visit Honduras to recover their language and build networks with other Garifuna communities, and still come home for holidays to celebrate family and culture. While there has been a significant disruption in Orinoco as a result of those forces, these new routes that emerge as a result of integration into the global economy represent opportunities for the resurgence of Garifuna identity in places where it was wavering, with Miss Arlene's museum a testament to that.

These acts show that the articulation, performance, and translation of the Garifuna as members of a larger ethnic Garifuna Nation are having positive impacts on the Garifuna in Nicaragua, speaking to the pride that Miss Patricia mentions at the beginning of the chapter. However, England questions whether or not the Garifuna will ever be recognized as politically equal to territorialized Indigenous nations or nation-states.[38] The Garifuna of Nicaragua still must negotiate their rights and identity within the challenging political reality of Nicaragua, where their access to land and assertion of Garifuna identity represents a challenge to the Sandinista Party. In spite of this, there are stronger ties beyond Nicaragua, connecting Orinoco and Marshall Point to Honduras, and those routes continue from Honduras to New York City, forming the infrastructure of the Garifuna Nation that transcends national borders and allows for Garifuna identity to persist in the face of the many factors that would see its vitality fade away.

Conclusion: Hope Going Forward

In the Pearl Lagoon region of Nicaragua, multiple forces—neoliberal economic policies and practices, technological changes, and indifferent or antagonistic state policies—have come in to the region since Father Chepe lived there in the 1990s and have so fundamentally altered life as to render many aspects unrecognizable when we first returned to Orinoco in 2015. That passive acceptance of outside cultural influence, or the dilution of giffiti to which Leonard refers is a real threat, as the Garifuna of Orinoco endured a process of acculturation that took away the Garifuna language from all but the elders, reduced the frequency of the wala-gallo ceremony, saw young people ship out for the cities and beyond, and felt the impact of the transnational drug routes that brought cocaine into the community to devastating effect. The Catholic church, once packed beyond capacity for the Saturday evening vigil during Holy Week, is now a much humbler affair, with our research team making up half of the congregation during our visits.

As such, the Garifuna of Nicaragua are a case of how language and other cultural practices can ebb to the point of disappearing, and of how these processes of acculturation and assimilation can prove devastating to key aspects of a culture and a place. However, this case is also evidence that those routes that so often take people away from the communities while allowing exogenous forces in can also prove to be sources of new hope for resilience through exchange programs, language classes, documentaries shared and viewed on YouTube, and new chances for articulation, performance, and translation of culture that persist in the face of colonial and neocolonial forces that the Garifuna have resisted for centuries.

In New York, a consistent reaction when we said we worked with Garifuna in Nicaragua was one of surprise. Many did not know there were Garifuna in Nicaragua until they saw a YouTube documentary about them, and were shocked and thrilled to see videos we shared of Garifuna cultural practices still in use in Orinoco. Yet, against all odds, there they are: Eric, Kelsey, Mateo, and others who are

119

reconnecting to their roots, allowing them to grow deeper as they resist and grow from routes, inspiring a belief that the ancestors are still indeed there, anchored in St. Vincent but protecting the Garifuna within the borders of a transnational, digital, and growing Garifuna Nation.

There is hope in research allowing for uprooted roots to reconnect and bring community members back home, be it physically, spiritually, or permanently. As Leonard shares, "For reason of high school and higher education teachings I began to be disconnected from the communities, and to be distracted by other cultures and practices as I live in the cities. This kind of exposure influenced my behavior, and cultural identity. I found myself drifting from family ties and values. And so when I launched out to be part of this research endeavor, I decided to embrace all of it because it is enabling me to reconnect myself to my roots. The research process has enabled me to reflect on the nature of our Garifuna people. It has allowed me to have a greater clarity of the high spirit of perseverance that characterizes us as a people. This tells me that in spite that we are a small in number, we are a great people and have a lot to offer to the world."

In Crotona Park, we asked one of the young drummers from Bodoma Cultural Band, no more than thirteen years old, what his favorite word in Garifuna was. Under a blazing hot sun, he looked up thoughtfully, and paused for a moment before answering. His answer captured this deeply held sentiment: "Keimoun múnadoun," he said, "Let's go home."

CHAPTER SEVEN

Unlearning/Relearning:
Decolonial Methodologies

Serena Cosgrove

"I carry a privilege I cannot negate."[1]

—WALTER MIGNOLO and CATHERINE WALSH, *On Decoloniality: Concepts, Analytics, Praxis*

Introduction

This chapter describes our research methodology: decolonial research at the service of Garifuna persistence. Today, when even the well-meaning efforts of researchers can reify exclusion, facilitate acculturation, or contribute to the exotification of Indigenous groups, there must be an explicit *unlearning* and *relearning* when it comes to the *how* of research—the research methodology that will be applied—so these exclusionary practices aren't reaffirmed by the research process. Echoing Mignolo and Walsh, we authors acknowledge that we are not experts, rather engaged and open (re)learners.[2] Research that supports Indigenous persistence has to be political and therein also decolonial, and by that I mean "affirming subjectivities that have been devalued by narratives of modernity."[3] This chapter is our attempt to be transparent about the how of research so the reader can critically assess the what or findings of the research. This chapter describes the methodological considerations—grounding ourselves in a critical historical analysis, practicing reflexivity, and engaging with the community—that led the authors to choose a set of particular methods—participant observation, interviews, and focus groups.

Carrying out decolonized research with peoples on the margins is not an attainable goal if one comes from a privileged background and the privileges are directly linked to the marginalization of the people one is studying.[4] In my case as a cisgender, white anthropologist from the United States, many of my privileges are tied to the exclusion of Indigenous peoples, an exclusion "produced by a post-1492 planetary system" that has only been exacerbated by U.S. foreign policy and economic extractive interests in Nicaragua.[5] However, just because the goal cannot be fully reached doesn't mean researchers can't commit to a decolonial agenda and partner with local researchers and the communities where they're working to support strategies of community persistence be they for community projects or political incidence. I write this in recognition that the economic, political, and epistemological processes that have pushed Indigenous and Afro-descendant peoples to the margins of society have been unfolding for centuries and will not be unmade by one researcher or one research team's best efforts. As long as we live in a world in which groups like the Garifuna have to persist against forces that seek to destroy their cultural, spiritual, and natural worlds and fight for their individual and collective rights, there will be a need for research that uses critical, participative methodologies committed to decolonial praxis.

This chapter focuses on the methodological issues raised by our research team in our attempt to document the persistence of Garifuna culture in Nicaragua in conversation with community members and leaders. Given that "(s)haring knowledge is also a long-term commitment," this research includes a Garifuna sociologist who lives in the region and also a researcher who lived with the Garifuna in the early 1990s and lives in Nicaragua.[6] Our guiding research question focuses on the adaptations and persistence of Nicaraguan Garifuna culture in the face of isolation, poverty, state extraction, abandonment, and repression. What are the reflections of community members in Orinoco and the other Pearl Lagoon communities about being, articulating, performing, and translating what it means to be Garifuna today? What are factors that encroach on Garifuna survivance such as the current political crisis, state repression, settler incursion, and the drug trade? How do pressures to seek employment, education, and other services affect Garifuna communities, particularly youth?

This research requires critically examining the epistemologies of Eurocentric disciplines so we can (re)learn by grounding our knowledge in the persistence of the peoples who have survived Western imperialism and colonization; this necessitates a set of decolonial methods that accompanies, is in solidarity, and commits to knowledge creation with and for the communities with whom we're working.[7] Not only does this type of research entail efforts to decolonize our own worldviews so as to better unlearn some of our own biases and then learn from our research partners, but it also compels us to put research communities at the center of our research endeavor and co-create knowledge with them that advances their persistence in an age of cultural threat and ongoing genocidal policies.

In addition to the work of decolonizing our own worldviews, this research also commits to decolonizing the institutions of higher education that employ and sponsor us. I say this for two reasons. First off, universities in the Americas were founded by colonizers as a place where Western epistemology and Eurocentric disciplines could be replicated or as Mignolo and Walsh argue, "(to secure) the coloniality of knowledge."[8] But universities today can "redirect the trend and decolonize and/or dewesternize."[9] For example, SU, the UCA, and the BICU need to pursue recruitment and retention policies that guarantee access and graduation rates of Indigenous and other students from minoritized backgrounds as well as provide students with training for careers that they can use for the persistence of their communities if they so choose.

As researchers who understand that qualitative methods are going to be the most useful for drawing close to our research participants and their variously positioned subjectivities, we chose ethnographic methods in which we embed ourselves in the community and participate in daily life for extended visits. For the ethnographic chapters that you've read in this book, we spent time in Orinoco, which also included frequent visits to Marshall Point, San Vicente, La Fe, and Brown Bank during 2015, 2016, 2017, 2018, and 2019, for a total of nine months. We didn't always travel as a group; in fact, many of the visits were comprised of mini-research pods: Serena and Leonard, Andy and Father Chepe, Andy and Leonard, and the group as a whole on a couple of occasions. We also carried out three multi-week visits to New York City in 2016, 2017, and 2018: one by Serena, one by Andy and Leonard, one by Andy and Father Chepe, and the final one in mid-2018 by Andy. Father Chepe, Andy, and Serena spent two weeks in Honduras in March 2018. Andy also carried out participant observation in meetings with Caribbean students at the UCA in Managua and the Caribbean coast during 2017 and 2018. Leonard carried out visits to all the Pearl Lagoon Garifuna communities in 2019 to gather historical and demographic data. This ethnographic approach means that we learn about the community through conversation and shared experiences, developing our conclusions in conjunction with our community partners. Ethnography grounds us in the lived realities of our research participants and leads to a text that is thick and rich with description and centers our research participants.

In brief, this chapter describes the actions and reflections we've used to implement decolonial concepts through an acknowledgment of the colonizing histories that have marked the Caribbean coast of Central America in general, and Nicaragua, in particular. Then, the chapter explores how Western social science epistemologies—ways of knowing—have to be interrogated for their imperial and colonizing legacies in order to begin to build a research methodology that puts Garifuna ways of knowing at the center and can serve community persistence and resurgence. Connecting epistemology to methodology and showing how data gathering and knowledge making are interconnected, the chapter also describes the particular methods of participant observation, interviews, and focus groups we used and how this process and the data it generates can, in turn, serve community activism and struggle.

Unpacking Colonial and Neocolonial Histories

Present-day research methodologies with minoritized groups must be grounded in a critical engagement with the past so that the connections between colonial, neocolonial, and internal colonial histories and a postcolonial present are explicit. *"Coming to know the past* has been part of the critical pedagogy of decolonization."[10] This history and our complicity means that as researchers we need to examine how we may have benefited from these histories and clarify with our research partners and participants how we are learning from them. For Father Chepe, a Jesuit Catholic priest and university leader from the Pacific coast of Nicaragua who is carrying out research on the Caribbean coast, he acknowledges how the Pacific coast has benefited from exploiting Caribbean coast resources and has to show with his actions that he is committed to a different set of power relations between the coasts. Father Chepe has to examine what it means to be a Catholic priest working with an Afro-Indigenous group: how has Catholicism contributed to the colonizing forces that have marginalized the Garifuna? Father Chepe has to think about how as a mestizo from the Pacific side of the country he can use his individual actions to support a more inclusive Nicaragua that centers communities that have been marginalized. For Leonard, a Garifuna researcher who lives in Bluefields and was raised with frequent visits to Orinoco, he has to reflect on how he negotiated the pressures to raise his children as Creoles rather than Garifuna. It turns out that sometimes people who have their roots in Indigenous communities get opportunities to leave their communities, decide to marry and raise children in places with more opportunities than their communities of origin, and then don't transmit their native language or traditions because these practices will only serve to further marginalize their children.[11] As researchers from the United States, Andy and I have to transmit a commitment to relearning given the charged history and centuries of intervention by U.S. foreign policy and economic interests that have preferenced U.S. capital and strategic interests over the wellbeing of Nicaraguans. We need to listen not lecture because *gringos* have told Nicaraguans what to do and how to run their country for centuries. We have to get out of our own way: listening is a great strategy. When researching, we need to focus on conversation and observation, immersing ourselves in the data, never just jumping to conclusions. A grounding in the historical, political, social, and economic forces that have affected Garifuna communities provides us with a foundation upon which to develop a set of research methods that might be able to center Garifuna survivance.

Decolonial Epistemologies and Methodologies

Analogous to how colonial, neocolonial, and postcolonial histories inform a present moment that in turn exacerbate the marginalization of groups like the Garifuna, Western epistemologies—positivistic ways of knowing in which the knower is disassociated from the known—and methodologies—ways of gathering data—have been used for centuries to reify the distance between groups, particularly the distance between researchers and groups forced to the margins of their societies.[12] The late eighteenth-century emergence of the social sciences connected knowledge production to the expansion of capitalist modes of production and the European colonization of much of the global south. Addressing this complicity and inequality is necessary if one wishes to accompany marginalized groups in the Americas because "the ways in which scientific research is implicated in the worst excesses of colonialism remains a powerful remembered history for many of the world's colonized peoples."[13] Anthropology, for example, developed as a discipline along with the expansion of European colonization. In her powerful ethnography of post-civil war Guatemala, Diane Nelson discusses this tension in the discipline of anthropology: "there's a mutilation inherent in our anthropological vocation, in the difficult spanning of our double worlds, caught between field and home, embodied knowledge gathering and the violent abstraction of transforming it into text."[14] As anthropologists and researchers from other disciplines in the social sciences such as sociology and international studies, our research team has paid particular attention to how we span the divides between our academic formation, our home institutions, and the field. We must seek to create bridges to facilitate increased exchange and movement between communities on the margins and universities. Transdisciplinary research in which multiple disciplinary perspectives push past disciplinary borders means we can partner with community activists and civil society efforts as a goal for overcoming the epistemic limitations of disciplinary knowledge.

If research is to serve peoples on the margins, it is crucial to critique and transform extractive epistemologies—those that just seek data for personal or disciplinary advancement. This critical assessment is important when considering north-south relations and is utterly necessary when preparing to carry out research with Afro-Indigenous Garifuna communities whose epistemologies and spiritualities comprise complementary ways of knowing, including different conceptions of time, being, and the relationship between the human and natural world. Researchers must pursue ways of knowing that incorporate local knowledges, cosmovisions, and struggles for autonomy, grounding knowledge in the community and then putting it at the service of the community. Decolonial research means "choos[ing] the margins" as Tuhiwai Smith calls it and "has the responsibility to open, widen, intercede in, and act from decolonial fissures and cracks, and to make cracks within the spaces, places, institutions, and structures" of power.[15] This is the way to work with historically minoritized groups. This means challenging the panoptic eye of Western research, incorporating local epistemologies and cosmovisions, and co-developing a research agenda serving the needs of the community. Researchers have to decenter themselves, consider their biases, and doublecheck that their theoretical frameworks center the communities they are serving. As someone who is privileged, I have to constantly recommit to this process because it's hard enough to draw close authentically, and even harder to get past my own biases. Every day I have to recommit and check my privilege because if left unexamined, it limits my ability to observe.

As academic epistemologies often reinforce colonial and neocolonial agendas, the worldviews of researchers trained in particularizing disciplines often preference individual explanatory frameworks over collective frames. "The individual, as the basic social unit from which other social organizations and social relations form, is another system of ideas which needs to be understood as part of the West's cultural archive."[16] This can lead to the imposition of individualistic, bootstrap theories on local communities blaming community members for the structural causes of their own exclusion and poverty. The Western cultural assumption that people are responsible for the situations they find themselves in often permeates data analysis and ignores systemic power relations in which Indigenous and Afro-descendant communities are embedded; it also preferences individual rights over community rights and survival. "Individualistic research not only fails to undermine prevailing ideologies that hold individuals—especially women [or Indigenous peoples]—responsible for their own misery but usually grants these ideologies scientific legitimacy."[17] Obviously, the error here is the misconception that the community is inhabited by Western autonomous individuals. The systemic causes of exclusion can fade as individuals' actions are brought to the foreground. This tendency turns the focus away from the context of power relations that sustain genocidal treatment of minoritized groups and their ways of life, such as national or foreign extraction of natural resources from Indigenous lands, settler incursion, monocultural educational systems, and the state abandonment, collusion, and repression involved in all these actions and "blames individual survivors."[18] Many of the communities where we are working in and around Pearl Lagoon have a significant problem with teenage pregnancy and adolescent drug use. Frequent conversations with community leaders in Orinoco draw our attention to the challenges facing youth: "They see so few options for themselves here in the community. The only salaries here in the Orinoco are for a couple of nurses and teachers."[19] These community problems will not be solved solely, for example, with increased access to birth control and sanctions for youth using and selling drugs. The decisions of youth are intimately tied to the exclusion and power structures that restrict options for thriving in their communities. It is important to challenge these individualizing tendencies through a grounding in a critical analysis of history and the power relations in which Indigenous communities struggle, which often involves criticizing state policies and economic extractive practices as well as applying collective frameworks rather than relying solely on individualistic causal analysis.

Elevating the voices of Mateo, Kelsey, Miss Rebecca, and other residents of Orinoco and the communities where we've carried out research in Nicaragua, Honduras, and the United States is crucial to temper the biases, motives, and power dynamics inherent to ethnographic, anthropological fieldwork. As a reminder, our research group includes Andy, a recent college graduate and cisgender white man from the United States; Father Chepe, a mestizo Jesuit Catholic priest who is the president of a prominent university in Managua; Leonard, a Garifuna sociologist born in Orinoco who is also a Moravian pastor and lawyer; and Serena, a white, cisgender, middle-aged woman from the United States. We all have our own motives, biases, and perspectives that we must navigate as we research and write. However, we hope that the collaborative process of researching, writing, and discussing the themes that have emerged with our research partners has helped us better traverse our biases in order to produce a nuanced, humanizing portrait of Garifuna communities in Nicaragua.

Reflexivity and Probing Researcher Positionalities

One of the principal tools for questioning research agendas and putting the communal interests of excluded communities at the center of research, is reflexivity—a critical analysis by researchers of their positionalities, unconscious biases, ideologies, and worldviews—which interrogates the role of the researcher in the research process and knowledge production. Reflexivity is "a process that challenges the researcher to explicitly examine how his or her own research agenda and assumptions, subject location(s), personal beliefs,. . . [and] emotions enter into their research."[20] I would add the phrase "institutional agendas" to Hsiung's quote because as members of a multi-university partnership, we have to be tracking the agendas of our universities and holding them accountable to develop and sustain inclusive programs for marginalized communities.

For each one of us, reflexivity demanded that we probe our positionalities as educated professionals. We also committed to being in touch with how our own privilege can cloud observation. Upon reading Diane Nelson's self-critique after feeling momentarily frustrated with having to wait during a fieldwork moment, we too recognized an important theme applicable to us as well: "Pondering my disgruntlement forced me to acknowledge how stupid privilege makes me."[21]

Reflexivity is not just a private personal analysis, nor a self-flagellating end in itself. Rather it is an ongoing commitment to critical engagement with privilege and history when preparing for and when carrying out research. Grappling with these issues must inform research design but also how we implement our research methods. As Riach reminds us, "conceptualizing reflexivity as something that is practiced within (rather than upon) the interview and consequently emerging through socialized activity opens up a new avenue of reflexive consideration in relation to all participants in the research process."[22] In addition to applying reflexivity to the researcher's own biases and positionalities, Riach encourages researchers to treat research participants as reflexive subjects as well. Research participants, like for example Mateo, the healer and bush doctor of Orinoco, have subject positionalities within their own communities as well. They may benefit from gender hierarchies, traditional leadership positions, or access to opportunities that other community members don't. Mateo is seen as a power-ful person in his community given his role as Garifuna healer and leader within the local Catholic church, but the fact that he struggles with basic reading and writing skills means that he is often passed over when important roles need to be filled in the community. When I am participating in an interview with Mateo, I seek "sticky moments," endeavoring to frame the interview as a conversation in which the participants can "step outside of a traditional interview protocol."[23] Acknowledging research participants as reflexive subjects also means seeking opportunities to interact with them in their community roles; this means breaking down the barriers between researcher and researched. In my last conversation with Mateo, I was suffering from diarrhea; I sought treatment from Mateo. The conversation unfolded as we moved from the chairs of the porch to the kitchen to prepare my medicine. Indeed, the interview with Mateo is probably best described as an ongoing conversation, which unfolds over multiple visits and different activities, including my imbibing of his tea made from medicinal plants to cure my intestinal parasites. When I become a patient seeking medical treatment from Mateo, which he prepares with medicinal plants his ancestors have helped him identify and gather, we're granted an opening to confront the limitations of researcher and researched and enter into a different way of creating knowledge. And maybe this exchange opens the way for Mateo to tell me when my questions are off-base or discomforting.

Shortening the distance between researcher and researched can only be achieved in a granular present in which the researcher embraces "sticky moments" and demonstrates transparency and flexibility about research objectives, where the researcher seeks to learn from the research participant as they play their roles in the community, and in which the researcher and research participant converse— examining topics together—in a collaborative construction of knowledge and future actions.

Decolonial Methodologies and Methods
ETHNOGRAPHY

Disruptive conversations; critical questioning of positionalities, biases, and the research process; and extended, frequent field visits open the possibility for a decolonial research methodology. There must also be regular and ongoing temporal and spatial accompaniment that includes building relations through time as well as visiting different places for their geographical and strategic importance. In our case, this includes the nine months all together we spent gathering data, but it is also strengthened by Leonard's childhood in Orinoco and his conversations with his Garifuna ancestors. It also includes Father Chepe's time in Orinoco in the early 1990s and his friendships and commitment to the Garifuna communities of Honduras. It is also important to conduct research and visit archives to understand those who hold power, particularly state power, and who deploy it from political power centers such as Bluefields, Puerto Cabezas, or Managua and beyond. It also means researching the settler incursions and imposition of individual property rights on Indigenous lands. And finally, we must follow the diasporic experience. What do Garifuna in Nicaragua share with Garifuna in Honduras? What do Garifuna in the Bronx and Brooklyn share with Central American Garifuna? Accompaniment needs to be spatial, and by this I mean, spending time in Pearl Lagoon, Bronx, other Central American countries, and it needs to be sustained and engaged so we can have the time to develop these open-ended, ongoing conversations and shared experiences, or *covivencia*. It's one thing for me to learn about Garifuna spiritual practices in Orinoco, but when Yolanda, a twenty-four-year-old Garifuna who lives in the Bronx, tells me that "Religion has come in to destroy, but we know that the ancestors are here to help us," I am able to consider what this means about surviving the Americas and how formal, organized religion can perpetuate the repression of Garifuna cultural practices.[24]

Ethnography, and its methods of participant observation and extended, open-ended interviews, informs the methods we've chosen given the threats that the Garifuna are facing. The present moment in Nicaragua, with its historical disjunctures, cultural erasures, and political costs for marginalized communities like the Garifuna, is a complicated terrain for carrying out research. "The complexities of our times require ethnographic skills. This is a matter of opening up simplified accounts, making accountability possible at different granularities, signposting the labyrinths of possible inquiries for their relevance, their points of no return, their conceptual reruns, acknowledging in a politics of recognition pebbles of resistance that destabilize easy theories."[25] Carrying out research with communities who are persisting *a pesar de* centuries of exclusion, fighting for their own survivance, and often just trying to make ends meet means engaging complexity and asking hard questions. And throughout this unfolding process, researchers and research participants must participate in a critical dialogue about how to create common ground without eliding difference or forcing secrets to be divulged, without pretending some of us haven't benefited at the expense of others, without denying the existence of culpability, power relations, and complexity. As the visits continue to unfold, life stories deepen, expand, and enmesh us, and our writing must include this thick description. Mateo's life story began when he would follow his grandfather out into the bush; and even though his parents weren't able to support him to get an education, today he's accompanied by his grandson who attends school in the community and follows his grandfather as he gathers medicinal plants for the variety of illnesses that afflict the community. Mateo talks with his ancestors and shows his grandson what the ancestors are showing him. Mateo is introducing his grandson to their ancestors, and they, in turn, are revealing the location of plants to them. And now our research team is participating in the building of Mateo's clinic as the healing powers of his medicinal plants move through our own very bodies. When I have drunk you in, you are part of me, and I am part of you. We are beholden to each other in this commitment to persistence and meaning making in the twenty-first century. This is the thick possibility of a decolonial, engaged ethnography.

METHODS

So, what did we actually do when we were in the field, on an extended visit to the communities? Our primary methods were interviews and participant observation. Interviews were often unstructured, seeking their orientation in the specific day and activities we were carrying out, and sometimes semi-structured. Unstructured interviews were ad hoc, situational, often part of an ongoing conversation that would get taken up again. In this case, there wasn't an interview guide per se. Rather, guiding questions informed the overall arc of the research, and then the researcher and research participants would agree on the topics of the session based on the objectives of the day and prior conversations. Sometimes, we looped back around to topics we covered previously probing and deepening a prior exchange or interaction. Other times, we would recap a prior conversation and ask what had been left out of the past conversations. I liked talking with Miss Rebecca; I couldn't get enough of her insights into her community from a long career as the community nurse and her leadership role in the Anglican Church. But as much as I had specific topics about women and youth I wanted to talk about, Miss Rebecca had things she wanted to accomplish that day. So, often we ended up talking about the teenage pregnancy problem in the community as we were making traditional Garifuna dishes—for which she'd had me purchase the specialty or more expensive ingredients.

Sometimes we used a semi-structured interview format when different members of our research team were having different conversations with research participants, and we wanted to assure that at least a similar group of questions got asked of all research participants. The semi-structured interview also worked well for us when carrying out conversations with people who do not have a lot of time. In fact, given time limitations, sometimes we employed the group interview or focus group method when visiting Garifuna communities in Honduras to gather as many perspectives as possible in a short period of time. These focus groups involved preparing an interview guide beforehand but allowing the multiple interventions of participants to take the conversation where they wanted it to go. We did not tape interviews or focus groups preferring to take extensive, handwritten notes instead. For instance, our interview guide for Garifuna men and women in the Bronx included the following questions:

1. Have you been able to maintain contact with your community of origin and family members still living there?

2. Are there Garifuna practices that you have been able to maintain while being far away from your community of origin?

3. What practices are maintained, and what practices are more often forgotten in New York?

4. What are the most significant challenges that you face in living your Garifuna identity in New York City?

5. How often do you travel to Central America? Where do you go and where do you stay?

6. How do you self-identify ethnically here in the United States?

This way we were able to carry out multiple interviews with Garifuna in the United States over time and without all being together, taking advantage of trips that got us to the New York City area.

Participant observation, on the other hand, is conscious presence. We participated in the events of the community that day or week or season. We entered into what the community was experiencing. This meant getting up before dawn to walk out to Mateo's plot of land, gathering plants, and bringing them back into town to be turned into medicine. It meant spending the day making bami (manioc flour tortillas) by soaking, grating, and wringing out the manioc to making the tortillas and putting them on the *comal* (metal griddle). It meant cleaning the cemetery in preparation for Holy Week. It meant attending religious ceremonies and participating in rituals when invited. Participant observation requires a divided consciousness: while simultaneously engaging in the activity, you do have to reserve part of yourself for taking mental or handwritten notes about what is transpiring around you.

As fieldworkers, our main source of data was the set of fieldnotes we wrote up at the end of every day. For every hour in conversation, there was a minimum of an hour of writing afterward. Fieldnotes included observations of what has happened, but they also detailed insights into what had transpired within the researcher that day. If I'm ill that day, it's important to flag that; I am going to be a different observer when I feel ill compared to when I'm healthy. When we reread those fieldnotes, we know that they were informed by that day's viewpoint. When it came time to analyze data, the same reflexive questions and vulnerability that informed preparation for research and actual research were employed to avoid the assumption that "the researcher, the method, and the data are separate entities rather than reflexively interdependent and interconnected."[26] Fieldnotes were read and reread with an eye to key themes, topics, and words; folks must be visited and asked to explain yet again what remains elusive. But even with our commitments, the Mateo of our fieldnotes, the Mateo of these chapters, can never be the robust, complex man he is in real life; it's a version, a statue, a frozen moment.[27] This is not Mateo, but our re-collections of his words and a re-construction or translation of his performance of Garifuna culture. Our interpretation of the data is a leap, a creative jump from data to conclusion as we search for key themes and their examples in the field notes to substantiate our claims. "The empirical is difficult to tag here because realities and elusiveness exist in the same space.[28]" Humility and sustained, reflexive reading and re-reading of field notes were necessary for data analysis and developing the actions that would follow from the research. Our final field visits involved double checking initial conclusions with key research participants and making adjustments based on their feedback. Obviously, we will share this book with the research participants who so generously provided their time to talk with us about what it means to be Garifuna in Nicaragua today, and listen carefully to their reflections on the published book.

Thinking about what comes after analysis and what use research conclusions can serve is important for a number of reasons. "Simple justice demands that the researcher reciprocate for the participants' trouble by sharing research results."[29] In her summary of Donna Haraway's classic appeal, Jennifer Goett, writing about the rural community of Monkey Point to the south of Bluefields, exhorts us to, "insist on better, richer, more critical, and power-savvy accounts of the world that have the ability to translate situated knowledges across power-differentiated communities."[30] This means a commitment to disseminating this ethnography of Garifuna persistence for its ability to inspire survivance in other similar groups, but it also means getting this book into the hands of people who should be doing more to support communities on the margins. Decolonial research means "choosing the margins" and putting data to work with Indigenous communities: moving from "studying about" to "thinking with."[31] We have also committed to directing all royalties from the sale of this book to increasing the educational opportunities for Garifuna youth from the Pearl Lagoon communities we visited.

Demonstrating Responsive Research

When the presidents of our three universities signed agreements to collaborate, they committed to working and learning collaboratively; this meant being open to being changed by what these relationships would bring. As Nicaragua faces continued student protests and government repression, it means that Seattle University has to be in solidarity with our Nicaraguan university partners. The UCA must acknowledge that they too have contributed to the discrimination that emanates from Managua toward the Caribbean coast and seek to implement policies that include students from the Caribbean coast. Both the UCA and the BICU have to examine how they may contribute to outbound migration (shipping out) from the communities by offering educational opportunities that will only lead to jobs in the cities. All three of our institutions, with their commitments and contradictions, must endeavor to match commitments to actions, even if that means acknowledging failing and then re-committing. Together we have raised funds to promote intercultural exchange, action research, and programming that brings the universities to the communities instead of always making community members leave for the city. And most importantly, the youth and leadership of the coastal communities we accompany need to be stakeholders in co-determining not just research priorities but institutional priorities. This means providing training in research methods and accompaniment in addition to actual research by putting privilege at the service of the communities and speaking truth to power when governments and state offices don't respect or implement laws designed to protect Indigenous autonomy or state officials and security forces repress Indigenous activism. This commitment also necessitates putting our data at the service of community priorities and making sure that this book supports the educational priorities of Garifuna communities. This commitment means putting resources behind our words and lobbying for accountability in this decolonial present in which Indigenous autonomy and collective livelihoods are constantly threatened.

This research project is part of a larger effort by our universities to be more sensitive to and inclusive of marginalized groups, particularly Indigenous and Afro-descendant peoples and their communities throughout the Americas. This means that in our conversations and community engagement we practice checking our privilege and biases, be it from a U.S. perspective contemplating a Nicaraguan perspective, or a Managua perspective contemplating Caribbean coastal realities, or a privileged coastal reality considering the challenges being faced by Indigenous, Afro-descendent, and Afro-Indigenous communities.

Unanswered Questions, Future Research Questions

When we came together as an intercultural, intergenerational, and inter-university research team in 2015, we were inspired by an initial research question about the persistence of the Garifuna communities of Nicaragua *a pesar de* all the challenges they've had to face. As we finish the writing of this book, we realize that while we've answered some questions, a whole new set of questions have presented themselves. May these new questions inspire future research with the Garifuna of Nicaragua!

This project has been an inter-university research project conducted with Garifuna communities. What are other methodologies, activities, and initiatives that universities can undertake with Indigenous communities in order to co-create knowledge?

In the course of our research, citizen protest and state repression in Nicaragua have led to the exodus of many young people from the country, the imprisonment of others, and the death or disappearance of hundreds of Nicaraguans, many on the Caribbean coast. The increase in state repression across the country raises vital questions about how this situation is affecting the Garifuna communities of Pearl Lagoon. Not only does increased state repression affect people, the consolidation of state power means that the extraction of natural resources and the influx of settlers continues apace. What does community survivance for the Pearl Lagoon communities look like in the face of this continued influx with an increase in state repression? Because interlocking forms of difference exacerbate exclusion, we remain concerned about the wellbeing of youth as well as women and other community members who experience other forms of social difference. What do their survivance strategies look like today?

Will repression in Nicaragua affect how the Garifuna communities of Pearl Lagoon are interacting with Garifuna communities in Honduras and beyond to learn the Garifuna language, for example? How will their sense of a pan-Garifuna identity evolve? And for the Garifuna in general, what political, economic, and social obstacles will they face as they continue to articulate a cross-border Garifuna nation that reaches from Central America to the United States and beyond?

Given the increase of Nicaraguan migration, it makes us wonder if outbound Garifuna are following routes to Costa Rica and the Caribbean or if they too are joining other Central Americans on the exodus north. If so, are they joining Garifuna friends and family in the United States? Maybe it's time to visit New York City again.

NOTES

TIMELINE

1. Christopher Taylor, *The Black Carib Wars*, 7.
2. Virginia Kerns, *Women and the Ancestors: Black Carib Kinship and Ritual,* 20.
3. Kerns, 20.
4. Taylor, 25.
5. Taylor, 25.
6. Edmund T. Gordon, *Disparate Diasporas*, 33.
7. Nancie González, "Garifuna Settlement in New York: A New Frontier," 265. Linda M. Matthei and David A. Smith, "Flexible Ethnic Identity, Adaptation, Survival, Resistance: The Garífuna in the World-system," 223.
8. Gordon, 33; Gordon, 96–97.
9. Taylor, 25.
10. Taylor, 27.
11. Taylor, 29.
12. Taylor, 52.
13. Taylor, 33.
14. Gordon, 33.
15. Taylor, 21.
16. Gordon, 33.
17. Taylor, 52.
18. Gordon, 34.
19. Matthei and Smith, 224; Taylor, 51.
20. Taylor, 76.
21. Taylor, 107.
22. Gordon, 35.
23. Taylor, 109.
24. Kerns, 19; Taylor, 165–166.
25. Matthei and Smith, 224.
26. González, 256; Matthei and Smith, 224.
27. Sharlene Mollett, "A Modern Paradise: Garifuna Land, Labor, and Displacement-in-Place," 35; Matthei and Smith, 224.
28. Kerns, 43; Matthei and Smith, 224.
29. Taylor, 174.
30. Taylor 175–176.
31. Depending on the sources, there are different names used by scholars and historians to refer to the Garifuna such as the Black Caribs.
32. Matthei and Smith, 224.
33. Taylor, 176.
34. Gordon, 40–41.
35. Gordon, 41.

36. Gordon, 44.
37. Kerns, 44.
38. Gordon, 41.
39. William D. Davidson, "The Garifuna of Pearl Lagoon: Ethnohistory of an Afro-American Enclave in Nicaragua," 34.
40. Gordon, 54.
41. Taylor, 177.
42. Gordon, 57.
43. Gordon, 55.
44. Leo Joseph, "Informe de viaje realizado a las comunidades Garífunas de la cuenca de Laguna de Perlas entre los días 2-6 de septiembre del 2019." Gordon, 60–61.
45. Davidson, 38.
46. González, 261.
47. Matthei and Smith, 225.
48. Gordon, 66.
49. Leo Joseph.
50. Leo Joseph.
51. Leo Joseph.
52. Leo Joseph; Davidson, 38.
53. Mollett, 35.
54. Matthei and Smith, 225–226.
55. Keri Vacanti Brondo, "'A Dot on a Map': Cartographies of Erasure in Garifuna Territory," 187.
56. Edmund T. Gordon, *Disparate Diasporas*, 11–12.
57. Mollett, 36.
58. Brondo, 187.
59. Taylor, 180.
60. Brondo, 186.
61. Brondo, 185.
62. Mollett, 28.
63. Brondo, 189.
64. Brondo, 186.

PREFACE

1. The panga is the main source of transportation for people living in the communities of Pearl Lagoon as well as the main vehicle for fishing. Via panga, one is connected to the other communities as well as having access to Pearl Lagoon town, Bluefields, and beyond.
2. James Chaney, "Malleable Identities: Placing the Garínagu in New Orleans"; Sarah England, *Afro-Central Americans in New York City: Garifuna Tales of Transnational Movements in Racialized Space*; Paul Christopher Johnson, "On Leaving and Joining Africanness through Religion: The 'Black Caribs' across Multiple Diasporic Horizons."
3. Nina Glick-Schiller, "From Immigrant to Transmigrant: Theorizing Transnational Migration."
4. Miguel González, "Leasing Communal Lands... In 'Perpetuity' Post-Titling Scenarios on the Caribbean Coast of Nicaragua," 77.

5. Jane Freeland, "Intercultural-Bilingual Education for an Interethnic-Plurilingual Society? The Case of Nicaragua's Caribbean Coast."
6. Centro Nicaragüense de Derechos Humanos, "Voces campesinas contra el proyecto del Canal."
7. Teresa V. Catter, "Intercultural Bilingual Education in Nicaragua: Contexualisation for Improving the Quality of Education."
8. Community member, interviewed by Father Chepe, January 1, 2016.

INTRODUCTION

1. Community member, interviewed by Leonard Joseph, September 4, 2019.
2. Community member, interviewed by Leonard Joseph, September 4, 2019.
3. Community member, interviewed by Leonard Joseph, September 4, 2019.
4. Community member, interviewed by Leonard Joseph, September 4, 2019.

CHAPTER ONE: PERSISTING

1. Irene Watson, "Aboriginal Sovereignties: Past, Present and Future (Im)Possibilities," 35.
2. James Clifford, *Returns: Becoming Indigenous in the Twenty-First Century*, 43.
3. Sarah England, *Afro-Central Americans in New York City: Garifuna Tales of Transnational Movements in Racialized Space*, 13.
4. James Chaney, "Malleable Identities: Place the Garínagu in New Orleans," 127.
5. Linda Tuhiwai Smith, *Decolonizing Methodologies: Research and Indigenous Peoples*, 7.
6. Clifford, *Returns*.
7. Gaurau Dibie and Johnston Njoku, "Cultural Perceptions of Africans in Diaspora and in Africa on Atlantic Slave Trade and Reparations," 404.
8. Philip Curtin, *The Atlantic Slave Trade: A Census*, 4–13.
9. Edmund T. Gordon and Mark Anderson, "The African Diaspora Toward an Ethnography of Diasporic Identification," 288.
10. Walter Mignolo and Catherine Walsh, *On Decoloniality: Concepts, Analytics, Praxis,* 101.
11. Gordon and Anderson, 290.
12. All names of research participants have been changed to protect their identities. The only exception is when research participants have public leadership positions and gave us permission to use their names.
13. Clifford, *Returns*.
14. Virginia Kerns, *Women and the Ancestors: Black Carib Kinship and Ritual.*
15. Donna Haraway, "Situated Knowledge: The Science Question in Feminism and the Privilege of Partial Perspective," 588.
16. Juliet Hooker, "'Beloved Enemies': Race and Official Mestizo Nationalism in Nicaragua," 15.
17. Nancie L. González, "Garifuna Settlement in New York: A New Frontier," 77.
18. England, 35.
19. Paul Christopher Johnson, "On Leaving and Joining Africanness through Religion: The 'Black Caribs' across Multiple Diasporic Horizons," 181.
20. José Idiáquez, *El culto a los ancestros en la cosmovisión Garífuna de Nicaragua.*
21. Christopher Taylor, *The Black Carib Wars*, 51–81.
22. Taylor, 164.

23. Linda M. Matthei and David A. Smith, "Flexible Ethnic Identity, Adaptation, Survival, Resistance: The Garifuna in the World-system," 222.
24. Taylor, 165–166.
25. N. González, 256; Taylor, 167–168.
26. Taylor, 175–176.
27. Taylor, 174.
28. Taylor, 176.
29. Joseph O. Palacio, *The Garifuna: A Nation Across Borders*, 69.
30. Carlos Vilas, *Del colonialismo a la autonomía: Modernización capitalista y revolución social en la costa atlántica*, 52–53.
31. Vilas, 53.
32. Vilas, 53.
33. Edmund T. Gordon, *Disparate Diasporas: Identity and Politics in an African-Nicaraguan Community*, ix.
34. Gordon, 39.
35. George Evans, "The Deaths of Somoza," 38; J. Soloman & سولومون, ج., "Tortured History: Filibustering, Rhetoric, and Walker's "War in Nicaragua" / التاريخ المعذب: القرصنة والإبلاغة وكتاب ووكر نع الحرب في نيكاراجوا," 105.
36. Gordon, *Disparate Diasporas*.
37. Gordon, 63.
38. Richard Sobel, "Contra Aid Fundamentals: Exploring the Intricacies and the Issues."
39. Pierre Frühling, Miguel González, and Hans Petter Buvollen, *Etnicidad y nación: El desarrollo de la autonomía de la costa atlántica de Nicaragua (1987–2007)*, 42.
40. Gordon, 145.
41. William Blum, "Killing Hope: U.S. Military and CIA Interventions since World War II," 293.
42. Frühling, González, and Buvollen, 73.
43. Hooker, 15.
44. Jennifer Goett, *Black Autonomy: Race, Gender, and Afro-Nicaraguan Activism*, 180.
45. Charles R. Hale, "Neoliberal Multiculturalism: The Remaking of Cultural Rights and Racial Discrimination in Latin America," 499.
46. Clifford, 42.
47. Gerald Vizenor, *Native Liberty: Natural Reason and Cultural Survivance*, 85.
48. Goett, 185.
49. Chandra Talpade Mohanty, "Under Western Eyes: Feminist Scholarship and Colonial Discourses," 333.
50. Paul Gilroy, *The Black Atlantic: Modernity and Double Consciousness*, 2.
51. Peter Wade, "Rethinking 'Mestizaje': Ideology and Lived Experience," 240.
52. Wade, 240.
53. Mignolo and Walsh, 7.
54. Mignolo and Walsh, 181.
55. Wade, 243. See also Gordon, 125.
56. Lisa Slater, "A Meditation on Discomfort," 339.
57. Leanne Betasamosake Simpson, *As We Have Always Done: Indigenous Freedom through Radical Resistance,* 48–49.
58. Mignolo and Walsh, 24.

59. Mignolo and Walsh, 69.
60. Clifford, *Returns*; Gilroy, *Black Atlantic*.
61. Gilroy, 6.
62. Clifford, 73.
63. Nina Glick-Schiller, "From Immigrant to Transmigrant: Theorizing Transnational Migration."
64. Glick-Schiller, 48.
65. Clifford, 51.
66. David Welchman Gegeo, "Cultural Rupture and Indigeneity: The Challenge of (Revisioning 'Place' in the Pacific."
67. Clifford, 59.
68. Slater, 341.

CHAPTER TWO: FRAMING

1. Kimberlé Crenshaw, *Background Paper for the Expert Meeting of the Gender-Related Aspects of Race Discrimination*, 13.
2. According to Tuhiwai Smith, "Imperialism tends to be used in at least four different ways when describing the form of European imperialism which 'started' in the fifteenth century: (1) imperialism as economic expansion; (2) imperialism as the subjugation of 'others'; (3) imperialism as an idea or spirit with many forms of realization; and (4) imperialism as a discursive field of knowledge." *Decolonizing Methodologies: Research and Indigenous Peoples*, 22.
3. Walter Mignolo and Catherine Walsh, *On Decoloniality: Concepts, Analytics, Praxis*, 1.
4. Crenshaw, *Background Paper*, 8.
5. Patricia Hill Collins and Sirma Bilge, *Intersectionality*, 36.
6. Kimberlé Crenshaw, "Mapping the Margins: Intersectionality, Identity Politics, and Violence Against Women of Color"; Crenshaw, *Background Paper*; Patricia Hill Collins, *Black Feminist Thought: Knowledge, Consciousness, and the Politics of Empowerment*. See also Patrick R. Grzanka, *Intersectionality: A Foundations and Frontiers Reader*, and Collins and Bilge, *Intersectionality*.
7. Crenshaw, *Background Paper*, 1.
8. Crenshaw, *Background Paper*, 5.
9. Collins and Bilge, 4.
10. Collins and Bilge, 7.
11. On single issue commitments, Sarah A. Radcliffe, *Dilemmas of Difference: Indigenous Women and the Limits of Postcolonial Development Policy*, 64. Collins and Bilge, 3. On intersectionality and biased data analysis, Serena Cosgrove, "'Who Will Use My Loom When I Am Gone?' An Intersectional Analysis of Mapuche Women's Progress in Twenty-First Century Chile."
12. Collins and Bilge; Cosgrove, "'Who Will Use My Loom?'"; Richard Delgado and Jean Stefancic, *Critical Race Theory: An Introduction*, 57–62; Sarah A. Radcliffe, "Geography and Indigeneity I: Indigeneity, Coloniality and Knowledge"; Radcliffe, *Dilemmas of Difference*.
13. Crenshaw, *Background Paper*, 8.
14. Grzanka, 100.
15. Crenshaw, *Background Paper*, 14.

16. José Idiáquez, *El culto a los ancestros en la cosmovisión de los Garífunas de Nicaragua*, 179.

17. Orson, interviewed by Andrew Gorvetzian and Leonard Joseph, January 22, 2018.

18. Grzanka, 16.

19. Collins, *Black Feminist Thought*; Crenshaw, *Background Paper*, 13.

20. Serena Cosgrove, *Leadership from the Margins: Women and Civil Society Organizations in Argentina, Chile, and El Salvador*.

21. Grzanka, 54.

22. Radcliffe, *Dilemmas of Difference*, 7.

23. James Clifford, *Returns: Becoming Indigenous in the Twenty-First Century*, 150.

24. Clifford, 55.

25. Mignolo and Walsh, 5–6.

26. Mignolo and Walsh, 17.

27. Irene Watson, "Aboriginal Sovereignties: Past, Present and Future (Im)Possibilities."

28. Mignolo and Walsh, *On Decoloniality*.

29. Mignolo and Walsh, 114.

30. Mignolo and Walsh, 159.

31. Crenshaw, *Background Paper*, 7.

32. Crenshaw, *Background Paper*, 7.

33. Collins and Bilge, 28.

34. Hale, "Neoliberal Multiculturalism: The Remaking of Cultural Rights and Racial Discrimination in Latin America," 13.

35. Grzanka, xix.

36. Crenshaw, "Mapping the Margins," 1243; Mignolo and Walsh, *On Decoloniality*.

37. Clifford, 69.

38. Clifford, 252. Culture—one of the English language words with the most meanings—is "shared meanings" according to Hall and often used to refer to Indigenous societies. But in this book, we shy away from using "culture" more broadly preferring to locate our usage socially and spatially by talking about the cultural practices of Garifuna in particular localities. Stuart Hall, "On Postmodernism and Articulation: An Interview with Stuart Hall," 1.

39. Stuart Hall, "On Postmodernism and Articulation: An Interview with Stuart Hall," 53.

40. Clifford, 61–62.

41. Clifford, 53.

42. Mignolo and Walsh, 74.

43. Hale, "Does Multiculturalism Menace? Governance, Cultural Rights and the Politics of Identity in Guatemala," 499.

44. Clifford, 45–46. See Charles Hale, "Does Multiculturalism Menace?" and *Más que un Indio: Racial Ambivalence and Neoliberal Multiculturalism in Guatemala*.

45. Clifford, 47.

46. Gerald Vizenor, *Native Liberty: Natural Reason and Cultural Survivance*, 85.

47. Clifford, 133.

48. Clifford, 48.

49. Clifford, 48.

CHAPTER THREE: ROOTING

1. "We only survived because we had medicina ancestral from our African and Indigenous ancestors. . . Fueron buscando el mar y el rio como el lugar donde vivían en San Vicente que les había dado sus ancestros. . . La naturaleza, el mar, el monte son el rostro de dios." Focus group, facilitated by Serena Cosgrove, March 25, 2018.
2. Luz Solís, interviewed by Andrew Gorvetzian, August 7, 2018. This quote was delivered as is in both languages.
3. Sharlene Mollett, "A Modern Paradise: Garifuna Land, Labor, and Displacement-in-Place," 29.
4. Andy, interviewed by Andrew Gorvetzian, August 4, 2018.
5. Christopher A. Loperena, "Honduras Is Open for Business: Extractivist Tourism as Sustainable Development in the Wake of Disaster?"; Keri Vacanti Brondo, "'A Dot on the Map': Cartographies of Erasure in Garifuna Territory"; Mollett, "A Modern Paradise."
6. Leonard Joseph, written reflection, July 2017.
7. Mateo, interviewed by Andrew Gorvetzian, July 3, 2016.
8. Charles, interviewed by José Idiáquez and Andrew Gorvetzian, April 14, 2017.
9. J. Martínez Cruz, Glenda Godfrey, and Salvador García, "Living in Community: Primeras aproximaciones al buenvivir de las poblaciones afrodescendientes en la cuenca de Laguna de Perlas, RACCS," 93–94.
10. Kelsey, interviewed by Serena Cosgrove and José Idiáquez, December 9, 2015.
11. Miss Rebecca, interviewed by Andrew Gorvetzian, April 11, 2017.
12. Lenin, interviewed by Andrew Gorvetzian and Leonard Joseph, January 26, 2018.
13. Miguel González, "Leasing Communal Lands. . . In 'Perpetuity' Post-Titling Scenarios on the Caribbean Coast of Nicaragua," 70.
14. González, "Leasing Communal Lands," 71.
15. Nora Sylvander, "Saneamiento Territorial in Nicaragua, and the Prospects for Resolving Indigenous-Mestizo Land Conflicts," 167.
16. Joe Bryan, "For Nicaragua's Indigenous Communities, Land Rights in Name Only," 58.
17. For information on this history, see Sarah Howard, "Autonomía y derechos territoriales indígenas: El caso de la RAAN."
18. "Algo sé y aunque vivimos aislados, cuando encuentro algún periódico o revista en Bluefields traigo muchas cosas para leer. Aquí estamos muy lejos de los pañas. Pero cada vez se están tomando el Caribe. Esos robos de tierra no lo hacia Somoza. Robaba la pesca, la madera, hacia inversiones con los creoles, pero no se metía con las tierras. Eso es nuevo de Ortega que parece que le quiere ganar a Somoza y el ladrón Alemán." Community member, interviewed by José Idiáquez, April 7, 2016.
19. Mollett, 29.
20. Community member, interviewed by Serena Cosgrove, July 12, 2015.
21. Leonard Joseph, interviewed by Serena Cosgrove, July 12, 2015.
22. Miss Blanca, interviewed by Serena Cosgrove and José Idiáquez, March 22, 2016.
23. Dolene Miller, interviewed by Serena Cosgrove, July 14, 2015.
24. Dolene Miller, interviewed by Serena Cosgrove, July 14, 2015.
25. Miss Patricia, interviewed by Andrew Gorvetzian, April 12, 2017.
26. Mateo, interviewed by Andrew Gorvetzian, April 14, 2017.

27. Bryan, 63.

28. James Mittleman, *The Globalization Syndrome: Transformation and Resistance,* 166.

29. Kelsey, interviewed by Serena Cosgrove and José Idiáquez, December 9, 2015.

30. "Estoy muy molesta con el Gobierno Regional y con la gente de Ortega que está en el pacífico. Ellos son los que están haciendo el problema con la tierra de los indígenas. Son gente de Ortega y lo triste es que los mismos sandinistas que son garífunas o miskitos se han unido con esos políticos de Managua que nunca se han interesado por nosotros. Y los políticos garífunas, miskitos, y creoles reciben dinero por la tierra comunal y después vienen los problemas. Ellos reciben dinero de los que tienen negocios de drogas y de los que están con Ortega, pero los muertos no son los de Managua: somos la gente de los pueblos autónomos. Y dicen que los indígenas tenemos derechos, pero eso es mentira. Sólo se acuerdan que existimos ahora que vienen las elecciones." Community member, interviewed by José Idiáquez, December 9, 2015.

31. Community member, interviewed by Serena Cosgrove, July 12, 2015.

32. "El partido del gobierno esta haciendo daño a los pueblos Indígenas y Afro. Nosotros los Garifunas, los Miskitos, los Ramas, y la población Costa somos gente excluida y el gobierno está dispuesto a todo por quitarnos nuestras tierras. Lo están logrando de la manera más sucia. Echando a pelear a campesinos con indígenas. Y los terratenientes/políticos que están detrás no aparecen porque son cobardes. Son los pobres los que morimos." Community member, interviewed by José Idiáquez, January 15, 2017.

33. Bryan, "For Nicaragua's Indigenous Communities, Land Rights in Name Only"; Miguel González, "Securing Rights in Tropical Lowlands"; González, "Leasing Communal Lands"; Sylvander, "Saneamiento Territorial in Nicaragua."

34. Bryan, 63.

35. Mateo, interviewed by Andrew Gorvetzian, April 14, 2017.

36. Community member, interviewed by Serena Cosgrove, July 12, 2015.

37. Miss Heidy, interviewed by Serena Cosgrove, July 12, 2015.

38. Virginia Kerns, *Women and the Ancestors: Black Carib Kinship and Ritual,* 22.

39. Keri Vacanti Brondo, *Land Grab: Green Neoliberalism, Gender, and Garifuna Resistance in Honduras,* 80.

40. Miss Heidy, interviewed by Serena Cosgrove, July 12, 2015.

41. Miss Magda, interviewed by Serena Cosgrove, July 12, 2015.

42. Kerns, 191.

43. Miss Magda, interviewed by Serena Cosgrove, July 12, 2015.

44. Jennifer Goett, *Black Autonomy: Race, Gender, and Afro-Nicaraguan Activism,* 171.

45. Kerns, 92.

46. Mateo, interviewed by Andrew Gorvetzian, April 14, 2017.

47. Kelsey, interviewed by Serena Cosgrove and José Idiáquez, December 9, 2015.

48. "Estamos más afuera que adentro. 75% de nuestra realidad va para afuera. Ahora quieren quitarnos la tierra por ley. Buscan a nuestras playas. Nuestra espiritualidad se vincula con el mar. La curación está en la playa. Más bello después de la familia es la playa. Si nos ven tirando basura en la playa, somos chanchos." Community member, focus group facilitated by Serena Cosgrove, March 25, 2018.

49. "Ir a la playa, sentir este aire es curación para nosotros. Aquí es donde encuentro el dios negro que conozco. Me siento aquí, ante esta agua, siento el aire de nuestros

ancestros y esto nos da solución a nuestros problemas." Community member, focus group facilitated by Serena Cosgrove, March 25, 2018.

50. "Si perdemos nuestra lengua y la tierra, perdemos todo lo que es nuestro. Lo bueno es que hay líderes con esta conciencia que están emergiendo." Community member, focus group facilitated by Serena Cosgrove, March 26, 2018.

51. Brondo, "'A Dot on the Map,'" 188.

52. "Sufrimos también una escasez de creatividad en cuanto al uso sostenible de la tierra. Hay que tener mayor vínculo entre nuestras ideas y la tierra, tenemos que pensar en como se puede desarrollar actividades y asistencia técnica para trabajar la tierra." Community member, focus group facilitated by Serena Cosgrove, March 28, 2018.

53. "Bien uso de la tierra necesita formación en una forma organizativa. Mucha gente se deprime, no tiene que hacer y se mete con drogas y alcohol y luego los derribados. No es fácil con la pesca. Sí, tenemos el derecho de pescar, pero hay poco pescado." Community member, focus group facilitated by Serena Cosgrove, March 28, 2018.

54. "Ninguno de mis hijos va a trabajar la tierra. ¿Tiene sentido contratar alguien a trabajarlo? Entiendo la tentación de pensar en venderla." Ernesto, interviewed by Serena Cosgrove. March 28, 2018.

55. Brondo, "'A Dot on the Map,'" 187.

56. Loperena, 628.

57. Loperena, 625.

58. "Turismo es amenaza a la tierra ancestral, triste que unos jóvenes profesionales formados son los que traicionan mas porque hacen negocio de tierra por dinero." Community member, focus group facilitated by Serena Cosgrove, March 26, 2018.

59. "Estamos peores que antes a causa de estos procesos. La privatización de playas en Honduras ha creado una situación en que uno corre el riesgo de ser disparado si pasa por una playa privada." Dr. Quisha González, interviewed by Andrew Gorvetzian and Leonard Joseph, April 24, 2018.

60. "Muchas veces son los mismos Garífuna quienes venden la tierra. La pobreza crea problemas que hace que la gente tenga que vender sus terrenos. La tierra no se vende, no se puede vender. Hay que esforzarse para vender la tierra. Pero ya que alguien lo compre y se hace dueño, intenta acaparar con todo. 'Dominio pleno' significa que tenemos que cuidar la tierra." Community member, focus group facilitated by Serena Cosgrove, March 28, 2018.

61. Brondo, "'A Dot on the Map,'" 196; Bryan, 63.

62. "It's been a highway of growth. Esto es debido al éxodo de Garifuna de Honduras, un hostigamiento por territorios, falta de empleo. Ahora nos encontramos en una situación en que hay que crear para poder sobrevivir." Milton, interviewed by Andrew Gorvetzian. July 27, 2018.

63. Kenia Smith, interviewed by Andrew Gorvetzian and Leonard Joseph, April 23, 2018.

64. Andy, interviewed by Andrew Gorvetzian, August 4, 2018.

65. Leonard Joseph, written reflection, July 2017.

CHAPTER FOUR: BELIEVING

1. "Lo importante es que los Garífunas cuando tocan a uno, tocan a todos. Todavía hay gente que no lo entiende. Religión ancestral—la presencia de nuestros ancestros en la vida diaria, y la lucha por la tierra, no la podemos separar de la espiritualidad. Es

una espiritualidad de combate. No porque queramos ser conflictivos, sino porque toda nuestra historia ha sido de lucha, ha sido de despojo, y ha sido de huir para sobrevivir. La espiritualidad es ecológica. Tenemos que defender nuestros recursos naturales." Sister Soyapa, interviewed by Serena Cosgrove, March 25, 2018.

2. Mateo, interviewed by Andrew Gorvetzian and Leonard Joseph, January 24, 2018.

3. Agustín, interviewed by José Idiáquez, January 22, 1992.

4. Isidro, interviewed by José Idiáquez, February 4, 1992.

5. Isidro, interviewed by José Idiáquez, July 11, 1992.

6. According to Bauman, "The great human invention culture (perhaps the greatest of all, a meta-invention, an invention that sets off inventiveness and makes all other inventions possible) manages to redefine in some way the horror of death as a driving force of life. It shapes the meaning of life on the basis of the absurdity of death." *Vidas desperdiciadas: La modernidad y sus parias*, 126–127.

7. Casáldaliga and Vigil say it this way: "All human beings have to face the mystery of our own existence. We are forced to opt for values that give meaning and consistency to our lives. It is not the religious practices that we do, perhaps with a lot of superficiality, that shapes us as people. It is spirituality that ultimately strengthens us as human beings because it impels us to live, to fight, to serve others." *Espiritualidad de la liberación*, 23–31.

8. Raúl Mora, "Rito, Mito, Símbolo," 57.

9. Virginia Kerns, *Women and the Ancestors*, 148.

10. Kerns, 149.

11. Paul Christopher Johnson, "On Leaving and Joining Africanness through Religion: The 'Black Caribs' across Multiple Diasporic Horizons," 189–190.

12. See Kerns, *Women and the Ancestors*.

13. Dominga, interviewed by José Idiáquez, November 10, 1992.

14. Clara Smith, interviewed by José Idiáquez, November 12, 1992.

15. Mateo, interviewed by José Idiáquez and Andrew Gorvetzian, July 4, 2016.

16. Mateo, interviewed by José Idiáquez and Andrew Gorvetzian, July 4, 2016.

17. Esperanza, interviewed by José Idiáquez, May 1992.

18. Kerns, 2.

19. Jacinto, interviewed by José Idiáquez, March 10, 1992.

20. Vernan, interviewed by Andrew Gorvetzian and Leonard Joseph, January 2018.

21. Mr. Cecil, interviewed by José Idiáquez, April 13, 2017.

22. Doña Ana, interviewed by José Idiáquez, February 15, 1993.

23. Miss Blanca, interviewed by José Idiáquez, January 10, 2018.

24. Freddy Estrada, interviewed by José Idiáquez, August 22, 1992.

25. Agustín, interviewed by José Idiáquez, Agustin, October 22, 1992.

26. Leonard Joseph, interviewed by José Idiáquez, October 21, 2018.

27. Martin, interviewed by Leonard Joseph, November 20, 2018.

28. Hugo José Suárez, *Creyentes urbanos: Sociología de la experiencia religiosa en una colonia popular de la ciudad de México*, 330–331.

29. Ignacio Ellacuria, "Teología política," 63–65.

30. Community member, focus group facilitated by Serena Cosgrove, March 25, 2018.

31. Don Isidro, interviewed by José Idiáquez, February 8, 1992.

32. Mateo, interviewed by Andrew Gorvetzian and Leonard Joseph, January 22, 2018.

33. Maria José Alvarez and Martha Clarissa Hernández, *Lubaraun*, documentary film.
34. Francesc Torralba, *La espiritualidad*, 19.
35. Father Tomas, interviewed by Serena Cosgrove, José Idiáquez, and Andrew Gorvetzian, March 28, 2018.
36. Luz, interviewed by Andrew Gorvetzian, August 7, 2018.
37. Community member, interviewed by Serena Cosgrove and José Idiáquez, March 25, 2018.
38. Luis, Facebook, August 7, 2018.
39. Visit to Santa Fe, Honduras, March 23, 2018.
40. Paul Christopher Johnson, "Diaspora Conversion: Black Carib Religion and the Recovery of Africa," 36.
41. Community member, focus group facilitated by Serena Cosgrove, March 25, 2018.
42. Kenya, interviewed by Serena Cosgrove and José Idiáquez, March 23, 2018.
43. Suárez, *Creyentes urbanos*; H. Daniel Levine, "The Evolution of the Theory and Practice of Rights in Latin American Catholicism"; Niklas Luhmann, *Sociología de la religión*.
44. Mateo, interviewed by Andrew Gorvetzian, March 27, 2017.

CHAPTER FIVE: ROUTING

1. Orson, interviewed by Andrew Gorvetzian and Leonard Joseph, January 22, 2018.
2. Marlon Howking, Selmira Flores, and Andrew Gorvetzian, "Hegemonía: Subalternidad en la educación del Caribe de Nicaragua. La experiencia de jóvenes creoles, miskitu y mestizos del Caribe estudiantes de la UNAN, UAM, UNI y UCA en Managua," 15.
3. University student, focus group facilitated by Andrew Gorvetzian, June 28, 2016.
4. David Harvey, *The Condition of Postmodernity*, 293.
5. J. Martinez Cruz, Glenda Godfrey, and Salvador Garcia, "Living in Community: Primeras aproximaciones al buenvivir de las poblaciones afrodescendientes en la Cuenca de Laguna de Perlas, RACCS," 101.
6. Linda M. Matthei and David A. Smith, "Flexible Ethnic Identity, Adaptation, Survival, Resistance: The Garifuna in the World-system," 217.
7. See Nancie L. González, "Garifuna Settlement in New York: A New Frontier"; Joseph O. Palacio, *The Garifuna: A Nation across Borders*; Aisha Khan, "Migration and Life-cycle of Garifuna (Black Carib) Street Vendors"; Felix G. Coe and Gregory J. Anderson, "Ethnobotany of the Garifuna of Eastern Nicaragua"; Virginia Kerns, *Women and the Ancestors: Black Carib Kinship and Ritual*; Kenny Fernández Castillo, "Apuntes sobre la migración Garífuna en relación a la caravana migrante de hondureños de 2018."
8. Eric, interviewed by Andrew Gorvetzian and Leonard Joseph, January 25, 2018.
9. Eric, interviewed by Andrew Gorvetzian and Leonard Joseph, January 25, 2018.
10. James Clifford, *Returns: Becoming Indigenous in the Twenty-First Century*, 61–62.
11. Matthei and Smith, 220.
12. Eric, interviewed by Andrew Gorvetzian and Leonard Joseph, January 25, 2018.
13. Eric, interviewed by Andrew Gorvetzian and Leonard Joseph, January 25, 2018.
14. William V. Davidson, "The Garifuna of Pearl Lagoon: Ethnohistory of an Afro-American Enclave in Nicaragua," 43.
15. Coe and Anderson, 92.

16. José Idiáquez, *El culto a los ancestros en la cosmovisión de los Garífunas de Nicaragua*, 183.
17. Idiáquez, *El culto,* 196.
18. Martinez Cruz, Godfrey, and Garcia, 33.
19. Community member, interviewed by Andrew Gorvetzian and Leonard Joseph, January 2018.
20. Martinez Cruz, Godfrey, and Garcia, 33.
21. Idiáquez, *El culto.*
22. Howking, Flores, and Gorvetzian, "Heremonía," 15.
23. Martinez Cruz, Godfrey, and Garcia, 39.
24. Community member, interviewed by Andrew Gorvetzian, April 2017.
25. Community member, interviewed by Serena Cosgrove and Leonard Joseph, December 2016.
26. Miss Rebecca interviewed by Andrew Gorvetzian and José Idiáquez, April 11, 2017.
27. Karla Lewis, "Influences on Garifuna Youth Education," 11.
28. Mateo, interviewed by Andrew Gorvetzian and Leonard Joseph, January 2018.
29. Community member, interviewed by Serena Cosgrove and José Idiáquez, December 9, 2015.
30. J. L. Rocha, "De la costa han salido en barcos los Ship-out caribeños."
31. Community member, interviewed by Serena Cosgrove and José Idiáquez, December 9, 2015.
32. Community member, interviewed by Andrew Gorvetzian and Leonard Joseph, January 24, 2018.
33. Coe and Anderson, 92.
34. Community member, interviewed by Andrew Gorvetzian, January 26, 2018.
35. Community member, interviewed by Serena Cosgrove and José Idiáquez, December 10, 2015.
36. William Brownfield, "International Narcotics Control Strategy Report, Volume 1, Drug and Chemical Control," 471; Community member, interviewed by Serena Cosgrove, July 2, 2016.
37. Community member, interviewed by Andrew Gorvetzian and Leonard Joseph, January 22, 2018.
38. Antonia, interviewed by Serena Cosgrove, December 16, 2015.
39. Sarah England, *Afro-Central Americans in New York City: Garifuna Tales of Transnational Movements in Racialized Space*, 90.
40. Kenia, interviewed by Serena Cosgrove and José Idiáquez, December 10, 2015.
41. Community member, interviewed by Serena Cosgrove and José Idiáquez, December 2016.
42. Community member, interviewed by Andrew Gorvetzian and Leonard Joseph, January 2018.
43. Clifford, 53.
44. Kelsey, interviewed by Andrew Gorvetzian, April 11, 2017.
45. Orson, interviewed by Andrew Gorvetzian and Leonard Joseph, January 22, 2018.
46. Orson, interviewed by Andrew Gorvetzian and Leonard Joseph, January 22, 2018.
47. Paul Christopher Johnson, *Diaspora Conversion: Black Carib Religion and the Recovery of Africa*; Clifford, *Returns.*
48. Leonard Joseph, interviewed by Serena Cosgrove, José Idiáquez, and Andrew Gorvetzian, 2017.

49. Ray, interviewed by Andrew Gorvetzian and Leonard Joseph, January 22, 2018.

50. Rosalind Shaw, *Memories of the Slave Trade: Ritual and Historical Imagination in Sierra Leone*, 46.

51. Mateo, interviewed by Andrew Gorvetzian, April 14, 2017.

52. Mateo, interviewed by Andrew Gorvetzian, April 12, 2017.

53. "Me gusta compartir mis conocimientos con las demás personas, y como garifuna, me siento muy orgullosa de mis raíces, y amo mi cultura. También apuesto por una evangelización enculturada, con eso me refiero a que debemos agradecer a Dios desde donde verdaderamente somos, desde nuestras raíces. . . Aquí en Nicaragua han perdido realmente parte de su cultura, de su identidad de ser Garifuna. El elemento fundamental que perdieron fue la lengua maternal, entonces eso es algo que me ha llamada mucho la atención y es una de las cosas por las cual estoy aquí, quiero apoyar en el rescate de la lengua maternal entre los garifuna de Nicaragua. Entendamos quienes somos, de donde son nuestras raíces, y cual es la importancia de rescatar nuestra lengua maternal, porque por nuestra cosmovisión nos identifica donde sea que nos encontremos, entonces, ya que ellos como Garifuna aquí en Nicaragua han perdido la mayor parte de la cultura, primero la lengua, segundo, parte de la danzas que enriquecen nuestra cultura. . . estar fuera de tu casa, y estar fuera de tu país no es fácil, y la verdad, siento que con la fe en Dios y en nuestros ancestros he aprendido perseverar." Esther, @NegrasSomos, Facebook video, February 4, 2018, https://www.facebook.com/watch/?v=877961305699059.

54. Kenny Fernández Castillo, "Monserrat Figueroa, la joven que enseña lengua garífuna en Nicaragua."

55. Matthei and Smith, 220.

56. Kelsey, interviewed by Serena Cosgrove and José Idiáquez, December 9, 2015.

57. Orson, interviewed by Andrew Gorvetzian and Leonard Joseph, January 22, 2018.

58. Ivan, interviewed by Andrew Gorvetzian and Leonard Joseph, January 23, 2018.

59. Harvey, 292.

60. Community member, interviewed by Andrew Gorvetzian and Leonard Joseph, January 26, 2018.

61. Community member, interviewed by Andrew Gorvetzian and Leonard Joseph, January 26, 2018.

62. Ramos, interviewed by Andrew Gorvetzian and Leonard Joseph, January 22, 2018.

63. Orson, interviewed by Andrew Gorvetzian and Leonard Joseph, January 22, 2018.

64. Community member, interviewed by José Idiáquez and Andrew Gorvetzian, February 8, 2017.

65. Esther, interviewed by José Idiáquez and Andrew Gorvetzian, February 8, 2017.

CHAPTER SIX: ROOTING, ROUTING, AND BELIEVING

1. Community member, interviewed by Andrew Gorvetzian, July 27, 2018.

2. See Sarah England, *Afro-Central Americans in New York City: Garifuna Tales of Transnational Movements in Racialized Space*, Paul Christopher Johnson, *Diaspora Conversion: Black Carib Religion and the Recovery of Africa*, and Paul Christopher Johnson, "On Leaving and Joining Africanness through Religion: The 'Black Caribs' across Multiple Diasporic Horizons."

3. Miss Patricia, interviewed by Andrew Gorvetzian and Leonard Joseph, January 20, 2018.

4. Community member, interviewed by Andrew Gorvetzian and Leonard Joseph, January 2018.

5. Community member, interviewed by Andrew Gorvetzian, August 7, 2018.

6. England, 218.

7. England, 219–220.

8. "'If I turn up dead one day, don't be surprised,' his father recalled him saying as the pair stared out at Bluefields Bay one blustery afternoon. It was not the first time Gahona, a crusading Nicaraguan journalist known for his investigative reports on police abuse and drug trafficking, had made such remarks. 'I can't remember how many times he told me they were going to kill him,' said his father, also called Ángel." Carl David Goette-Luciak, "How a Journalist's Death Live on Air became a Symbol of Nicaragua's Crisis."

9. "Quiero volver a Honduras. Hay mucho que hacer allá con todo lo que he aprendido aquí. Me vuelvo loco aquí. La mayoría quiere volver a Honduras para evitar la mierda de aquí." Community member, interviewed by Andrew Gorvetzian and Leonard Joseph, April 22, 2018.

10. Community member, interviewed by Andrew Gorvetzian and Leonard Joseph, April 23, 2018.

11. Community member, interviewed by Andrew Gorvetzian and Leonard Joseph, April 23, 2018.

12. Community member, interviewed by Andrew Gorvetzian, August 4, 2018.

13. Andy, interviewed by Andrew Gorvetzian, August 4, 2018.

14. Community member, interviewed by Andrew Gorvetzian, August 4, 2018.

15. Community member, interviewed by Andrew Gorvetzian, August 4, 2018.

16. Community member, interviewed by Andrew Gorvetzian, August 5, 2018.

17. Community member, interviewed by Andrew Gorvetzian, August 5, 2018.

18. David González, "Garifuna Immigrants in New York."

19. Johnson, *Diaspora Conversion*, 20.

20. Community member, interviewed by Andrew Gorvetzian, April 22, 2018.

21. England, 68.

22. "Hacemos mucho con pocos recursos, y nos sentimos satisfechos de que el gobierno nos apoya, porque somos una minoría. Siempre estamos pensando en regresar. Nos da nostalgia. Trabajamos con jóvenes allá y acá para que no migren más, pero es difícil cuando fuente de trabajo no tenemos para los jóvenes. También, la discriminación ha tenido un papel muy negativo para los jóvenes, nos ha destruido como personas. Las mujeres tenemos más visión, nos preocupamos más, igual que Barauda. Las mujeres empujamos, a veces los hombres se quedan ahí no tan convencidos. Se va perdiendo la tradición porque hay que adaptarse y eso a mi me duele. And then when things don't work out, there's the temptation to get involved in 'actividades ilicitas.' Quisiéramos sobrevivir en nuestra tierra, pero aun ahí hay problemas." Bartolomé Colón, interviewed by Andrew Gorvetzian and Leonard Joseph, April 24, 2018.

23. "No importa si se maneja bien el inglés, lo más importante es saber como moverse en este espacio para organizar y hacer lo que se tiene que hacer para su comunidad." Mirtha Colón, interviewed by Andrew Gorvetzian, July 20, 2018.

24. England, 68.

25. Milton, interviewed by Andrew Gorvetzian, July 27, 2018.

26. "Este trabajo es muy importante para mantener nuestra cultura, porque si no lo hacemos se va a perder, por toda la política que hay aquí. Por eso es importante hacer lo que estamos haciendo." Bodoma, interviewed by Andrew Gorvetzian, August 1, 2018.

27. "Los jóvenes están perdiendo la cultural totalmente. No hablan, me responden en español. No vienen a la misa, estoy segura que no habría jóvenes aquí." Community member, interviewed by Andrew Gorvetzian, August 5, 2018.

28. Community member, interviewed by Andrew Gorvetzian, August 5, 2018.

29. Luz Solís, interviewed by Andrew Gorvetzian, August 7, 2018.

30. Luz Solís, interviewed by Andrew Gorvetzian, August 7, 2018.

31. "No puedo decir mucho por los ancestros. Cuando era niña mi mama no me llevó a las reuniones con los ancestros, dijo que era para gente mayor. Por eso nunca he ido a una reunión. A veces sí pongo comida para los ancestros, para mi abuela y abuelo. Pero mi mama se sentía vergonzosa. Los ancestros le tocaron a ella y se metió con otra iglesia donde se le fue desapareciendo el miedo a los ancestros. Logró rechazar a los ancestros. Mis hijos no saben de los ancestros. Con muchas divisiones en el mundo, ¿qué va a hacer uno? La cultura se pierde." Community member, interviewed by Andrew Gorvetzian and Leonard Joseph, April 27, 2018.

32. Christopher Anthony Loperena, "A Divided Community: The Ethics and Politics of Activist Research," 332. Emphasis added.

33. "En mi humilde opinión yo soy garífuna y amo mis raíces. Pero según la Biblia que es clara esta tal tradición no es de Dios y no le agrada a Dios. Precisamente hoy estuve escuchando a un padre católico. Que habló sobre todo esto. Y dijo todo claro. Sobre estos puntos, a Dios no le agrada." Community member, interviewed by Andrew Gorvetzian, August 10, 2018.

34. Luz Solís, interviewed by Andrew Gorvetzian, August 7, 2018.

35. Luz Solís, interviewed by Andrew Gorvetzian, August 7, 2018.

36. Miss Arlene, interviewed by Andrew Gorvetzian and Leonard Joseph, January 25, 2018.

37. Kenny Fernández Castillo, "Monserrat Figueroa, la joven que enseña lengua garífuna en Nicaragua."

38. England, 226.

CHAPTER SEVEN: UNLEARNING/RELEARNING

1. Walter Mignolo and Catherine Walsh, *On Decoloniality: Concepts, Analytics, Praxis*, 21.

2. Mignolo and Walsh, 245.

3. Mignolo and Walsh, 146.

4. I feel great resonance with Catherine Walsh, an academic from the United States committed to unlearning and relearning, when she acknowledges the dilemma of her privilege and accompanying biases and yet still reaffirms her commitment to decolonial research and pedagogy: doing it "and not expecting that I will ever be able to fully surmount (the dilemma)." Mignolo and Walsh, 21.

5. Diane Nelson, *Who Counts? The Mathematics of Death and Life after Genocide*, 8.

6. Linda Tuhiwai Smith, *Decolonizing Methodologies: Research and Indigenous Peoples*, 16.

7. Tuhiwai Smith, *Decolonizing Methodologies*.

8. Mignolo and Walsh, 198.

9. Mignolo and Walsh, 200.

10. Tuhiwai Smith, 36.

11. Serena Cosgrove, *Leadership from the Margins: Women and Civil Society Organizations in Argentina, Chile, and El Salvador*; Serena Cosgrove, "'Who Will Use My Loom When I Am Gone?' An Intersectional Analysis of Mapuche Women's Progress in Twenty-First Century Chile."

12. Mignolo and Walsh, 112.

13. Tuhiwai Smith, 1.

14. Nelson, 33.

15. Tuhiwai Smith, 198–216; Mignolo and Walsh, 84.

16. Tuhiwai Smith, 51.

17. Michelle Fine, "The Politics of Research and Activism: Violence against Women," 552.

18. Fine, 551.

19. Community member, interviewed by Serena Cosgrove and José Idiáquez, July 12, 2015.

20. Ping-Chun Hsiung, "Teaching Reflexivity in Qualitative Interviewing," 212.

21. Nelson, 248.

22. Kathleen Riach, "Exploring Participant-centered Reflexivity in the Research Interview," 358.

23. Riach, 361.

24. Yolanda, interviewed by Serena Cosgrove, November 11, 2016.

25. James Faubion and George Marcus, *Fieldwork Is Not What It Used to Be: Learning Anthropology's Method in a Time of Transition*, viii.

26. Natasha Mauthner and Andrea Doucet, "Reflexive Accounts and Accounts of Reflexivity in Qualitative Data Analysis," 414.

27. Lynn Stephen describes how video and audio—even texts—"freez[e] the moment," taking people out of their original context. Stephen, *We Are the Face of Oaxaca: Testimony and Social Movements*, 17.

28. Faubion and Marcus, 40.

29. N. Patrick Peritore, "Reflections on Dangerous Fieldwork," 362.

30. Jennifer Goett, *Black Autonomy: Race, Gender, and Afro-Nicaraguan Activism*, 187.

31. Mignolo and Walsh, 28.

BIBLIOGRAPHY

Acosta, María Luisa. "El impacto de la ley del gran canal interoceánico de Nicaragua sobre los pueblos indígenas y afrodescendientes de Nicaragua." *Aportes al Debate/Academia de Ciencias de Nicaragua*. Managua: Serie Ciencia, Técnica y Sociedad, 2015.

Alvarez, María José, and Martha Clarissa Hernández, dir. *Lubaraun: Al encuentro. . . Encountering*. Nicaragua: Luna Films, 2014.

Ampié, Mauro, and Gonzalo Carrión. "Hay una indiferencia criminal de las autoridades ante la violencia en el Caribe." *Envío* 36, no. 420 (2017): 13–21.

Aparicio, José Manuel. "La lectura creyente de la naturaleza como creación." *Cuidar de la tierra, cuidar de los pobres: "Laudato Si" desde la teología y con la ciencia*. Santander, Spain: Sal Terrae, 2015.

Baracco, Luciano. *Indigenous Struggles for Autonomy: The Caribbean Coast of Nicaragua*. Lanham: Lexington Books, 2019.

Barth, Fredrik, ed. *Ethnic Groups and Boundaries: The Social Organization of Culture Difference*. Boston: Little Brown and Company, 1969.

Bauman, Zygmunt. *Vidas desperdiciadas: La modernidad y sus parias*. Barcelona: Paidós Ibérica, 2005.

Blanco, Emelinda, and José Francisco Ávila. *Diagnóstico institucional de las asociaciones Garífunas en New York*. New York: Inter-American Development Bank, 2006.

Blum, William. *Killing Hope: U.S. Military and CIA Interventions since World War II*. London: Zed Books, 2014.

Boccara, Guillaume. "The Mapuche People in Post-Dictatorship Chile." Études *Rurales*, no. 163/164 (2002): 283–303.

Boff, Leonardo. *Iglesia: Carisma y poder. Ensayos de eclesiología militante*. Santander, Spain: Editorial Sal Terrae, 1984.

———. *Quinientos años de evangelización: De la conquista espiritual a la liberación integral*. Santander, Spain: Editorial Sal Terrae, 1992.

Brondo, Keri Vacanti. "'A Dot on the Map': Cartographies of Erasure in Garifuna Territory." *Political and Legal Anthropology Review* 41, no. 2 (2018): 185–200. http://doi.org/10.1111/plar.12272.

———. *Land Grab: Green Neoliberalism, Gender, and Garifuna Resistance in Honduras*. Tucson: University of Arizona Press, 2013.

Brownfield, William. "International Narcotics Control Strategy Report, Volume 1, Drug and Chemical Control." *United States Department of State, Bureau for International Narcotics and Law Enforcement Affairs*. Washington, DC, 2010.

Bryan, Joe. "For Nicaragua's Indigenous Communities, Land Rights in Name Only." NACLA Report on the Americas 51, no. 1 (2019): 55–64. http://doi.org/10.1080/10714839.2019.1593692.

Casaldáliga, Pedro, and José María Vigil. *Espiritualidad de la liberación*. Santander, Spain: Editorial Sal Terrae, 1992.

Castillo, José María. *Espiritualidad para insatisfechos*. 5th ed. Madrid: Editorial Trotta, 2011.

———. *Simbolos de libertad: Teología de los sacramentos*. Salamanca: Ediciones Sigueme, 1992.

Castillo Fernández, Kenny. "Apuntes sobre la migración Garífuna en relación a la caravana migrante de hondureños de 2018." *Diarios del Terruño: Reflexiones sobre migración y movilidad* 7, no. 1 (2019): 122–133. Latindex.

———. "Monserrat Figueroa, la joven que enseña lengua garífuna en Nicaragua." *Kenny Castillo (personal blog)*, 2019. August 20, 2019. https://kennycastillo.com/montserrat-figueroa1/.

Catter, Teresa V. "Intercultural Bilingual Education in Nicaragua: Contextualisation for improving the quality of education." *International Review of Education* 57, no. 5–6 (2011): 721–735. http://doi.org/10.1007/s11159-011-9258-0.

Centro Nicaragüense de Derechos Humanos. "Voces campesinas contra el proyecto del Canal," *Envío* 35, no. 416–417 (2016): https://www.envio.org.ni/articulo/5276.

Chaney, James. "Malleable Identities: Placing the Garínagu in New Orleans." *Journal of Latin American Geography* 11, no. 2 (2012): 121–44. http://doi.org/10.1353/lag.2012.0049.

Clifford, James. *Returns: Becoming Indigenous in the Twenty-First Century*. Cambridge: Harvard University Press, 2013.

Coe, Felix G., and Gregory J. Anderson. "Ethnobotany of the Garífuna of Eastern Nicaragua." *Economic Botany* 50, no. 1 (1996): 71–107.

Collins, Patricia Hill. *Black Feminist Thought: Knowledge, Consciousness, and the Politics of Empowerment*. New York: Routledge, 2000.

———. "It's All in the Family: Intersections of Gender, Race, and Nation." *Hypatia* 13, no. 3 (1998): 62–82.

Collins, Patricia Hill, and Sirma Bilge. *Intersectionality*. Malden, MA: Polity Press, 2016.

Cosgrove, Serena. *Leadership from the Margins: Women and Civil Society Organizations in Argentina, Chile, and El Salvador*. New Brunswick, NJ: Rutgers University Press, 2010.

———. "'Who Will Use My Loom When I Am Gone?' An Intersectional Analysis of Mapuche Women's Progress in Twenty-First Century Chile." In *Bringing Intersectionality to Public Policy*, edited by Julia Jordan-Zachery and Olena Hankivsky. New York: Palgrave-Macmillan, 2018.

Cosgrove, Serena, and José Idiáquez, S. J. "Intersectionality and Women's Leadership: Garifuna Women Responding to Challenges on the Caribbean Coast." Paper presented at the Annual Meeting of the National Women's Studies Association, Montreal, Canada, November 2016.

Crenshaw, Kimberlé. *Background Paper for the Expert Meeting on the Gender-Related Aspects of Race Discrimination*. New York: United Nations, 2000.

———. "Mapping the Margins: Intersectionality, Identity Politics, and Violence Against Women of Color." *Stanford Law Review* 43, no. 6 (1991): 1241–1299.

Curtin, Philip. *The Atlantic Slave Trade: A Census*. Madison: University of Wisconsin Press, 1969.

Davidson, William V. "The Garifuna of Pearl Lagoon: Ethnohisotry of an Afro-American Enclave in Nicaragua." *Ethnohistory* 27, no. 1 (1980): 31–47.

Delgado, Richard, and Jean Stefancic. *Critical Race Theory: An Introduction*. New York: New York University Press, 2012.

Desai, Gaurau, and Supriya Nair. *Postcolonialisms: An Anthology of Cultural Theory and Criticism.* New Brunswick, NJ: Rutgers University Press, 2005.

Dibie, Robert, and Johnston Njoku. "Cultural Perceptions of Africans in Diaspora and in Africa on Atlantic Slave Trade and Reparations." *African & Asian Studies* 4, no.3 (2005): 403–425. http://doi.org/10.1163/156920905774270457.

Durkheim, Emile. *Las formas elementales de la vida religiosa.* Madrid: Akal editor, 1982.

Eldelman, Marc, and Angelique Haugerud. *The Anthropology of Development and Globalization: From Classical Political Economy to Contemporary Neoliberalism.* Malden, MA: Blackwell Publishing, 2005.

Eliade, Mircea. *Mito y realidad.* Madrid: Ediciones Guadarrama, 1973.

———. *Occultism, Witchcraft, and Cultural Fashions: Essays in Comparative Religions.* Chicago: University of Chicago Press, 1976.

Ellacuria, Ignacio. *Teología política.* San Salvador: Secretariado Social Interdiocesano, 1973.

England, Sarah. *Afro-Central Americans in New York City: Garifuna Tales of Transnational Movements in Racialized Space.* Gainesville: University of Florida Press, 2006.

Evans, George. "The Deaths of Somoza." *World Literature Today* 81, no. 3 (2007): 36–43.

Faubion, James, and George Marcus, eds. *Fieldwork Is Not What It Used to Be: Learning Anthropology's Method in a Time of Transition.* Ithaca, NY: Cornell University Press, 2009.

Fine, Michelle. "The Politics of Research and Activism: Violence against Women." *Gender and Society* 3, no. 4 (1989): 549–558.

Freeland, Jane. "Intercultural-Bilingual Education for an Interethnic-Plurilingual Society? The Case of Nicaragua's Caribbean Coast." *Comparative Education* 39, no. 2 (2003): 239–260. http://doi.org/10.1080/03050060302553.

Frühling, Pierre, Miguel González, and Hans Petter Buvollen. *Etnicidad y Nación: El Desarrollo de la Autonomía de la Costa Atlántica de Nicaragua (1987–2007).* Guatemala City: F & G editores, 2007.

Garrido, Javier. *Proceso humano y gracia de Dios: Apuntes de espiritualidad cristiana.* Santander, Spain: Editorial Sal Terrae, 1996.

Gegeo, David Welchman. "Cultural Rupture and Indigeneity: The Challenge of (Re)visioning 'Place' in the Pacific." *The Contemporary Pacific* 13, no. 2 (2001): 491–507.

Gilroy, Paul. *The Black Atlantic: Modernity and Double Consciousness.* Cambridge, MA: Harvard University Press, 1993.

Girardi, Giulio. *La Conquista permanente: El cristianismo entre paz del imperio y paz de los pueblos.* Managua: Ediciones Nicarao, 1992.

Glick-Schiller, Nina. "From Immigrant to Transmigrant: Theorizing Transnational Migration." *Anthropological Quarterly* 68, no. 1 (1995): 48–63.

Gobat, Michael. *Confronting the American Dream: Nicaragua under U.S. Imperial Rule.* Durham, NC: Duke University Press, 2005.

Goett, Jennifer. *Black Autonomy: Race, Gender, and Afro-Nicaraguan Activism.* Stanford, CA: Stanford University Press, 2017.

Goette-Luciak, and Carl David. "How a Journalist's Death Live on Air Became a Symbol of Nicaragua's Crisis." *Guardian.* May 29, 2018. https://www.theguardian.com /world/2018/may/29/nicaragua-journalist-killed-live-on-air-angel-gahona.

González, David. "Garifuna Immigrants in New York." *Lens* (blog). *New York Times* July 24, 2015. https://lens.blogs.nytimes.com/2015/07/24/garifuna-immigrants-in-new-york/.

González, Faus José Ignacio. "La constitución idolátrica del ser humano." *Idolatrías de Occidente*. Córdoba, Argentina: Universidad Católica de Córdoba, 2005.

González, Miguel. "Leasing Communal Lands. . . In 'Perpetuity': Post-Titling Scenarios on the Caribbean Coast of Nicaragua." In *Indigenous Struggles for Autonomy: The Caribbean Coast of Nicaragua*: 75–97. Lanham, MD: Lexington Books, 2019.

———. "Securing Rights in Tropical Lowlands." *AlterNative: An International Journal of Indigenous Peoples* 8, no. 4 (2012): 426–446.

González, Nancie L. "Garifuna Settlement in New York: A New Frontier." *The International Migration Review* 13, no. 2 (1979): 255–263.

Gordon, Edmund T. *Disparate Diasporas: Identity and Politics in an African Nicaraguan Community*. Austin: University of Texas Press, 1998.

Grzanka, Patrick R., ed. *Intersectionality: A Foundations and Frontiers Reader*. Boulder, CO: Westview Press, 2014.

Gutiérrez, Gustavo. *Textos de espiritualidad: Selección e introducción de Daniel G. Groody*. Lima: Instituto Bartolomé de las Casas, 2013.

Hale, Charles R. "Does Multiculturalism Menace? Governance, Cultural Rights and the Politics of Identity in Guatemala." *Journal of Latin American Studies* 34 (2002): 485–524.

———. *Más que un Indio: Racial Ambivalence and Neoliberal Multiculturalism in Guatemala*. Santa Fe, NM: School of American Research, 2006.

———. "Neoliberal Multiculturalism: The Remaking of Cultural Rights and Racial Discrimination in Latin America." *PoLAR: Political and Legal Anthropology Review* 28, no. 1 (2005): 10–28.

———. *Resistance and Contradiction: Miskitu Indian and the Nicaraguan State, 1894–1987*. Stanford, CA: Stanford University Press, 1994.

Hall, Stuart. "On Postmodernism and Articulation: An Interview with Stuart Hall." Edited by Lawrence Grossberg. *Journal of Communication Inquiry* 10, no. 2 (1986): 5–27.

———. *Representation: Cultural Representations and Signifying Practices*. Thousand Oaks, CA: Sage Publications, 1997.

Haraway, Donna. "Situated Knowledges: The Science Question in Feminism and the Privilege of Partial Perspective." *Feminist Studies* 14, no. 3 (1988): 575–599.

Harvey, David. *The Condition of Postmodernity*. Cambridge, MA: Blackwell, 1990.

Hondagneu-Sotelo, Pierette. "Why Advocacy Research?: Reflections on Research and Activism with Immigrant Women." *The American Sociologist* 24, no. 1 (1993): 56–68.

Hooker, Juliet. "'Beloved Enemies': Race and Official Mestizo Nationalism in Nicaragua." *Latin American Research Review* 40, no. 3 (2005): 14–39.

Howard, Sarah. "Autonomía y derechos territoriales indígenas: El caso de la RAAN." In *Demarcación territorial de la propiedad comunal en la costa caribe de Nicaragua*, edited by Alvaro Rivas and Rikke Broegaard, 38–61.

Howking, Marlon, Selmira Flores, and Andrew Gorvetzian. "Hegemonía: Subalternidad en la educación del Caribe de Nicaragua. La experiencia de jóvenes creoles, miskitu y mestizos del Caribe estudiantes de la UNAN, UAM, UNI y UCA en Managua." Managua: Nitlapan instituto de investigación y desarrollo, 2019.

Hsiung, Ping-Chun. "Teaching Reflexivity in Qualitative Interviewing." *Teaching Sociology* 36, no. 3 (2008): 211–226.

Idiáquez, José, SJ. "Cómo ven el mundo los Garífunas," *WANI*, No. 27, Julio–Diciembre (2001): 13–27.

———. *El culto a los ancestros en la cosmovisión de los Garífunas de Nicaragua*. Managua: Instituto Histórico Centroamericano, 1994.

Incer Barquero, Jaime. *Descubrimiento, conquista y exploración de Nicaragua: Cronicas de fuentes originales seleccionadas y comentadas por Jaime Incer Barquero*. Managua: Fundación VIDA, 2006.

Johnson, Paul Christopher. *Diaspora Conversion: Black Carib Religion and the Recovery of Africa*. Berkeley: University of California Press, 2007.

———. "On Leaving and Joining Africanness through Religion: The 'Black Caribs' across Multiple Diasporic Horizons." *Journal of Religion in Africa* 37, no. 2 (2007): 174–211. http://doi.org/10.1163/157006607X188911.

Kerns, Virginia. *Women and the Ancestors: Black Carib Kinship and Ritual*. Champaign: University of Illinois Press, 1983.

Khan, Aisha. "Migration and Life-cycle of Garifuna (Black Carib) Street Vendors." *Women's Studies* 13 (1987): 183–198.

LaFeber, Walter. *Inevitable Revolutions: The United States in Central America*. New York: W.W. Norton, 1993.

Land, Clare. *Decolonizing Solidarity: Dilemmas and Directions for Supporters of Indigenous Struggles*. London: Zed Books, 2015.

Levine, H. Daniel. "The Evolution of the Theory and Practice of Rights in Latin American Catholicism." *Religious Responses to Violence: Human Rights in Latin America–Past and Present*, edited by Alexander Wilde. South Bend, IN: University of Notre Dame Press, 2016.

Levitsky, Steven, and Daniel Ziblatt. *How Democracies Die*. New York: Crown Publishing, 2018.

Lewis, Karla. "Influences on Garifuna Youth Education." Paper presented at the Annual Meeting of the American Educational Research Association, Montreal, Canada, April 19–23, 1999.

Loperena, Christopher A. "Honduras Is Open for Business: Extractivist Tourism as Sustainable Development in the Wake of Disaster?" *Journal of Sustainable Tourism* 25, no. 5 (2017): 618–633.

Loperena, Christopher Anthony. "A Divided Community: The Ethics and Politics of Activist Research." *Current Anthropology* 57, no. 3 (2016): 332–346. http://doi.org/10.1086/686301.

Luhmann, Niklas. *Sociología de la religión*. Mexico City: Universidad Iberoamericana, 2009.

Martinez Cruz, J., Glenda Godfrey, and Salvador Garcia. "Living in Community: Primeras aproximaciones al buenvivir de las poblaciones afrodescendientes en la cuenca de laguna de perlas, RACCS." *Bluefields Indian and Caribbean University and United Nations Population Fund,* 2016.

Matthei, Linda M., and David A. Smith. "Flexible Ethnic Identity, Adaptation, Survival, Resistance: The Garifuna in the World-system." *Social Identities* 14, no. 2 (2008): 215–232.

Mauthner, Natasha, and Andrea Doucet. "Reflexive Accounts and Accounts of Reflexivity in Qualitative Data Analysis." *Sociology* 37, no. 3 (2003): 413–431.

Mignolo, Walter, and Catherine Walsh. *On Decoloniality: Concepts, Analytics, Praxis.* Durham, NC: Duke University Press, 2018.

Mittleman, James. *The Globalization Syndrome: Transformation and Resistance.* Princeton, NJ: Princeton University Press, 2000.

Mohanty, Chandra Talpade. "Under Western Eyes: Feminist Scholarship and Colonial Discourses." *Boundary* 2, no. 12/13 (1984): 333–358. http://doi.org/10.2307/302821.

Mollett, Sharlene. "A Modern Paradise: Garifuna Land, Labor, and Displacement-in-Place." *Latin American Perspectives* 41, no. 6 (2014): 198–140.

Mora, Raúl. "Rito, mito, símbolo." *Christus* 534 (1980): 57–67. Mexico City: Centro de Reflexión Teológica.

Nelson, Diane. *Who Counts? The Mathematics of Death and Life after Genocide.* Durham, NC: Duke University Press, 2015.

Ortega Hegg, Manuel, y Marcelina Castillo. *Religión y política: La experiencia de Nicaragua.* Panama City: Casa Editorial Ruth, 2006.

Palacio, Joseph O. *The Garifuna: A Nation across Borders.* Benque Viejo del Carmen, Belize: Cubola Productions, 2005.

Palacio, Joseph, R. Judith Lumb, and Carlson Tuttle. "El poder de la demarcación: El primer deslidamiento en Barranco, Belice." In *Política e identidad: Afrodescendientes en México y América Central,* edited by Odile Hoffmann. Mexico City: INAH/UNAM/CEMCA/IRD, 2010.

Peritore, N. Patrick. "Reflections on Dangerous Fieldwork." *The American Sociologist* 21, no. 4 (1990): 359–372.

Prakash, Gyan. *After Colonialism: Imperial Histories and Postcolonial Displacements.* Princeton, NJ: Princeton University Press, 1995.

Programa de las Naciones Unidas para el Desarrollo (PNUD) Nicaragua. *Informe de desarrollo humano 2005: Las regiones autónomas de la Costa Caribe.* Managua: PNUD, 2005.

Radcliffe, Sarah A. *Dilemmas of Difference: Indigenous Women and the Limits of Postcolonial Development Policy.* Durham, NC: Duke University Press, 2015.

———. "Geography and Indigeneity I: Indigeneity, Coloniality and Knowledge." *Progress in Human Geography* (2015): 1–10. http://doi.org/10.1177/0309132515612952

Riach, Kathleen. "Exploring Participant-Centered Reflexivity in the Research Interview." *Sociology* 43, no. 2 (2009): 356–370.

Rivas, Alvaro, and Rikke Broegaard, eds. *Demarcación territorial de la propiedad comunal en la Costa Caribe de Nicaragua.* Managua: CIDCA-UCA, 2006.

Rocha, José L. "De la costa han salido en barcos los Ship-out caribeños." *Envío,* no. 333 (2009): 10.

Rueda Estrada, Verónica. *Recompas, recontras, revueltos y rearmados: Posguerra y conflictos por la tierra en Nicaragua, 1990-2008.* Mexico City: Instituto de Investigaciones Dr. José María Luis Mora and Universidad Nacional Autónoma de México, 2015.

Santidrián, Pedro R. *Diccionario básico de las religiones.* Navarra, Spain: Editorial Verbo Divino, 1993.

Scott, James C. *Weapons of the Weak: Everyday Forms of Peasant Resistance.* New Haven, CT: Yale University Press, 1985.

Seelke, Claire, Liana Wyler, and June Beittel. *Latin America and the Caribbean: Illicit Drug Trafficking and US Counterdrug Programs.* Washington, DC: Congressional Research Service, 2010.

Shaw, Rosalind. *Memories of the Slave Trade: Ritual and Historical Imagination in Sierra Leone.* Chicago: University of Chicago Press, 2002.

Simpson, Leanne Betasamosake. *As We Have Always Done: Indigenous Freedom through Radical Resistance.* Minneapolis: University of Minnesota Press, 2017.

Slater, Lisa. *Anxieties of Belonging in Settler Colonialism: Australia, Race and Place.* London: Routledge, 2018.

———. "A Meditation on Discomfort." *Australian Feminist Studies* 32, no. 93 (2017): 335–343. https://doi.org/10.1080/08164649.2017.1407635.

Sobel, Richard. "Contra Aid Fundamentals: Exploring the Intricacies and the Issues." *Political Science Quarterly* 110, no. 2 (1995): 287.

Solomon, J., & نومولوس ,ج. "Tortured History: Filibustering, Rhetoric, and Walker's "War in Nicaragua' / التاريخ المعذب: التصرفنة والغلابة وكاتكو ركوو عن الحرب في نيكاراجوا." *Alif: Journal of Comparative Poetics* no. 31 (2011): 105–132. http://www.jstor.org.proxy.seattleu.edu/stable/23216049.

Stephen, Lynn. *We Are the Face of Oaxaca: Testimony and Social Movements.* Durham, NC: Duke University Press, 2013.

Suárez, Hugo José. *Creyentes urbanos: Sociología de la experiencia religiosa en una colonia popular de la ciudad de México.* Mexico City: UNAM, Instituto de Investigaciones Sociales, 2015.

Sylvander, Nora. "Saneamiento Territorial in Nicaragua, and the Prospects for Resolving Indigenous-Mestizo Land Conflicts." *Journal of Latin American Geography* 17, no. 1 (2018): 166–194.

Taylor, Christopher. *The Black Carib Wars.* Oxford, UK: Signal Books Ltd, 2012.

Torralba, Francesc. *La espiritualidad.* Translated by Ramón Sala Gili. Lleida, Spain: Editorial Milenio, 2014.

———. *Inteligencia espiritual: "Vivimos en un desierto espiritual."* 8th ed. Barcelona: Plataforma Editorial, 2016.

Tuck, Eve, and K. Wayne Yang. "Decolonization is not a metaphor." *Decolonization: Indigeneity, Education, and Society* 1, no. 1 (2012): 1–40.

Tuhiwai Smith, Linda. *Decolonizing Methodologies: Research and Indigenous Peoples.* 2nd ed. London: Zed Books, 2012.

Vilas, Carlos. *Del colonialismo a la autonomía: Modernización capitalista y revolución social en la Costa Atlántica.* Managua: Editorial Nueva Nicaragua, 1990.

Vizenor, Gerald. *Native Liberty: Natural Reason and Cultural Survivance.* Lincoln: University of Nebraska Press, 2009.

Wade, Peter. "Rethinking 'Mestizaje': Ideology and Lived Experience." *Journal of Latin American Studies* 37, no. 2 (2005): 239–257.

Watson, Irene. "Aboriginal Sovereignties: Past, Present and Future (Im)Possibilities." In *Our Patch,* 23–44, edited by Suvendrini Perera. Curtin, Western Australia: Network Books, 2007.

Wheelock Roman, Jaime. *La Mosquitia en la Revolución.* 2nd ed. Managua: Colección Blas Real Espinales, 1981.

Wieviorka, Michel. *El espacio del racismo.* Barcelona: Paidós, 1991.

ACKNOWLEDGMENTS

As a group of people who have learned so much from the Garifuna communities of Nicaragua and beyond, we begin by acknowledging our ancestors: we wouldn't be here if not for them, their intercession, and support, as four people in multiple countries worked full-time jobs and managed to find time to carry out research.

We are particularly grateful to the Garifuna communities of Pearl Lagoon in Nicaragua for receiving us with patience, humor, and hospitality. In the course of our research in Orinoco, we were repeatedly welcomed into the house of Miss Rebecca, who treated us like family. She passed away in 2019; Orinoco will not be the same without her. We surely hope she's become one of our ancestor spirits and will celebrate with us when this book is finally published.

Thanks also to Father Cacho and his sister Hermana Soyapa in Honduras: they introduced us to the communities of La Fe and Guadalupe and then took us to their family home in the village of Sangrelaya where we were treated like long-lost family members. We are indebted to the *Coalición Mexicana* in the Bronx, Jairo and Claudia, for taking time from their work with other immigrant groups to introduce us to Garifuna families in the Bronx. To all the Garifuna people in Nicaragua, Honduras, and the New York City area who received us in their homes, met with us in churches, and talked with us outside next to the sea: thank you for your *confianza, hospitalidad, y cariño*. Your trust, hospitality and friendship have helped us learn about what it means to be Garifuna today. Your daily conversations with your ancestors keep you connected to the past, persistent in this current moment, and full of faith for what will come. You are our inspiration at a time when we see few signs of hope for the political landscapes of Nicaragua, Honduras, and the United States. Thank you.

A special shout out to anthropologist Dr. Irina Carlota (Lotti) Silber at the City College of New York in New York City: you have been a colleague and friend to Father Chepe and Serena, and a mentor to Andy. Not only have you served as a discussant on multiple conference panels and given us feedback on initial presentations about this data, you have generously yet critically read our manuscript. From your belief that our manuscript was articulating a new theory of persistence and needed to get published, to reminding us to trust that the ethnographic stories would explicate the dense theory that needed to be woven into unpacking Indigeneity, Black Indigenous Central America, diaspora, and decoloniality, thank you. Also in New York City, special thanks to Dr. Victoria Sanford at Lehman College for inviting Serena to give a talk about Garifuna persistence. The warmth, enthusiasm, and hospitality of you and your colleagues was needed encouragement during early phases of analysis and writing.

Deep heartfelt gratitude to the anonymous reviewers who read early versions of this manuscript. Your comments helped us improve and expand multiple sections of this book. Sarah England, thank you for seeing the value of telling the Garifuna story from the Nicaraguan perspective; your own work in Honduras and New York City was extremely important as we endeavored to unpack commonalities and differences between Nicaragua and other Central American countries as well as to understand the Garifuna in diasporic dimensions. Ultimately, however, we authors are responsible for the content of this book and any errors that it may contain. We are aware that our scholarship rides on the shoulders of other scholars throughout the Americas and beyond whose research questions, data, and analysis have encouraged us to ask our questions and contribute our theory of Nicaraguan Garifuna persistence. Thank you!

The work of Australian researchers confronting Eurocentric epistemology and applying a more expansive, Indigenous-inspired vision has helped us to situate this story in a global decolonial set of academic works. Thank you to Dr. Lisa Slater for coming to Seattle to share her new book, *Anxieties of Belonging in Settler Colonialism: Australia, Race and Place*. Your book led us to the work of Irene Watson, an Aboriginal legal theorist, which helped frame chapter 1.

All of us are grateful to the support of our institutions and families. This project would not have come to fruition if not for the support of the Bluefields Indian and Caribbean University (BICU); the Universidad Centroamericana (UCA) in Managua, Nicaragua; and Seattle University (SU). At the BICU, thanks to former rector, Gustavo Castro, for encouraging Leonard to take this project on. At the UCA, the Rector's Cabinet embraced our topic and encouraged us to share our insights as the research unfolded. Seattle University president, Father Steve Sundborg, SJ, welcomed our research team to campus and supported this project. Serena also thanks Provost Shane Martin and SU colleague Joe Orlando for their commitment and support of the partnership between the UCA in Managua and SU. And to Serena's colleagues at Seattle University in International Studies, and the broader College of Arts and Sciences, she gives her gratitude for reading and discussing coloniality and decoloniality over multiple years. A special shout out to Isabeau J. Belisle Dempsey, research assistant extraordinaire: thank you for your thoughtful summaries of important sections of the literature review as well as your preparation of the Garifuna timeline. Also, thank you to Michael Ninen for research assistance in the final stage of manuscript preparation. Serena also extends gratitude to the Institute of Catholic Thought and Culture at Seattle

University for research support and the opportunity to participate in the Inclusion Reading Group in 2017–2018 and 2018–2019.

Leonard couldn't have done this without Jeannette, his children, and grandchildren. Father Chepe hopes that his niece Raquel and nephew Juan find this book useful for expanding their understanding of what it means to be Nicaraguan. Andy thanks his mom and dad, Nancy and Joe, and siblings, Joey and Sarah, for their patience and love, in addition to Fiore, his partner, for her constant companionship and for sharing stories of persistence from Garifuna families migrating to the United States, and the many friends at the UCA and throughout Nicaragua for all of their support during this project. Serena thanks Marty and hopes that the next generation, Alexandra and Meme, will read this book and be moved by Garifuna persistence. Deep gratitude to Shady Cosgrove whose own writing process and sisterly love is always an inspiration and motivation and to Marlene Kenney for your commitment to inclusion and overcoming trauma in Indigenous communities around the world.

This book would probably never have come to fruition if not for a serendipitous encounter with the University of Cincinnati Press. We are grateful to the staff of UCP, particularly Elizabeth Scarpelli and Sarah Muncy, for ushering this book through the publishing process from idea to proposal to manuscript to published book in English and Spanish.

And finally, to you our reader: may this story of Garifuna persistence in Nicaragua inspire you to unlearn and relearn and celebrate the persistence of Afro-Indigenous, Indigenous, and Afro-descendant groups along the length of the Americas.

Simplemente, gracias a todos, todas, y todes por su comprensión y compromiso.

INDEX

Ortega, Daniel
  on assimilation of Indigenous people, 24
  calls for removal of, xix, 102–3
  and land displacement of Indigenous
    population, 39, 50
  protests against government of, 46
  support for tourism, 90

P
palm trees (Sconfra), 5
panga, xv, xvi, 47, 54, 87, 99
Panama Canal, xix
Pañas (Garifuna term for mestizos), 19, 36,
  49–51, 60
Paris, Treaty of (1763), x, 20
participant observation, 121, 123, 129–33
Patricia, Miss, 50, 101, 119
Pearl Lagoon
  Catholicism established in, 7
  changes in lifestyle from 1990s to 2015,
    119
  founding of communities surrounding,
    3–4
  Garifuna communities under
    Sandinistas, 24–25
  Garifuna immigration to, 21
  language classes in primary school, 118
  loss of Garifuna culture in, 85
  Moravian Church arrives 1849, xi
  research visits to, 123
  timber and fishery products sold in, 11
Pentecostals, 71, 72, 84
Peralta, Miss, 117
performance, xxiv, 32, 41–43, 83, 118–19
persistence
  articulation, performance, and
    translation, 40–43
  and community flexibility, xx
  and decolonial research, 38, 121–24
  diaspora's impact upon, 29
  of Garifuna in Nicaragua, Honduras and
    New York City, 99–120
  and Garifuna land in Honduras, 56–58
  and Garifuna land in Nicaragua, 46–47
  impact upon youth, xxii, xxv, 30, 80–98
  and indigenous commuting, 18

influence of nature and ancestors upon,
  21
and postcolonial present, xxiii, 26, 38,
  113, 124
theory of, 26–29
placenta, 65
political intersectionality, 36
population growth, 11
postcolonial present
  and conflict with national mestizo
    government, 26
  and decolonial future, 113
  and Garifuna persistence, xxiii, 26, 38,
    113, 124
  and intersectionality, 36–37
  "postcolonial" as controversial term,
    37
potreros (fields to run cattle on), 52
poverty
  causes of, 10, 23, 26, 33, 38, 47, 54
  community blamed for, 126
  effect upon youth migration, 30
  of inhabitants of Caribbean coast, xx
  as a result of intersectionality, 33
  and sale of land, 58
pregnancy, 56, 90, 126
protect the land *(proteger las tierras)*, 45
Protestant religion, 64. *see also specific
  denominations*
pulali (sweet atole or gruel), 9

R
RACCN. *see* Autonomous Region of the
  Caribbean Coast - North
RACCS. *see* Autonomous Region of the
  Caribbean Coast - South
Radcliffe, Sarah, 37
Rama people, xix, xxii, 18, 53
Ray (musician and teacher), 92
Reagan, Ronald, 24
Rebecca, Miss, xvi, xxiii, 19, 47, 51, 56,
  88
Red Caribs
  intermarriage with Garifunas, 20
  as local Indigenous group on St.
    Vincent, xvi

ABOUT THE AUTHORS

Serena Cosgrove is a Sociologist and Anthropologist. She is an Associate Professor of International Studies and the Director of Latin American Studies at Seattle University; she currently serves as the Faculty Coordinator for SU's Central America Initiative. Her previous books include the co-authored book, *Understanding Global Poverty: Causes, Capabilities, and Human Development* (2018), and *Leadership from the Margins: Women and Civil Society Organizations in Argentina, Chile, and El Salvador* (2010).

José Idiáquez is an Anthropologist, a Jesuit priest, and the President of the Universidad Centroamericana in Managua, Nicaragua. His previous books include *En Búsqueda de Esperanza: La Migración Ngäbe a Costa Rica y su Impacto en la Juventud (In Search of Hope: Ngäbe Migration to Costa Rica and its Impact on Youth)* in 2012 and *El Culto a los Ancestros en la Cosmovisión Religiosa de los Garífunas de Nicaragua (The Worship of the Ancestors in the Religious Cosmovision of the Garifuna of Nicaragua)* in 1997.

Leonard Joseph Bent is Garifuna; he is a Sociologist and Attorney of Law. He taught Sociology and was the director of the Training and Development Program at the Bluefields Indian and Caribbean University until his retirement in 2018. Currently, he is a consultant and practices law.

Andrew Gorvetzian is a graduate student in Anthropology at the University of New Mexico. Prior to his studies at UNM, he taught at the Universidad Centroamericana in Managua, Nicaragua and at the United World College in Montezuma, New Mexico.